MW00993359

"The first book on BPMN that I can enthusiastically recommend... It teaches you about the elements of BPMN, but much more important, it teaches you how to use BPMN, how to approach problems, [with] guidelines for what constitutes a good BPMN style.... If you want to learn to use BPMN, this is the book to buy and study."

Paul Harmon
Executive Editor, BPTrends
Author, *Business Process Change*

"Balanced, digestible guidance and insight for business people. *BPMN Method and Style* demystifies BPMN's deceptively sophisticated concepts, laying the foundation for rich, meaningful collaboration between "the business" and IT. This well organized book is an invaluable reference to those using BPMN, regardless of their tool of choice. I highly recommend it."

Wolfgang Hilpert
Senior Vice President, SAP AG
NetWeaver Solution Management – SOA & BPM

"A very valuable book for anyone interested in BPM modeling... The book's pattern-based approach enables quick application of the acquired knowledge, while anti-patterns show and help protect against typical pitfalls."

Matthias Kloppmann
IBM Distinguished Engineer, Chief Architect BPM Technology

"An excellent basic framework, showing which features are useful at each layer of refinement. This book could have been aptly named *BPMN Bible for Business Analysts*."

Manoj Das
Director, BPM Product Management, Oracle

"Bruce Silver has logged more time teaching people BPMN than anyone else on the planet. Here he combines that experience with a unique approach to process modeling and the result is a book that shows you how to design/document processes with clarity and precision."

Robert Shapiro
Chairman, WfMC Conformance Working Group (BPMN Portability)
Manager, ProcessAnalytica LLC, and SVP Research, Global 360

"comprehensive method for those that take [BPMN] to the next level."

Alexander Grosskopf
Author, *The Process*

For Junell

BPMN METHOD AND STYLE

Bruce Silver

CODY-CASSIDY PRESS

BPMN Method and Style

By Bruce Silver
ISBN 978-0-9823681-0-7

Published by Cody-Cassidy Press, Aptos, CA 95003 USA
Contact
        info@codycassidy.com
        +1 (831) 685-8803

Library of Congress Control Number: 2009904709
Library of Congress Subject Headings
Workflow -- Management.
Process control -- Data processing -- Management.
Business -- Data processing -- Management.
Management information systems.
Reengineering (Management)
Information resources management.
Agile software development.

Cover design by Leyba Associates

1.0

TABLE OF CONTENTS

Preface vii

Part I. Method and Style 1

1. HOW DOES A MODEL MEAN? 3
   UNLOCKING BPMN'S SECRETS 4
   THE QUESTIONS BPMN ASKS 5
   LEVELS OF BPMN USE 6

Part II. Level 1: Descriptive BPMN 9

2. BPMN LEVEL 1 BY EXAMPLE 11
3. ARE YOU IN? 19
   WHY DOES IT MATTER? 23
4. LEVEL 1 MODELING PALETTE 25
   POOL 25
   LANE 26
   TASK 27
   SUBPROCESS 27
   START EVENT 28
   END EVENT 28
   EXCLUSIVE GATEWAY 29
   PARALLEL GATEWAY 29
   SEQUENCE FLOW 30
   MESSAGE FLOW 30
   DATA OBJECT, MESSAGE, AND DATA STORE 31
   TEXT ANNOTATION 33
   LINK EVENT PAIR (OFF-PAGE CONNECTOR) 33
5. BPMN METHOD: LEVEL 1 35
   STEP 1. DEFINE PROCESS SCOPE 35
   STEP 2. CREATE THE TOP LEVEL DIAGRAM FOR THE HAPPY PATH 36
   STEP 3. ADD TOP-LEVEL EXCEPTION PATHS 39
   STEP 4. EXPAND SUBPROCESSES TO SHOW DETAIL AT CHILD LEVEL 41
   STEP 5. ADD INTERMEDIATE MESSAGE FLOWS TO EXTERNAL POOLS (OPTIONAL) 42
   WHAT ABOUT DATA? 45

6. ELEMENTS OF BPMN STYLE: LEVEL 1 47
    PRINCIPLES OF COMPOSITION.. 47
    ELEMENTARY RULES OF USAGE.. 53

Part III. Level 2: Analytical BPMN 57

7. BPMN'S DEEPER MEANINGS 59
    STEPPING UP TO BPMN LEVEL 2 59
    STARTING AND COMPLETING.. 59
    SENDING AND RECEIVING 61
    AUTOMATED TASKS 64
    DECISIONS AND RULES 66

8. USING SUBPROCESSES 69
    THE VALUE OF SUBPROCESSES 69
    SUBPROCESS TYPES 71

9. START AND END EVENTS 75
    START EVENTS.. 75
    END EVENTS 79

10. INTERMEDIATE EVENTS 83
    CLASSIFYING INTERMEDIATE EVENTS... 84
    TIMER INTERMEDIATE EVENTS 87
    MESSAGE INTERMEDIATE EVENTS 89
    ERROR INTERMEDIATE EVENTS 91
    ESCALATION INTERMEDIATE EVENTS 94
    SIGNAL EVENTS 96
    EVENT SUBPROCESSES 100
    NON-INTERRUPTING EVENTS IN BPMN 1.X 104

11. BRANCHING AND MERGING PATTERNS... 107
    EXCLUSIVE BRANCH... 107
    PARALLEL SPLIT 109
    CONDITIONAL SPLIT... 110
    MERGING AND JOINING 112
    OTHER BRANCH AND MERGE PATTERNS... 117

12. EXCEPTION HANDLING PATTERNS.. 119
    CATEGORIZING EXCEPTIONS 119
    INTERNAL BUSINESS EXCEPTION... 120
    USER ACTION... 121
    FAULT.. 122
    TIMEOUT 122
    UNSOLICITED EXTERNAL EXCEPTION 124
    SOLICITED RESPONSE EXCEPTION 129
    RETHROWING EXCEPTIONS 131
    INTERPRETING EXCEPTION HANDLING PATTERNS IN THE DIAGRAM 137
    EXCEPTION PROPAGATION PATTERNS 139

13. REPEATING ACTIVITIES AND POOLS 145
    LOOPING ACTIVITIES.. 146

MULTI-INSTANCE ACTIVITIES..148
MULTI-INSTANCE POOLS...149
MODELING BATCH PROCESSING 151

14. TRANSACTIONS...153
WHAT ARE TRANSACTIONS? 153
COMPENSATION EVENTS AND COMPENSATING ACTIVITIES 154
CANCEL EVENT..155
COMPENSATION THROW-CATCH 155
USING COMPENSATION..156

15. BPMN METHOD: LEVEL 2 159
STEP 6. REFINE BRANCH/MERGE NOTATION 160
STEP 7. REFINE FOR CHANNEL-DEPENDENT START 161
STEP 8. REFINE FOR ITERATIVE BEHAVIOR...162
STEP 9. REFINE EXCEPTION HANDLING PATTERNS 163

16. ELEMENTS OF BPMN STYLE: LEVEL 2 169

17. MODEL SERIALIZATION AND INTERCHANGE 181
THE MODEL INTERCHANGE PROBLEM 181
BPMN AND MODEL PORTABILITY 184

Part IV. Level 3: Executable BPMN 187

18. WHAT IS EXECUTABLE BPMN? 189

19. DATA 191
DATA OBJECTS, PROPERTIES, AND DATA STORES 191
DATA INPUTS AND OUTPUTS..192
DATA ASSOCIATIONS 193
DATA MAPPING 193
EXAMPLES 193

20. SERVICES AND MESSAGES..197

21. HUMAN TASKS..203

22. FOR FURTHER LEARNING 207

23. INDEX 209

24. ABOUT THE AUTHOR 213

Why are you reading this book? Is it because BPMN is cool? No, BPMN is not cool or sexy. Neither is it elegant or especially profound. In fact, it looks a lot like plain old flowcharting that has been around forever.

I hope you are reading this because you want to improve how you manage your business processes, document how they really work, and then make them work better: faster, with fewer errors, more compliant with regulations and policies, and easier to change. Modeling your processes is the first step to all that, and today BPMN has emerged as the "right" way to do process modeling.

Why BPMN?

Why is BPMN – which stands for Business Process Modeling Notation – the right way? For starters, it is a standard. It is not owned by a tool vendor or consulting company. You pay no fee or royalty to use it. Because BPMN is a standard, the cost of process modeling tools has dropped by an order of magnitude. In fact, some very good BPMN tools are free. That means you can afford to deploy process modeling and a "culture of process" broadly across your organization – even across your industry.

Tool affordability is only a small part of the story. While BPMN's similarity to flowcharting notation makes it friendly and familiar to business users, its unique advantages lie in features missing from traditional flowcharting. Each shape and symbol has a precisely defined meaning, with rules about what can connect to what and what those connections signify. That means others, inside or outside your company, can understand the diagrams you create without you being there to explain them. Actually, the diagram is just the surface layer of a complete XML language for process definition. Using that language, you can project process performance by running your model through a simulation engine, or even automate the process by executing your model on a process engine.

Moreover, BPMN adds a dimension absent entirely in flowcharts: support for *event-triggered behavior*. An event is "something that happens" while the process is underway: The customer calls to change the order. A service level agreement is in danger of being violated. An expected response does not arrive in time. A system is down. These things happen all the time. If your model is going to represent the "real" process and not just the idealized "happy path," it needs to say *what should happen* when those exceptions occur. BPMN lets you do that.

By combining business-friendliness with expressiveness for exception handling, BPMN has a real chance to achieve that elusive goal of business-IT alignment in BPM. From the beginning, BPMN was designed to be business-friendly. Its creators consciously rejected existing modeling standards like UML as too "IT-centric." They gave BPMN an overall look – swimlanes, with boxes and diamonds connected by arrows – that was already familiar to business. At the same time, they made sure the BPMN diagram could be more than just a sketch. They gave each shape precise operational semantics, so that the meaning of the diagram was not dependent on the modeler's whim, but standardized and subject to automated validation.

In addition to precisely defining the semantics of the diagram, BPMN specifies the technical details that the modeler can attach to each shape in the diagram, details that can be used to *execute* the model as an automated workflow! With BPMN version 1, most tools for designing and running executable processes – so-called BPM Suites – have used BPMN just for the "abstract" flow diagram, ignoring BPMN's execution-related attributes in favor of their own vendor-specific ones. This is changing. Beginning with BPMN 2.0, software giants like IBM, Oracle, and SAP have begun to make BPMN simultaneously a diagramming notation for process description and analysis, and an XML language for executable process design.

BPMN doesn't *require* you to create executable processes. In fact, most BPMN users today are simply documenting existing process flows and proposing "to-be" improvements, with little immediate thought of process execution. But, if you want, BPMN lets you take that to-be model and make it executable, without starting over.

In other words, BPMN provides a common language for describing process behavior, shareable by business and IT. We've never had that before.

Why This Book?

As you dig into it, you quickly realize that BPMN, while simple and business-friendly on the surface, can turn maddeningly complex when you want to harness its full expressive power. In fact, many BPMN examples you can find on the web – and even in BPMN books – are ambiguous, clumsy, or just plain invalid. That is the real motivation for this book.

I started BPMessentials.com in early 2007 to teach process modelers how to use BPMN correctly. Since then around 1000 students have taken the two-day course, either in the classroom or online. Initial versions of that training, based on BPMN 1.0, basically summarized the specification, with a bit extra on which elements were the important ones to know and how to project performance improvement using simulation. I found the "techies" in the class usually got it; the business folks sometimes struggled. Subsequent revisions of the training material, updated to BPMN 1.1, devoted more time explaining underlying concepts and practical tips on things not in the spec, what you might call the "art" of process modeling. That helped a lot, but students would still sometimes say, "I see how this works and I understand the value. But I'm not sure everyone on my team wants this level of detail in their models." With BPMN skills and objectives, one size does not fit all.

Now in its third year, my BPMN training continues to be shaped by the most basic student questions: *Is the customer part of the process or external to it? If a message can only express communication with external entities, how do I show communications inside the process? How can I show a possible ad hoc user action from the middle of an activity?* Basic questions like these have made me really stop and think. In a few areas, BPMN provides no good solution. In most cases, however, BPMN provides an answer, but you would not find it spelled out anywhere in the specification.

Out of my BPMN training experience I have gained two important insights, which form the central themes of this book (and of the latest version of the BPMessentials training):

1. Clarity and effectiveness of BPMN diagrams depend more on things *not stated in the spec* than on the official definitions and rules. I call those other things *method and style*. The BPMN spec proudly offers no guidance on either one, but they are critical to effective modeling.

2. While BPMN diagrams can indeed serve as the common process language shared by business and IT, that is not its only value or its only level of use. For example, detailed modeling of exception paths may not be necessary for business users trying to do basic process mapping and improvement. Those users get benefit from BPMN as well, but using a different method and style. There must be *multiple levels* of BPMN method and style in order to address the separate goals and concerns of business users, analysts and architects, and IT developers. The trick is *aligning* them so that each level is a refinement of the previous one. This allows groups at all skill levels to collaborate in BPM around a common view of the process.

These insights as a BPMN educator, an outside interpreter of the spec, were the original motivation for this book. But another important one arose only *after* I began writing it. It was essentially an accident. In the fall of 2008, one section of an early public draft[1] of the BPMN 2.0 submission to OMG was so tangled and obtuse that I rewrote it and sent it to the team drafting the submission. The team informed me that if I wanted them even to look at my language, I would need to sign a ten-page participation agreement and Fedex copies of it all over the world. Was that an invitation to join? OK, I took it!

Thus I became an active member of the BPMN 2.0 working group. This gave me a close-up view of how standards like BPMN are created and the thinking that goes into them. What I found in this case surprised me, since the team, led by IBM, Oracle, and SAP, was not thinking about the kind of process modeling my BPMessentials students were trying to do. Their focus was creating an executable process language behind the notation. In the revised specification, the execution tail would be wagging the modeling dog!

Actually, there is little cause for worry. The basic notation is mostly unchanged from BPMN 1.x, and includes some additions extremely useful for all process modelers. But the spec itself has increased an order of magnitude in technical complexity. Moreover, since its focus is on executable processes, the spec still does a poor job of explaining fundamental concepts as they

---

[1] "Public" to OMG members only.

relate to non-executable modeling. These remain matters of method and style. That makes a book like this one more important than ever.

The Missing Piece: Method and Style

So we come back to the central themes of this book: method and style. My goal is to explain how to create BPMN diagrams that stand on their own, that express the exception paths as clearly as the happy path, and that can be shared effectively by business and IT.

To do it, the book weaves three elements.

1. The notation

The first is the notation itself, what the various shapes and symbols mean, and rules about where each can be used. It starts with information defined in the BPMN specification, which you could download for free from the OMG website[2] or from www.bpmnstyle.com, the website for this book. A digest of the spec, however, is not everything you need to use BPMN effectively. Not even close.

BPMN is, after all, the work of a committee, a compromise. In fact, BPMN 2.0 is a negotiated settlement between rival committees! Consequently, it's a bit of a hodgepodge. It combines the notation for modeling business *processes* with an alternative notation, called *choreography*,[3] for modeling trading partner interactions, and forces them to share a common metamodel.

Even within the process modeling section, the spec fails to distinguish the elements needed for creating non-executable models from those only needed for process execution. Nor does it distinguish the important shapes and symbols – the ones all tools support and modelers actually use – from the unimportant ones, seldom used, and missing from the palette of most BPMN tools.

The notation contains redundant elements and patterns. There may be three different ways to express the same thing in the diagram. In addition, some diagram patterns are allowed that probably should be illegal, while for some other useful behaviors BPMN offers no solution at all. Most unfortunately, the narrative portions of the spec still fail to explain the deeper meaning of its most basic concepts, such as process, decision, event, sequence flow, or message.

Thus information provided in the BPMN spec is insufficient for learning to use the notation properly. Effective BPMN modeling requires understanding things *not* stated in the spec. This book shows you which elements and diagram patterns are the ones you really need to know, and when and how to use them. It explains the deeper meanings of the BPMN shapes, and reveals the hidden assumptions underlying them.

---

[2] See www.omg.org or www.bpmn.org.

[3] This is not the same as choreography as defined in BPMN 1.x. Message flow interactions between a process and external entities are now called *collaboration*. In BPMN 2.0, choreography is an entirely new conceptual/notational framework. It might become an important part of BPMN someday, but it is not a concern of process modelers today, and we ignore it in this book.

This will remove much of BPMN's mystery, but you still need more to use it effectively.

2. BPMN Method

If all members of your team are going to create BPMN models that can stand on their own, understandable without an accompanying narrative, you also need a consistent *method*. By method I mean a cookbook approach starting from a blank sheet of paper and leading to a complete BPMN model. OMG boasts that BPMN has no methodology, since how it is used depends on what you are trying to do. But confronted with a complex palette of shapes, symbols, and connectors, modelers *need* a methodology or they will get lost. That should not imply, however, a single method used across the board. The details of the method necessarily depend on the modeler's objective.

For that reason, the book describes three distinct levels of BPMN use, each with its own methodology.

- Level 1, or *descriptive BPMN*, limits the palette to a basic working set of shapes and symbols readily understood by any business person and supported by almost all BPMN tools. The Level 1 method starts from a blank sheet of paper and provides a basic framework for structuring the process model: *What starts and ends it? What does the instance represent? What are the basic steps in the so-called "happy path"? What steps are concurrent or conditional? Besides the happy path end state, what are the important exception end states of the process?* The Level 1 method relaxes some of BPMN's more restrictive rules without sacrificing semantic clarity. It also conditions the modeler to BPMN's top-down hierarchical style, important to handling complex real-world processes.

- Level 2, or *analytical BPMN*, draws on the full palette of BPMN shapes and symbols, but the method emphasizes the diagram elements and patterns most commonly used. It picks up where the Level 1 method leaves off. The primary emphasis is on events and exception handling, matching each type of event or exception to a specific *pattern* in the diagram. The method emphasizes consistency with the more technical meaning of the BPMN shapes, critical to the goal of a common process language shared by business and IT.

- Level 3, or executable BPMN, deals with the XML language underneath the shapes. It is brand new in BPMN 2.0, and as of this writing, tools implementing it have not yet been released. This book does not provide a Level 3 method, but illustrates how details such as data, services, messages, and human task assignment are specified and used in executable BPMN.

3. BPMN Style

The final element, *style*, reflects the "art" of process modeling. It is easy to create models that are perfectly valid according to the BPMN spec but are ambiguous, difficult for others to decipher. Style means consistent application of principles and best practices that allow diagrams to be readily understood even when they express complex behavior. Some of these principles and rules are implied by the spec even though they are not clearly spelled out. Others are admittedly personal preference.

It is perfectly fair for you to ask, "Who appointed you the arbiter of BPMN style?" And I would have to answer, "No one." But someone has to be the first to do it.

The style sections of this book are structured after Strunk and White's *The Elements of Style*, still a reliable set of principles for writing effective English prose. Even though that book goes back to Professor Strunk's lecture notes of 1919, it demonstrates that basic principles of style can stand the test of time. My book tries to apply similar principles to the creation of BPMN models, with the goals of clarity, expressiveness, and consistency with BPMN's precise technical meaning. There are separate chapters describing Level 1 and Level 2 modeling style.

BPMN Training

The book provides many examples, and I encourage readers to reproduce them using a software tool. It is difficult, if not impossible, to become proficient at BPMN simply from reading a book. Like any skill, you really learn BPMN only by *doing* it, working through the creation of diagrams that clearly express your intended meaning. But this book is meant only as *education*. It is not BPMN *training*.

There is an old joke about sex education vs. sex training that I won't repeat here. But you get the idea. Training involves practice, exercises and discussion of solutions, why certain ways work better than others. I provide such training, both online and in the classroom, through several channels: BPMessentials[4], BPMS Watch[5], the BPM Institute[6], and other venues, and others provide it as well. This book could be used as a reference for that training, or as a textbook in a college course on BPMN, but by itself it is not training.

BPMN Tools

The method assumes use of a software tool. BPMN diagrams can be drawn by hand, but serious modeling requires using a tool. With BPMN you have many to choose from, including good free ones. While BPMN is a standard, the tools are not all the same. Many of the free ones are essentially just drawing aids. They can reproduce the standard shapes and connectors but do not "understand" what they mean. They cannot, for example, validate your model, or create XML interchangeable with another BPMN tool.

The non-free tools are not all the same, either. Some support all of the BPMN shapes and symbols, while others – particularly those from vendors with a process execution engine – may support just a subset. Some tools adhere strictly to the symbols, markers, and semantics specified

---

[4] Online, classroom, and train-the-trainer. For more information, see www.bpmessentials.com

[5] Private classroom training and consulting. See www.brsilver.com/wordpress

[6] Public 2-day classes. See www.bpminstitute.org/index.php?id=523

by the standard, while others do not. Some allow you to create *collaboration diagrams* linking the process with external participants, while others do not. Some naturally support *hierarchical modeling* with subprocesses – essential to the method and style described in this book – more easily than others. Some let you *simulate* process performance without providing executable process components, or even providing technical detail of process activities, while others do not. Simulation is not part of the BPMN standard, so each tool does it differently.

Prior to version 2.0, the BPMN standard did not even attempt to specify requirements for "compliance". As a consequence, many tools claim to be BPMN-compliant but really are not. BPMN 2.0's section on "process modeling conformance" does little to improve things. It says that tools claiming such conformance must "support" all parts of the metamodel related to process modeling, even those just important for executable design. Strictly interpreted, no tool will likely be conformant for a long time. Loosely interpreted, it's no different than before. Other efforts to promote interoperability of BPMN tools are going on outside of OMG, and we discuss them in Chapter 17.

The diagrams used in this book were created using Process Modeler for Visio, an add-in to Microsoft Visio created by ITP Commerce[7]. This is the tool I use in my BPMessentials training. It supports all of the BPMN standard, and I had access to the new BPMN 2.0 shapes through a pre-release version. But in principle, the BPMN models you create should not depend on which tool you use. BPMN is a standard. That's the whole point.

Nevertheless, some readers will surely find that the BPMN tool they are currently using does not support all the shapes, symbols, and patterns described in this book. The most likely reason is that the book is based on version 2.0 of the BPMN standard, which at this writing is brand new. Tool vendors are often loath to advertise which version of the standard they support, so here is an easy way to tell.

If your tool can draw a shape that looks like this

but not a shape that looks like this

then it is based on BPMN 1.0. It is fine for BPMN Level 1, but not the best for BPMN Level 2, since events that send a message and those that receive a message both use the white envelope icon and are indistinguishable in the diagram.

If your tool can draw a shape that looks like this

---

[7] Pre-release of Process Modeler for Visio 6.0. See www.itp-commerce.com for more information.

or a shape with a black envelope like this

then it is based on BPMN 1.1 or later. This is a better choice for Level 2 modeling, since it uses the color of the icon to distinguish "throwing" events from "catching" ones, and adds a valuable new event type, called Signal.

BPMN 2.0 is even better. It adds an extremely valuable new class of *non-interrupting* events, describing common real-world behavior that was not easily captured in BPMN 1.x. It also formalizes the metamodel and execution semantics, important to software architects, and adds a standard XML interchange format, important for interchanging models between tools. If your tool does not yet support BPMN 2.0, don't worry. There are relatively few notational differences between BPMN 1.x[8] and 2.0, and even tools that claim BPMN 2.0 compliance still may not support all the new shapes and symbols. If your tool includes shapes that look like these

 or or (non-interrupting events)...

then it is definitely based on BPMN 2.0.

BPMN's Unlikely Road

The ability to go from documentation of as-is process flow to executable design of an improved to-be process, within the confines of a single notation, is unique to BPMN. Nevertheless, BPMN's road to widespread acceptance has been an unlikely one.

BPMN began as the visual design layer of a new type of "transactional workflow" system created by a consortium called BPMI.org, led by a dotcom-era startup named Intalio. Leveraging the distributed standards-based architecture of the web and web services, this new type of BPM would be a radical break from the proprietary workflow systems of the client/server era. One key difference would be making the process execution language – the code that runs on a process engine to automate and track the process flow – a *vendor-independent standard*. As it developed the language, called BPML, BPMI.org reached a peak of 200 members, essentially all the major software vendors except IBM and Microsoft.

Another difference would be business empowerment. "In a nutshell," recalls BPMI's founder Ismael Ghalimi, "it would allow less-technical people to build transactional applications by drawing simple flow charts."[9] BPML would not be coded by hand, but generated from a diagram, which would also be standardized: BPMN. Existing process diagramming standards like UML were rejected as too IT-centric. BPMI demanded something more business-friendly. Howard

---

[8] BPMN 1.2 is virtually unchanged from BPMN 1.1, which is more widely adopted. In this book I refer to them collectively as BPMN 1.x.

[9] For a firsthand account, see Why All This Matters, Ismael Ghalimi, http://itredux.com/2008/10/24/why-all-this-matters/

Smith and Peter Fingar fleshed out the promise of business-empowerment through BPMN in a seminal 2002 book, *BPM: The Third Wave*. Although the book has been criticized for blurring the line between vision and reality, it correctly predicted that empowering business people to manage their own processes would be critical to the evolution of BPM.

BPMI.org produced a spec for BPMN 1.0 in 2004. Ghalimi continues: "Among [the BPMI members were] very many process modeling tool vendors who loved the idea of a standard notation for processes, and very many workflow vendors who hated the idea of a standard language for executing them. The former understood that they could provide a lot of value around the core process modeling tool. The latter knew all too well that fragmentation of the market helped preserve the status quo…"

The central tension seen today within BPMN's stewardship thus was present from the beginning. Originally intended as a business-empowering tool for process automation, BPMN was instead embraced for non-executable process description and analysis, while BPML – the "code" it automatically generated – was seen as a threat by workflow automation vendors once they understood the implications of standardizing the runtime.

As it turned out, no one had anything to fear from BPML. IBM and Microsoft countered with BPEL, a slightly different language layered on top of the new web services standard called WSDL. In an instant those two vendors trumped 200, and BPML was effectively wiped out. In 2005, needing a new home, BPMI.org was absorbed into the Object Management Group, ironically home of the spurned alternative, UML. OMG formally adopted the BPMN 1.0 spec in 2006 and a minor update, BPMN 1.1, in January 2008.

It's a familiar cycle in the world of IT standards, one that normally leads to quiet oblivion. By the end of 2008, however, against all odds, BPMN turned out to be not on the road to oblivion but approaching a tipping point of mass adoption. And here, most ironically, the credit has to go to those proprietary workflow – today we would call them BPM Suite (BPMS) – vendors who supposedly hated BPML from the start! Along with Intalio, these vendors were the ones who developed and widely disseminated free BPMN tools and popularized the notion of business-IT collaboration via shared BPMN models. Savvion, TIBCO, Lombardi, Appian, BizAGI… thank you!

The explanation is simple. Smith and Fingar were right… sort of. Business empowerment *is* the key to BPM, and BPMN provides that – not the executable code, but the precise flow logic that code would have to implement. Even though the BPMN specification makes no explicit distinction between its elements that are part of the process *model* and those required for executable *design*, it is pretty obvious which is which. The "model" elements are essentially those displayed in the diagram; the execution-related elements don't appear in the diagram, but are captured in the XML underneath.

The BPM Suite vendors simply adopted the *modeling* parts of BPMN – the diagram – and ignored the *execution* parts. Executable details could be added to the process model, but each BPMS would do this in its own way. Thus BPMN 1.x today – as implemented by the majority of modeling tool and BPMS vendors and *as it is actually used in practice* – is not by itself executable, although it is incorporated in many vendor-specific executable design tools. And that suits the vast majority of process modelers just fine. Few are even thinking about execution in a BPMS, anyway. They are business analysts and process architects, not developers.

That summarizes the current situation, but it's not the end of the story. Now BPMN 2.0 is on its way. It will deliver at last a key missing piece, an XML interchange format for BPMN models. It's amazing that BPMN has achieved the success it has without that feature, but somehow that was never a priority at either BPMI.org or OMG. The new version will also connect BPMN with OMG's broader Model Driven Architecture (MDA) efforts by means of a formal *metamodel*.

In fact, it was OMG's original intention that this metamodel, called BPDM, would *redefine* BPMN 2.0, taking the emphasis off the particulars of the notation and placing it on abstract semantics that could be mapped to *any* process modeling language. That was a bit too abstract for three BPMS heavyweights – IBM, Oracle, and SAP – who countered with a rival proposal that formalizes the execution semantics of BPMN itself.[10] Their vision would return BPMN to its roots, as a business-friendly graphical front end to a standardized process execution language! In the end, the BPDM team withdrew their submission, electing to merge their ideas into the IBM-Oracle-SAP proposal, which is now BPMN 2.0.

The notation is mostly unchanged from BPMN 1.x, but there are some valuable new event types and, of course, the long-awaited XML interchange format. Most of the change from BPMN 1.x to BPMN 2.0 concerns executable BPMN, but even for non-executable modeling, BPMN 2.0 is a big step in the right direction.

In world of BPM tools, BPMN 2.0 marks a tipping point. BPMN 1.x adoption was spearheaded by the small BPMS "pureplay" vendors. With BPMN 2.0, the biggest software companies in the world are leading the charge. Going forward, if a process modeling tool uses some other notation, it will be seen as "proprietary," "legacy," or some other euphemism for software dinosaur. Somehow, against all odds, BPMN has become *the* important standard in BPM.

"Business Modeling" Is More Than BPMN!

Business architects and other BPM practitioners never cease to remind me that process modeling, as defined by BPMN, is only one component of the *business modeling* needed to properly describe, analyze, transform, and optimize a company's business processes. I don't disagree with this. BPMN really just describes processes in terms of their activity flows. That alone encompasses quite a lot, but admittedly more information is needed to do BPM.

So what is missing? I asked Brett Champlin, president of the Association of BPM Professionals (www.abpmp.org) and a BPM practitioner himself at a major insurance company, what

---

[10] Author's note: In December 2008, toward the end of the drafting cycle, I joined this submission team and have tried to represent the interests of business analysts and process architects – the actual users of BPMN today – in the final specification.

information, beyond that captured by BPMN, needs to be modeled to support a process manager in an enterprise BPM program. He gave me a long list, which I have rearranged as follows:

Enterprise or Line of Business
- High-level business context, describing the business's relationships to Competitors, Regulators, Suppliers, Business Partners, Customers, Community, etc.
- Strategic Objectives and Performance Metrics
- Controls and Constraints
- Markets, Customers
- Products (goods and services)
- Locations

Operational, Cross-Process
- Value Chains and Process Portfolios
- Operational Goals and Objectives
- Policies
- Performance Metrics and KPIs
- Organizational Structure and Roles.

Process-Specific
- Activity resource requirements
- Revenue and Costs, both activity-based and resource-based
- Job Aids (instructions for human performers)

Technical
- IT Systems
- Services
- Data

Each of these items can be described by one or more models and attachments, linked in some relationship to the BPMN model. The fact that BPMN itself does not include them is not, in my view, a deficiency. In fact, a single standard describing all of these models and their interrelationships would be nearly impossible to create. A key reason why BPMN is so widely accepted as a standard is that it does not attempt to do too much.

Business modeling, or BPM at the enterprise level, generally requires a suite of tools built around a *repository*, a database that maintains the relationships between all of the different models, along with governance and change impact analysis. So-called Business Process Analysis (BPA) suites link the BPMN to models of business rules, organizational roles, strategic goals and problems, and master data. Enterprise Architecture (EA) suites link the BPMN to technical models and executable artifacts. The boundaries between these tools and suites will likely blur as vendors begin to implement "executable BPMN" in version 2.0.

Keeping Up With BPMN Changes

As this book goes to press, BPMN 2.0 is entering the Finalization Task Force (FTF) phase, the final stage before official adoption by OMG. It could change a bit in that phase, but typically such changes are minor. In order to keep up with these changes, as well as news about tools that support BPMN 2.0, initiatives to promote BPMN tool interoperability, and other information relevant to the BPMN modeler, readers are referred to the website for this book, www.bpmnstyle.com.

Bruce Silver
June 2009

PART I.
METHOD AND STYLE

CHAPTER 1

How Does a Model Mean?

BPMN is a language for constructing business process models. It's not the only one in existence, but it is far and away the most widely adopted, by modelers and tool vendors alike. BPMN is a multi-vendor standard controlled by the Object Management Group. Using it requires no license or fee, and BPMN tools are generally low-cost. Some are free.

The N in BPMN stands for *notation*, because BPMN is at heart a diagramming standard. A BPMN model contains information that does not show in the diagram, but – for the majority of process modelers, at least – it's the diagram that counts most. Process modelers are a diverse lot, spanning a broad range of technical skill, business knowledge, and modeling objectives. BPMN's unique value is that it can be used by all of them and facilitates communication among them. Because it is based on notions familiar from traditional flowcharting, BPMN is considered business-friendly. At the same time, the notation is linked to a precisely defined semantic model. That means each shape used in the notation has a specific meaning, with defined rules about what is allowed to connect to what, and what each diagram element or pattern signifies. This makes BPMN useful and appealing to IT.

These aspects can be critical to enabling something even more powerful and rare: business-IT collaboration. They allow a diagram understandable by business – perhaps even created by business – to be incorporated directly within an automated implementation of a core business process. We've never had that before.

However, there is an inevitable tension between these aspects, familiarity and simplicity for business, expressiveness and semantic precision for IT. While BPMN has only three shapes – *activity* (rounded rectangle), *gateway* (diamond), and *event* (circle) – expressiveness and precision demand a myriad of subtypes of each, distinguished by border style, the symbols inside, and placement in the diagram. Thus what looks simple on the surface is in reality complex.

The BPMN specification and most books and training about BPMN focus on classifying the various shapes and symbols, defining what each one means. But, as John Ciardi wrote in his classic, *How Does a Poem Mean?*, "the language of experience is not the language of classification." Describing how a process *really* works, or *should* work, and communicating that effectively in a diagram require more than a dictionary definitions of the shapes and symbols. They also demand a consistent method and style, and that is what this book tries to present. In BPMN as in ordinary prose, clarity of expression is essential for effective communication, and it is a learnable skill

Unlocking BPMN's Secrets

While BPMN is widely adopted, few process modelers know how to use it correctly or effectively to achieve its promises of shared understanding and business-IT alignment. One reason is the specification itself.

Here is the great irony of BPMN. Most modelers today are using it for process description and analysis, not executable process design. Whether in IT or line of business, most BPMN users are non-technical, and they are rarely even considering the possibility of an automated implementation. However, BPMN's conceptual foundations assume "executable" processes. Automated execution is the hidden subtext of the BPMN spec, and it continues to shape OMG's vision for BPMN. While most modelers simply want their BPMN models to *describe* their processes, the authors of the BPMN specification are actually thinking about models that *control* process execution.

To be clear, BPMN does not insist process models be executable, but the technical meaning it assigns to the notation's shapes and symbols assume the perspective of a central execution engine. This unstated conceptual frame is one reason why many business users find BPMN's semantic distinctions so befuddling.

BPMN in practice can be used for both types of modeling. In fact, documentation and analysis of non-executable processes benefit greatly from BPMN's semantic precision and expressiveness. But that means finding common ground.

First, BPMN's core concepts and secret assumptions must be decoded.

Beyond its hidden "executable" orientation, BPMN is confusing to business users because the spec never explains its most basic concepts. For example, what exactly is a *process*? What does it mean for a participant to be *inside* vs. *outside* the process? What does it mean to *start* or *complete* an activity, and what does it mean for an activity to complete *normally*? Why does *sending* occur immediately but *receiving* implies a wait? What is the difference between *making* a decision and taking this path or that *based on* a decision, or a related question, what is the difference between a business rule and a routing rule? What does it mean for two activities to be *concurrent* versus *sequential*? What is the difference between *performing* some automated function like Check Credit and *requesting* it? What is the difference between branching based on *data* vs. branching based on an *event*?

The answers to these questions are critical to correct use of the notation. In fact, BPMN has answers to all of them, but you won't easily find them in the spec. Using the notation effectively depends on understanding and even accepting, BPMN's hidden assumptions, its conceptual framework. In other words, to really understand *what* a BPMN model means you first need to come to grips with the question, *how* does a model mean?

In BPMN, a process really means an *orchestration*. That is a sequence of activities in which the flow is *centrally controlled*. When an activity completes, the central controller – the process "engine" – commands or "enables" the next activity in the flow to start. The process model describes all the possible paths from creation of an instance of the process to its eventual completion, along with the logic that determines which path is taken. Software that actually does that in fact exists: It's called a *BPM Suite*, or BPMS, and there are dozens of them available. Even though most process modelers do not have a BPMS, or any other form of centralized orchestration engine, that figment or metaphor is baked deeply into BPMN.

The Questions BPMN Asks

When a company decides to "do" business process management, the first step is usually to model the current state process. The people doing it don't even call it modeling, but process "mapping" or "discovery". The map, model, or diagram – whatever you want to call it – is a kind of flowchart. It is organized into swimlanes representing roles or organizational units, with boxes representing activities linked to other boxes with lines and arrows. That's a flowchart, and BPMN is at heart just that.

The mapper might be inclined to describe the process like this: *First X happens, and then it typically goes to Y, and then finally we do Z.* That's fine. It describes what *usually* happens, leading to a successful end state. Let's call it the *happy path*. But companies don't decide to "do" BPM because of work that follows the happy path. Work that follows the happy path is rarely the reason why the process takes so long, costs so much, or has so many errors. So BPMN asks us to dig deeper.

It starts with really basic questions:

> *How does the process actually start? What event triggers it? Is there more than one possible way it could start?*

> *What determines when the process is complete? Are there different end states for the process, such as one signifying successful completion and others signifying failed or abandoned attempts?*

> *How does the process get from X to Y? Does the person doing Y somehow just "know" it's supposed to happen? You said it "typically" goes to Y, but where else might it go? And why?*

> *How do you know when X is done? Does X always end in the same way? Or besides the normal end states are there exception end states where you don't go on to Y? Are there rules that govern this?*

These are questions BPMN requires you to answer, because they relate to the inner logic of that imaginary "process engine." The mapper's first reaction might be, "Nothing is *making* the process go from X to Y. That's just what happens." But, of course, something is *always* making it go. The logic is just hidden, probably inside the head of whoever happens to be doing X for that particular instance. And there is tremendous value in surfacing that logic, making it explicit in a diagram that all stakeholders in the process can understand. Without that you can't really *manage* the process or improve its performance.

In my BPMessentials training, a student once asked me how to show in the diagram that a certain activity was expected to complete in five hours. I replied that that was not a question that BPMN asks. Instead, BPMN wants you to say *what happens* if the activity is *not* completed in five hours. Do you send a reminder? Notify the manager? Escalate the task? Cancel and abandon the process as a whole? Those are things that belong in the BPMN diagram.

In BPMN, a business process diagram just reveals the *order* of activities, *when* they happen, and under what conditions, including the exceptions. It does not describe, for example, *how* an activity is performed or *where* or *why*. In fact, BPMN barely touches on *what* the activity is or *who* performs it. Those are simply suggested by labels on activities and swimlanes in the diagram. That stands in stark contrast to Professor Scheer's famous ARIS "house," the complex framework of interlinked models describing the full gamut of who-where-what-when-how-why that has long defined "serious" business process modeling. It's not that those other questions are not important – for enterprise-level process governance or even for an ordinary process improvement project, they certainly are – but they are external to the orchestration, and thus outside the domain of BPMN. In fact, they are described by other models, linked to the BPMN model through a repository. BPMN's strength lies in not trying to do too much.

Levels of BPMN Use

In their BPMN reference guide[11], Stephen White and Derek Miers quote the epigram, *All models are wrong, some are useful.* By "wrong" they mean that a model is inherently an idealization, a simplification that leaves out inessential detail. Even restricting the information to the orchestration logic described by BPMN, what is essential or inessential depends on the modeler's purpose. And the purpose of a modeler trying to capture how the as-is process works is not the same as that of another modeler designing an executable process.

This is more than a question of detail. Process modeling for description and process modeling for execution may employ different interpretations of what the shapes and lines in the diagram actually signify. BPMN's strength comes from the fact that it can be used as both an idealized description of the sequence of activities in a process and a blueprint for automating that sequence of activities with an execution engine.

I find it helpful to classify use of BPMN in the real world at three levels, based on how the model is used. These levels reflect different interpretations of what – or how – the model means, to three distinct classes of BPMN users. These levels are not part of the BPMN specification, just part of my pedagogical approach. (Despite that disclaimer, OMG now includes my three-levels concept as "reference material" for its OCEB BPM certification exam!)

---

[11] BPMN Modeling and Reference Guide, Stephen A White, PhD and Derek Miers, Future Strategies, 2008.

Level 1

BPMN Level 1, or *descriptive modeling*, is what business-oriented process mapping is all about: simply documenting the process flow. BPMN Level 1 modeling uses a basic working set of BPMN elements, most familiar from traditional flowcharting, to describe the typical order of activities and what role or organizational unit performs, or is responsible for, each one. It may omit some exception paths, and may ignore some of the rules prescribed by the BPMN specification. The Level 1 modeler is also free to ignore BPMN's fiction of a controlling orchestration engine. Nevertheless, it is possible to apply a method and style to Level 1 modeling so that extending it to Levels 2 and 3 requires only refinement, not major structural change.

Level 2

BPMN Level 2, or *analytical modeling*, leverages the expressive power of the complete notation to describe the activity flow precisely, including the exception paths significant to key performance indicators. Level 2 models obey BPMN's defined semantics and are subject to its validation rules. However, Level 2 models are *non-executable*. They omit technical details – specification of data structures and expressions, for example – that would be required to execute the model on a process engine.

The BPMN specification does not clearly separate execution-related information elements in the model from the rest, but the distinction is straightforward. Level 2 models are essentially bounded by what you can see in the diagram. Diagram labels take the place of the missing technical details. For example, instead of using formal data expressions to specify the branching logic at a gateway, Level 2 models simply label the gateway and the paths out of it so that the business meaning is clear.

Thus BPMN Level 2 reflects a *business-oriented perspective*, and is understandable by business analysts and business architects, not just IT. Nevertheless, it requires disciplined thinking and attention to detail. It exploits BPMN's power to express the events and exceptions that govern real-world process performance and quality, and thus can be used to analyze process alternatives, both qualitatively by inspection and quantitatively by simulation analysis. It really is that long-sought *common process language shared by business and IT*.

Most business architects, business process analysts, and business analysts can learn to use BPMN at Level 2, but it is difficult for some business users. One reason for the difficulty is Level 2 forces the modeler to go along with BPMN's assumption (or pretense) of a central controlling engine that "makes" the process advance from one step to the next, even when there is none in reality. That mental leap is difficult for some, but it is the key to the making models complete and self-consistent.

There are actually two distinct use cases for BPMN Level 2. One is as just described: documentation of as-is and to-be process flow for purposes of analysis but not execution in a process engine. The modeler can leverage the expressive power of BPMN's full palette of activity, gateway, and event types to describe and analyze the operational behavior of the process, even if there is no intention to automate it.

The second use case is creating the business view of an executable process design in a BPMS. Here BPMN is used to define the process model underlying the executable design, but absent technical detail. Why is this not Level 3, executable BPMN? The reason is that the BPM Suite does not use BPMN for that executable detail. Instead, it layers its own execution-related attributes on top of the BPMN model. The executable design is thus vendor-proprietary, but the underlying flow model, as expressed in the BPMN diagram, complies with the BPMN standard, and remains visible to business throughout the implementation cycle.

This hybrid style is in fact the way the majority of BPM Suites work today, including those from Adobe, Appian, Cordys, Fujitsu, Lombardi, Oracle, SAP, Savvion, SoftwareAG, TIBCO, and Vitria. In fact, promotion of BPMN by these vendors is a key reason for its widespread adoption as a standard. However, the BPMN tools provided by BPMS vendors frequently deviate in various ways from the BPMN specification. They may omit activity, event, and gateway types that their process engine does not support, and may include other constructs not described by BPMN.

Level 2 modeling is the main focus of this book. Mastering it requires understanding of BPMN's hidden assumptions and the deeper meaning of its core concepts, and the book explains them. We also provide a method and style that bridges the gap between Level 1 models and the more disciplined approach required by IT, focusing on events and exception handling, using specific diagram patterns to identify distinct classes of exceptions.

Level 3

BPMN Level 3, or executable modeling, is brand new with BPMN 2.0. Whether it becomes the accepted standard for executable process design remains to be seen, although the undeniable influence of its principal backers, IBM, Oracle, and SAP, assures it will play a significant role.

BPMN Level 3 is similar to the second use case of Level 2, except that the executable detail is fully captured in BPMN standard attributes. It is part of OMG's broader goal of Model Driven Architecture (MDA), in which executable systems are governed by graphical models rather than "code." BPMN at Level 3 is ostensibly targeted at developers, not business architects or analysts. However, as BPM tools mature, we can expect to see them hide much of the technical complexity of executable process design, so that business process analysts and architects will be able to create robust process implementations with little or no developer support.

BPMN Level 3 begins with a Level 2 diagram and adds detail in the XML underneath the shapes and symbols. It transforms BPMN from a diagramming notation to an XML language for executable process design. As of this writing, tools supporting that language have not yet been released. Those tools will determine the method and style appropriate to Level 3, but we provide in this book a glimpse into how that language works to specify process data, service interfaces, and human task assignment.

PART II.
LEVEL 1: DESCRIPTIVE BPMN

CHAPTER 2

BPMN Level 1 By Example

Consider the process to handle an order. The company receives the order, checks the buyer's credit, fulfills the order, and sends an invoice. In BPMN, that looks like this:

Figure 2-1. Basic order process

The thin circle at the start of the process is called a *start event*. It indicates where the process starts. The thick circle at the end is called an *end event*, signifying the process is complete. The rounded rectangles are *activities*. Activities represent actions, specific work performed, as distinct from functions (e.g., Order Handling) or states (e.g., Order Received). To reinforce this, activities should be named in the form VERB-NOUN.

This diagram is not a complete description of the process. It simply describes the normal sequence of activities when nothing goes wrong, the so-called *happy path*. What could go wrong? Well, the buyer's credit might not be sufficient, or the goods might not be in stock. Those situations would represent failed orders. So a more complete representation of the process might look like this:

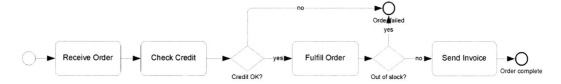

Figure 2-2. Order process with exception paths

The diamond shapes are called *gateways*. They represent branch points in the flow. BPMN provides a number of different gateway types, but this one – the most common, with no symbol inside – means take one path or the other based on some logical condition, such as *Is the buyer's credit OK?* or *Are the order items in stock?* The flow logic is indicated in the diagram by the combination of a label on the gateway and labels on the arrows, called *sequence flows*, out of the gateway. Gateways are a common way to separate *exception paths* from the happy path.

Note we now have two end events, one labeled *Order failed* and the other *Order complete*. BPMN does not require multiple end events like this, but it is best practice to use separate end events when the process can end in different *states*, such as one representing success and the other failure, and to label them appropriately.

Also notice that not all of the process's activities are performed for every instance of the process. If the credit check fails, for example, we do not fulfill the order. If the order items are not in stock, we do not send the invoice. This is common sense, and the BPMN indicates this explicitly.

BPMN also lets us show who performs each activity, using *swimlanes*, or to use the BPMN-specific term, *lanes* (Figure 2-3). Lanes typically represent roles or organizational units that perform activities in the process. They are drawn as subdivisions of the rectangle containing the process, called a *pool*. You sometimes see pools labeled with the name of an organization, but for pools that contain activity flows – some don't, as we will see later – it's best practice to label them with the name of the process.

We can also indicate the type of activity represented. It is generally useful to distinguish human tasks from automated ones, and these are indicated in the diagram by different task icons. Lanes really apply only to activities; we can place gateways and events wherever it's convenient in the diagram. Some people like to put systems in their own lanes as well, either one lane for all systems or one lane per system. I tend not to do that, but it's really a matter of preference.

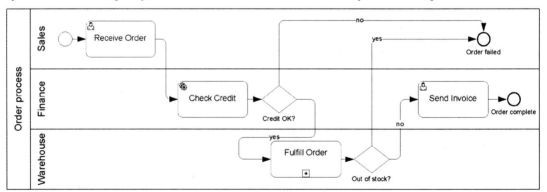

Figure 2-3. Order process in swimlanes

What type of activity is *Fulfill Order*? It does not have an icon representing a human or automated task, but a little [+] marker instead. That is a *subprocess*, one of BPMN's most important concepts. A subprocess is an activity containing subparts that can be expressed as a process flow. In contrast, a *task* is an activity with no defined subparts.

A subprocess is simultaneously an *activity*, a step in a process that performs work, and a *process*, a flow of activities from a start event to one or more end events. In the diagram, a subprocess can be rendered either *collapsed*, as a single activity shape, or *expanded* as a process diagram in its own right. BPMN tools typically let you toggle or hyperlink between those two views, allowing zoom in and out to view the process diagram at any level of detail.

One way to represent the expanded view of a subprocess is *inline* in the diagram, like so:

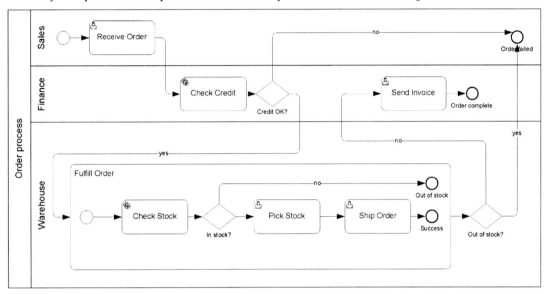

Figure 2-4. Order process including expanded subprocess

With inline expansion, the process flow is enclosed in an enlarged activity shape, the rounded rectangle. Figure 2-3 and Figure 2-4 mean exactly the same thing, but Figure 2-4 provides an additional level of detail. Note that the expanded view of *Fulfill Order* looks just like a process. It has a start event, a flow of activities, and end events. The start of the *Fulfill Order* process is triggered by the sequence flow into it, which, we can see from the diagram, occurs after *Check Credit* whenever the credit is OK. When *Fulfill Order* completes, the overall process continues on the sequence flow out of the subprocess.

Here we see the real benefit of using multiple end events to distinguish end states, in this case the *Out of stock* end state and the *Success* end state. By matching the label of the gateway following the subprocess (*Out of stock?*), it is clear the gateway is asking the question, "Did we reach the *Out of stock* end event?"

Inline is not the only way to render expanded subprocesses. In fact, except in simple cases, it is not even the best way. Note that Figure 2-4 takes up a lot more space on the page than Figure 2-3. For real-world processes, managing the page real estate in your diagram is a key concern. Showing all the details of an end-to-end process on one page usually isn't possible. One solution is to use off-page connectors to link to a continuation of the diagram on another page. BPMN provides a notation for this, called a *Link event*. But I recommend a different way – expanding the subprocess on another page of the diagram. Let's see how it works, and then talk about why it's the preferred way.

I call it *hierarchical expansion*, because it expresses the end-to-end process as a hierarchy of diagrams representing *process levels*. The level containing a collapsed subprocess is considered the *parent* of the *child level* containing the expanded view. BPMN tools typically allow the user to hyperlink between the parent- and child-level views of a subprocess.

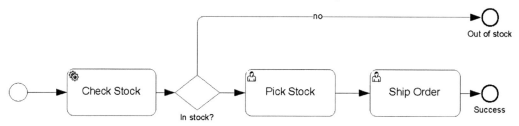

Figure 2-5. Subprocess expansion on a separate page

Figure 2-5 shows the child-level expansion of *Fulfill Order*. Note that it omits the pool shape, which is inherited implicitly from the parent. Remember, this is not a new process but a subprocess of *Order Process*. It also omits the enlarged activity shape surrounding the flow. A child-level expansion can contain lanes, although none are represented in Figure 2-5.

In a hierarchical diagram of *Order Process*, Figure 2-3 depicts the top level and Figure 2-5 depicts the child level. Both are part of a single process model. Each BPMN tool provides its own mechanism for holding the levels of a process model together. Typically, you can navigate between them using hyperlinks.

While inline expansion is useful in simple diagrams, for real-world modeling the hierarchical approach is better. One reason is it allows even a complex process to be captured end-to-end on a single page. That top-level view provides little detail about each component of the process, but it does show how those components – expressed as collapsed subprocesses – relate to each other, as well as how the process interacts with external entities. In other words, it expresses the big picture. You can then drill down into each subprocess at a child level, which can drill down further to a deeper child level, and so on. With hierarchical modeling, additional detail is provided in layers, and you can drill down, or zoom in, to view detail at any level without losing the integrity of a single end-to-end model.

Child-level subprocess expansion does add one bit of complexity when reading the model, in that linked elements may appear on different pages of the diagram instead of together on one page. For example, in Figure 2-4 the end event *Out of stock* and the gateway *Out of stock?* appear on the same page, while in the hierarchical model they appear on separate pages. Once you get used to the hierarchical method, this difficulty rapidly diminishes.

One mistake beginners make is repeating process logic external to the subprocess inside the expanded view. For example, Figure 2-6 is *incorrect* as a child-level expansion of *Fulfill Order*:

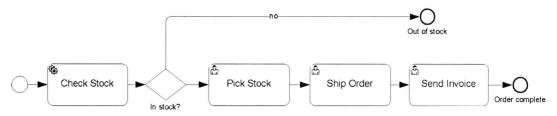

Figure 2-6. Incorrect expansion of the subprocess

The reason is *Send Invoice* is external to the subprocess. In the parent level diagram (Figure 2-3), it comes after *Fulfill Order* is complete. Modeling the expanded subprocess as in Figure 2-6 means the invoice is sent twice, once within *Fulfill Order* and then again afterward. That was probably not the modeler's intent. The way to think about it is that when the child-level expanded subprocess is complete, the flow continues on the sequence flow out of the collapsed subprocess at the parent level.

Taking another look at Figure 2-3, you might decide that simply ending the process if the requested item is out of stock is not really how you handle sales. In reality you would contact the customer and offer a replacement item. If the customer accepts the offer, go on to fulfill the order. That would look something like this:

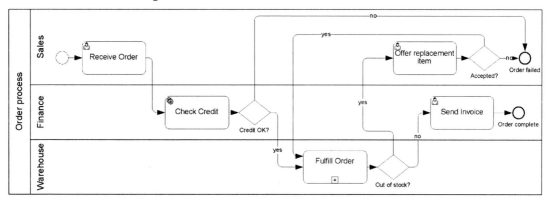

Figure 2-7. Loopback to handle exceptions

In BPMN, unlike process languages such as BPEL, a sequence flow may freely loop back to a previous step. In Figure 2-7, if the replacement offer is accepted, a gateway directs the flow back to *Fulfill Order*. Remember the process is not complete until an end event is reached.

The BPMN spec does not ascribe any significance to whether a sequence flow enters an activity from the left, right, top, or bottom, nor even whether pools and lanes run horizontally or vertically. These are really matters of personal style. I usually try to draw the flow left to right with sequence flows entering activities from the left and exiting from the right. It takes some rearranging to keep line crossings at a minimum, and sometimes it cannot be avoided. But keeping the diagram as neat and consistently organized as possible is important to the objective of shared understanding. Nothing is more frustrating than looking at a diagram someone else has created and being unsure where exactly the process starts and ends.

Now let's consider one last detail of our *Fulfill Order* subprocess. In order to expedite shipment, we'd like to make the shipping arrangements concurrently with picking the stock, that is, in parallel. We originally considered making these arrangements to be part of *Ship Order*, but technically that means we don't do it until after *Pick Stock* completes. At Level 1, it is not uncommon to ignore these "technical semantics" of BPMN, but BPMN does provide a way to show concurrent activities, and it's not too hard to understand.

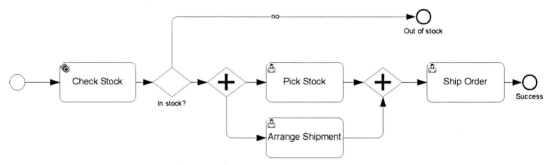

Figure 2-8. Parallel split and join

Figure 2-8 shows how it looks. Again it uses a gateway, in fact two of them, but with a marker inside. A gateway with a + icon inside is a *parallel gateway*, sometimes called an *AND-gateway*. A parallel gateway with one sequence flow in and two or more out is called a *parallel split* or *AND-split*. It means split the flow into parallel, i.e., concurrent, segments. Both *Pick Stock* and *Arrange Shipment* are enabled to start at the same time. If the same shipping clerk performs them both, they cannot be done literally simultaneously. Concurrent really means it does not matter which is done first.

We cannot combine this parallel gateway with the one that precedes it (*In Stock?*) because they mean different things. The *In Stock?* gateway is an exclusive decision, meaning take one path or the other. *After* we take the *yes* path, then the AND-split says we do *Pick Stock* and *Arrange Shipment* in parallel.

What about the second parallel gateway? A parallel gateway with multiple sequence flows in and one out is called an *AND-join* or *synchronizing join*. It means wait for *all* of the incoming sequence flows to arrive before enabling the outgoing sequence flow. In plain English, it means *Ship Order* cannot occur until both *Pick Stock* and *Arrange Shipment* are complete.

Labels on AND-splits and joins (and sequence flows connecting them) usually add no new information, so it is generally safe to omit them.

Unlike "block-structured" process languages, BPMN does not require all the paths out of a parallel split to be merged in a downstream AND-join. They can eventually lead to separate end events. In that case, the process or subprocess is not complete until *all* parallel segments have reached an end event.

You may be asking, where is the customer in this process? Technically, the customer is *external* to our process, not part of it. This is a subtle point, and one we will discuss at length later, but for now suffice it to say that the requester of a process is best modeled as an external participant, not as a lane within the process pool. We model external participants as additional pools in our diagram. But unlike the pool that contains our *Order Process*, the customer pool is empty. We call it a *black-box pool* – meaning customer's internal process is invisible to us – and label it with the name of the role or entity, in this case *Customer* (Figure 2-9).

The customer (like other external participants) interacts with the process by exchanging messages. In BPMN, the term *message* means any communication between the process and an external participant. We can indicate these communications in the diagram with another type of connector, called a *message flow*. A sequence flow is represented by a solid line and can only be drawn *within a pool*; a message flow, a dashed line with an unfilled arrowhead and little circle on the tail, can only be drawn *between two pools*.

In BPMN 2.0, Figure 2-9 is called a *collaboration diagram*. In addition to the activity flow of our internal *Order Process*, it shows the interaction of our process with external participants by means of message flows. Note that the message flows attach to the boundary of the black-box pool and directly to activities and events of our internal, or white-box, pool. (In BPMN 1.1, the pattern of message flows was called *choreography*, but in BPMN 2.0 choreography means a new, specialized type of diagram intended for B2B interactions, and the new term for message flow between pools is *collaboration*.)

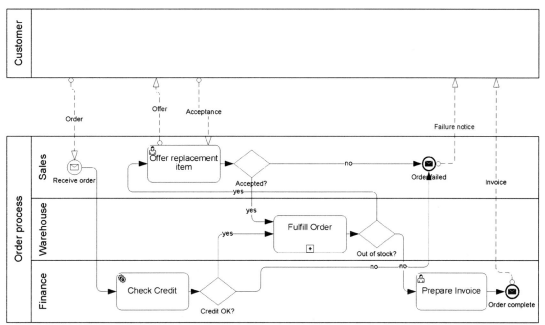

Figure 2-9. Order process in collaboration diagram

You may also have noticed there is an envelope icon inside the start and end events that receive and send the message flows. That icon defines start event *trigger* and end event *result* as messages. A *Message start event* signifies that a new instance of the process is created upon receipt of a message, in this case *Order*. A *Message end event* signifies that a message is sent when the end event is reached. Here we have one end event sending an *Invoice* and another sending a *Failure notice*. BPMN events that listen for, or *catch*, a trigger are shown with white icons; events that send, or *throw*, a result are shown with black icons.

The Message start event replaces the *Receive order* activity in Figure 2-7, and we have changed Figure 2-7's *Send Invoice* to *Prepare Invoice*. The "send" is done by the message end event. We only want to receive the order once, not twice, and similarly send the invoice once. We don't want to duplicate the action of a Message event with an activity that does the same thing.

Finally, we see message flows out of and into the human task *Offer replacement item*. A message flow signifies any communication between the process and external participants – a phone call, fax, or even face-to-face. Activities can send and receive message flows just as events can.

CHAPTER 3

Are You In?

One of the biggest surprises to Level 1 modelers is the idea that the Customer in the previous example is not considered part of the process, but external to it. Actually, the idea has been around since the Rummler-Brache diagrams of the 1980s, what business people today call swimlane diagrams. Geary Rummler was one of the first analysts of business performance from a process perspective and a great influence on the management discipline of BPM. Paul Harmon, editor of BPTrends and a former colleague of Rummler's, recounts[12]:

> An IBM researcher took Rummler's courses and was so impressed with the power of Rummler-Brache diagrams that he created an IBM process methodology called LOVEM. The acronym stood for Line of Vision Enterprise Methodology. The "line", in this case, referred to the swimlane line at the top of a Rummler-Brache diagram that divided the customer from the process and allowed the analyst to see exactly how the process interacted with the customer.

Inherent in analysis of process performance is the interaction of a process with its "customer." In Rummler-Brache and derivatives like LOVEM, the customer was drawn in the top swimlane, and communications across that line represented the customer's perspective on the process. In BPMN, the notation has changed slightly – we show external participants in separate pools – but the concept remains the same.

Still, there are some situations where the initiator of the process might be modeled as an internal participant. How do you know whether the initiator of a process should be modeled as an external pool or as a lane within the process? Here are some factors to consider.

What event marks the start of the process? Don't answer this too hastily. Think about it. In many processes, someone – the Customer – first creates a document that in effect triggers the process. It could be an order form, a loan application, an insurance claim, or a customer service request. Does the process start when the Customer begins to create that document, or when the document is submitted?

---

[12] Paul Harmon, BPTrends Advisor, December 8, 2008,
http://www.bptrends.com/publicationfiles/advisor20081209.pdf

Many beginners would model the first step of such a process with an activity like *Complete Order Form*. That means the process starts when the Customer begins filling out the form. In most cases that is not right, because the process actually starts later, when the completed form is *submitted*.

Why do I say that? Let's consider how the performance or quality of such a process is measured. *How long does the process take? How much does it cost? What percentage of instances have errors?* Usually a retailer, lender, insurance carrier, or customer service provider does not consider the time it takes the Customer to fill out the form, the cost of the Customer's time, or the errors the Customer might make in filling out the form to be part of the process metrics. Those factors might be important from a business standpoint, and the process provider may even provide an elaborate web application intended to make filling out the form quick, easy, and error-free. But the time spent in that application is not usually considered part of the process duration.

Moreover, a form started by the customer might never be submitted. How many times have you shopped online, maybe gotten all the way to the checkout page, and then decided not to submit the order after all? In that case, have you created an instance of the order process or not?

I say not. The order process begins when the order is *submitted and received*. The first step in the BPMN model should be an activity or event labeled *Receive Order*.

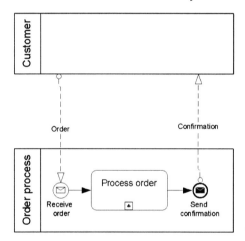

Figure 3-1. Process starts when order is received

> **Rule of thumb 1:** If the process starts upon receipt of a form or other document from a requester (e.g., Customer) and has no other interaction with the requester than returning some form of final status notice (e.g., confirmation/invoice or failure notice), then the requester/Customer should be modeled as an external black-box pool (Figure 3-1).

What about the situation where there are additional communications with the requester in the middle of the process? For example, in processing an insurance claim, the process might require the claimant to provide additional information. Is the claimant inside or outside the process?

Again, I think outside. The reason is that here the claimant is clearly an external business entity, distinct from the organization processing the claim.

Rule of thumb 2: If the requester's interactions with the process are as an external entity, not as part of the organization or team providing the process, the requester should be modeled as an external black-box pool (Figure 3-2).

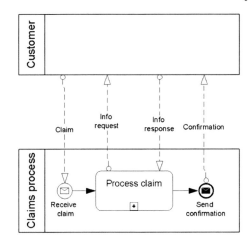

Figure 3-2. External participant as black-box pool

Now the picture gets cloudier. Every December, Managers prepare their annual budget requests, which are reviewed, revised, approved, and rolled up at the division level. Is the Manager internal or external to the process, and is creating the initial budget request part of the process or not?

Here I say internal to the process, so Manager is a lane in the process pool, not an external black-box pool. The reason is the budget process is triggered by an *internal rule*, in this case based on the calendar. It runs on a recurring schedule, let's say December 1 each year. Also, the Manager's time, cost, and quality in creating the initial budget request would likely be considered part of the overall process metrics.

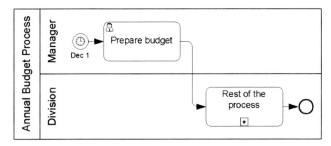

Figure 3-3. Initiation of a scheduled process

Rule of thumb 3: If process start is triggered by some internal rule, such as a preplanned schedule or monitored data condition, as opposed to an external request, then the performer of the process's initial activity should be modeled as a lane within the process pool. BPMN provides special start events, such as *Timer start* and *Conditional start*, to indicate such rule-based triggering (Figure 3-3).

The previous example was edging into a gray area, so now let's just jump into it entirely. An employee prepares a purchase requisition for a piece of capital equipment. The requisition requires a justification memo, which may need revision in order to be approved. For payment, accounting may need confirmation from the employee that the goods were received in good condition. Is the employee internal or external to this process?

It could go either way, depending on the modeler's intent and perspective. The process is initiated upon request, but the employee interacts repeatedly with the process, and is not part of an external entity. By that logic, the employee should be modeled as a lane in the process pool (Figure 3-4). The process would start with a *None start* event (no trigger icon inside), indicating participant-initiated, and filling out the purchase requisition may or may not be included as the first activity.

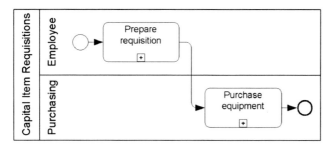

Figure 3-4. Initiation by a process participant

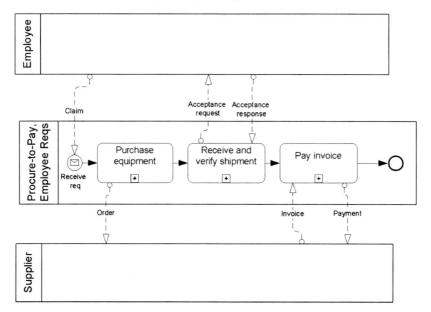

Figure 3-5. Another perspective on the purchase requisition process

That would make sense from the perspective of the employee's department or business unit. However, the corporate purchasing organization might look at that process differently. They might see the employee as Customer, external to the process. In fact, they would consider their process to start upon receipt of a completed, properly approved and authorized requisition, and probably have no interest in the employee's work to complete the form and secure the approvals. The company's Procure-to-Pay process would likely be modeled this way, with Employee (as requisitioner) in a separate black-box pool (Figure 3-5).

So in the end, how the process starts, and whether a participant is inside or outside, is really a matter of perspective.

Why Does It Matter?

The employee purchase requisition example highlights the issue of *process scope*: *When does the process start, and when is it complete?* There may be no single correct answer to this question. It is often a matter of perspective.

In process improvement projects, scope is an important but seldom discussed issue, and experts may disagree. For example, a consultant engaged in helping a project team streamline some aspect of the business may want to restrict the scope to a process within the control and responsibility of the project team and its sponsor. On the other hand, a business architect may argue that the only processes worth a serious improvement effort are "end-to-end," i.e., customer-facing, even though that may increase the cost and risk, or difficulty of gaining executive sponsorship.

BPMN stands happily outside this debate. It can be employed with business processes of any scope. However, firmly establishing the scope of the process being modeled is essential at the outset. That scope determines who is internal and who is external to the process, and matters to measurement of process cost, time, and quality.

The question of whether an entity is internal or external is more than philosophical. It is absolutely central to how the model works. And here we begin to take leave of Level 1 – where we could ignore some of BPMN's deeper meanings – and venture into the land of Level 2, or "real" BPMN.

At Level 1, the solid arrow connections between process activities, called *sequence flows*, can be simply interpreted as time ordering: This activity occurs after that one. But at Level 2, sequence flows represent a *flow of control*. They mean when an activity is complete, the sequence flow triggers the next activity to start. That doesn't mean the next activity "usually starts" or "could possibly start" but "starts." In an executable process, it means that the process engine would *command* that activity to start, invoking an automated task or making a human task appear in the assigned performer's worklist. Most BPMN models are not executable, but sequence flow still means that the activity at the arrowhead is triggered to start when the previous activity completes.

On the other hand, a signal from an external participant, represented by *message flow*, is not a flow of control. It is simply a *request*. A request is not a command. A message flow cannot perform any process action; only an activity in the process can do that. Besides, there may be nothing to receive the request. Some activity or event in the process is needed to *receive* a message flow before it can be acted upon. If the process instance has gone past that point already, the message flow is not received, and has no effect.

Other aspects of BPMN work differently between participants inside and outside the process. For example, we saw previously how an *AND-join gateway* can be used to wait for concurrent activities within the process to complete before continuing. What if one of the activities is *outside* the process, i.e., a response from an external participant? You can still wait for it, but it is modeled differently. We'll get to all that in due course. For now, suffice it to say you should take some time at the outset to think about the scope of your process and whether the initiator is internal or external to it before you start modeling it in BPMN.

CHAPTER 4

Level 1 Modeling Palette

Our Level 1 modeling method is based on a limited palette of BPMN shapes and symbols, a basic working set suitable for descriptive modeling. The set is easily understood by business users and is supported by almost all BPMN tools. Again, it must be emphasized that this palette, like many other recommendations of this book, is not part of the BPMN specification. It is a matter of method and style.

The following BPMN constructs comprise the Level 1 palette:

- Pool and Lane
- User task, Service task
- Subprocess, collapsed and expanded
- Start event (None, Message, Timer)
- End event (None, Message, Terminate)
- Exclusive and Parallel Gateway
- Sequence Flow and Message Flow
- Data Object, Data Store, and Message
- Text Annotation
- Link event pair (off-page connector)

Anyone in your organization who will be involved with process modeling should become familiar with them.

Pool

In BPMN 1.x, a *pool* meant a container for a *process*. Now, BPMN 2.0 says it is only defined for a *collaboration diagram* showing message flow between the process and external participants. In that context, the pool technically represents a *participant* in the collaboration. I don't think that is a particularly helpful definition, since you can have a model in which two collaborating pools represent the same business entity. But it remains true that a white-box poolcontains a single process, and that is still the best way to think about it.

The pool shape is a rectangular box (Figure 4-1). It can be either horizontal, with the label boxed off on the left, or vertical, with the label boxed off on the top. (Boxing off the label distinguishes a pool from a lane, which does not have its label boxed off.) In BPMN 1.x, you commonly see diagrams containing a single process enclosed within a pool. In some diagrams, the pool shape may not be drawn, but a pool is always there by default. In BPMN 2.0, things have changed. A diagram may not contain a single pool; to have pools, you need two or more of them. But as before, the pool shape for one white-box pool may be invisible in the diagram, just implied by default.

Figure 4-1. Pool

The pool label should name the *process* in the case of a white-box pool, and simply name the *participant* – role or business entity – in the case of a black-box (empty) pool.

BPMN attaches strict semantic rules to pools. It cannot contain multiple processes, just one. A sequence flow is confined within a single pool; it cannot cross the pool boundary, connecting to an element in another pool. Conversely, a message flow can only connect elements in separate pools, never two elements in the same pool.

Lane

A *lane* (Figure 4-2) is a subdivision of a process. In BPMN 1.x, lanes were optional and frequently omitted. In BPMN 2.0, at least one lane is always assumed to exist by default in the model, even if not drawn in the diagram. Like pool, a lane is drawn as a rectangular box, but its label – at the left for a horizontal lane or at the top for a vertical lane – is not boxed off. Lanes are a carryover from traditional swimlane flowcharts and have no semantics in BPMN. BPMN has no rules about sequence flows or message flows crossing lane boundaries.

Figure 4-2. Lane

BPMN 2.0 uses lanes as a way to organize flow elements belonging to different *categories*. Most often lanes represent *performer roles* or *organizational units*, but in principle any categorization may be used for lanes. A *lane set* specifies the categorization represented by the lanes in a particular diagram. A process can be defined with multiple alternative lane sets, each diagram representing a different way to divide the same semantic elements into lanes.

Lanes may contain nested *sublanes*. For example, a parent lane might represent a department, and sublanes roles within that department.

Task

A *task* is an atomic activity, meaning an activity that has no internal subparts defined by the model. It is represented by the activity shape, rounded rectangle, with the *task type* indicated by a small icon in the corner. BPMN defines a number of task types, but the Level 1 palette just includes the two most commonly used (Figure 4-3). A *User task* means a task performed by a person, i.e., a human activity. A *Service task* means an automated activity. A task type value of *None* – no task type icon displayed – means the task type is undefined. Tasks represent work performed – actions, not functions or states. They should be labeled VERB-NOUN.

Figure 4-3. User task (left) and Service task (right)

Subprocess

A *subprocess* (Figure 4-4) is a compound activity, meaning an activity with subparts that can be represented as a process, a flow of contained activities. A subprocess can be represented in multiple ways in the diagram. A *collapsed* subprocess is drawn using a standard-size activity shape with a [+] symbol at the bottom center. An *expanded inline* representation uses an enlarged activity shape to enclose a process diagram representing the subprocess activity flow.

You can alternatively expand the subprocess in a separate child-level diagram within the same model, or in an external model. This is called *hierarchical expansion*, with the collapsed subprocess shape drawn as part of the *parent process level* and the expansion in a separate diagram representing the *child process level*. In the child-level diagram, the enlarged activity shape (rounded rectangle) is not drawn. (BPMN distinguishes between an "embedded" subprocess, defined in the same model as the parent, and a reusable "global" subprocess, defined externally, but Level 1 modelers may ignore this distinction.)

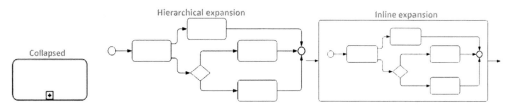

Figure 4-4. Collapsed and Expanded subprocess

The three representations shown in Figure 4-4 should be considered *multiple views of the same semantic element,* so they must be consistent. For example, if a collapsed subprocess receives a message flow, there must be an element of the expanded subprocess that receives the same message flow.

Start Event

A *start event* (Figure 4-5) indicates the start of a process or subprocess. It is drawn as a thin circle, and normally each process or subprocess has just one. In a top-level process, the symbol inside the start event signifies the *trigger,* meaning the signal that creates a new instance of the process.

Figure 4-5. Start events (None, Message, Timer)

A *None start event* (no symbol) in a top-level process technically means the trigger is unspecified. I recommend using it when the process is initiated by an internal participant. A subprocess MUST have a None start.

A *Message start event* (envelope symbol) signifies the process is triggered by a signal from outside the process. Best practice is to draw a message flow to the event from the external pool. A common use case is a request from the Customer. You may not use Message start in a subprocess.

A *Timer start event* (clock symbol) signifies the process is run on some predetermined schedule, either one-time or recurring.

End Event

An *end event* (Figure 4-6) indicates the end of a path in a process or subprocess. It is drawn as a thick circle, and frequently a process or subprocess may contain more than one. In fact, it is best practice to use more than one to identify distinct *end states.* If a process or subprocess includes parallel paths, each path must reach an end event in order for an instance to be complete.

An end event may be drawn with a symbol inside, indicating the *result* signal thrown when the event is reached. This is allowed both in top-level processes and subprocesses. In the Level 1 palette, only one end event type, Message, throws a result.

Figure 4-6. End events (None, Message, Terminate)

A *None end event* (no symbol inside) signifies that no result signal is thrown when the end event is reached.

A *Message end event* (black envelope symbol) signifies that a message is sent when the end event is reached. Best practice is to draw a message flow from the event to the external pool. A common use case is return of a response message to the Customer.

A *Terminate end event* (bulls-eye symbol) is a special case. Reaching Terminate in a process or subprocess immediately ends that process or subprocess, even if other parallel paths are still running. Note: Reaching Terminate in a subprocess only ends that subprocess, not the parent-level process. Terminate does not throw a result signal.

Exclusive Gateway

A gateway represents a control point in the sequence flow. An *exclusive gateway* (Figure 4-7), also called *XOR gateway,* with one sequence flow in and more than one sequence flow out, represents an *exclusive decision.* It means only one of the output sequence flows is to be followed, based on some condition.

Figure 4-7. Exclusive (XOR) gateway, shown in alternative representations

It is drawn as a diamond shape, either with no symbol inside or with an X symbol inside. There is no difference in meaning between the two; it is merely a matter of convention. The BPMN spec says you cannot mix the two conventions in a diagram. I recommend you just pick one convention and use it all the time. I personally use the one with no symbol inside.

Parallel Gateway

A *parallel gateway* (Figure 4-8) with one sequence flow in and more than one sequence flow out signifies a *parallel split* or *AND-split.* It means that *all* of the outgoing sequence flows are to be followed in parallel, unconditionally. It is distinguished from the exclusive decision gateway by the + symbol inside the diamond.

Figure 4-8. Parallel gateway

Each outgoing path thus represents a parallel (concurrent) thread of process activity. Parallel paths may be joined downstream or may lead to separate end events. Each parallel path must reach an end event in order for the process or subprocess complete. In most cases, using a gateway for parallel split is superfluous because multiple sequence flows drawn directly out of an activity or event means the same thing (Figure 4-9): after the activity or event completes, all paths are enabled concurrently.

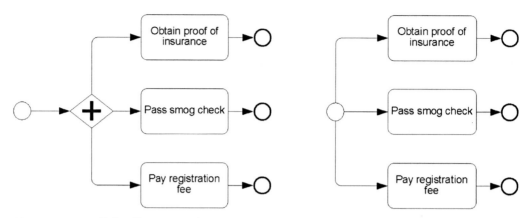

Figure 4-9. Parallel split gateway is technically redundant; left and right diagrams mean the same thing

A parallel gateway drawn with multiple sequence flows in and one out is called a *parallel join* or *AND-join*. It is a type of *synchronizing join* because it requires all of its incoming flows to arrive before enabling the outgoing flow. A parallel join may ONLY be used to merge paths that are unconditionally parallel. Typically this occurs only when the paths were originally the result of a parallel split, either using the parallel split gateway or multiple sequence flows out of an activity.

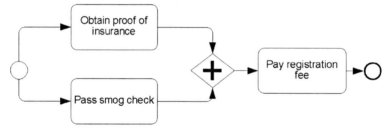

Figure 4-10. Parallel gateway must be used to join parallel paths

Sequence Flow

A *sequence flow* (Figure 4-11) is a solid line connector linking activities, gateways, and events within a single pool. Sequence flow represents *orchestration*: When the node at the tail of the sequence flow is complete, the node at the arrowhead is enabled to start.

Figure 4-11. Sequence flow

Message Flow

A message flow (Figure 4-12) is a dashed connector representing a signal (message) sent between two pools. It may not be used to connect two nodes within a pool.

Figure 4-12. Message flow

Data Object, Message, and Data Store

One of the biggest changes from BPMN 1.x to BPMN 2.0 concerns the modeling of data and data flow. In BPMN 1.x, data representation in the diagram was considered an *artifact*, effectively an annotation with no semantic rules. In BPMN 2.0, *data objects* and their connectors, called *data associations* (now distinguished from ordinary *association* connectors used with annotations), were upgraded to first-class objects in the BPMN semantic model. This change technically imposes new restrictions on where and how data objects and data associations may be used, although at Level 1 they may still be treated as artifacts.

In both BPMN 1.x and 2.0, data objects may be used to represent data or document flow between process activities and events. The symbol is a dog-eared page (Figure 4-13). Besides the *name* of the data object, the label may indicate its *state* by enclosing it in square brackets. In BPMN 1.x, a data object is linked either to a sequence flow, message flow, or activity using a dotted line connector called an *association*. When linked to a sequence flow or message flow, the association is *non-directional*, with no arrow. When linked directly to an activity or event, the association is *directional*, with an arrow to or from the activity or event. [Note: Data association and message flow connectors look similar and are easily confused. Message flow has a circle on the tail; data association does not. Message flow has a closed triangular arrowhead; data association has an open V-shaped arrowhead.]

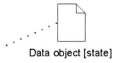

Data object [state]

Figure 4-13. Data object and data association

In BPMN 2.0, a data object represents a *variable*, and a data association represents a *mapping* between that variable and a data input or output of an activity or event. In the notation, this is expressed by the directional association of data objects directly to activities (or events). A non-directional association between a data object and a sequence flow, common in BPMN 1.x, in BPMN 2.0 is considered a *visual shortcut* that implies a specific equivalent direct association. That only works, however, if such an equivalent is unambiguously implied. For example, if the sequence flow connects to a gateway (Figure 4-14), the equivalent direct data association may be ambiguous from the visual shortcut. For that reason, you should only use the non-directional data association to a sequence flow when the source and target of the data flow are unambiguous.

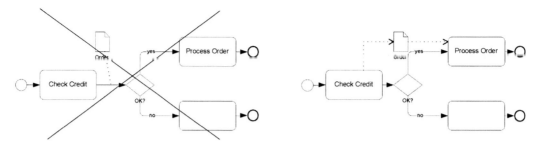

Figure 4-14. Use directional data association when the source and target are unclear using the visual shortcut

What about data association to a message flow? That has changed in BPMN 2.0 as well. You no longer use a data object for that; instead you use a *message* symbol, an envelope icon. It can be drawn linked to the message flow either with a non-directional data association or by directly overlaying the message symbol on top of the message flow (Figure 4-15). Technically, the message flow represents the *fact* of a signal exchanged between the process and an external entity. The message represents the *content* of that signal.

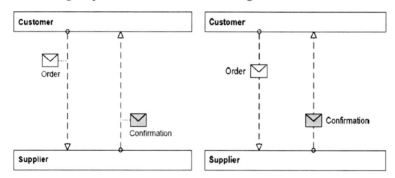

Figure 4-15. A message linked to a message flow represents the content of the inter-pool communication.

Messages are communications sent directly from one pool to another. That is a common way information flows between a process and the external environment, but it is not the only way. Another common way is via a shared *data store*, such as a file, database, or business application. For example, a process activity can query and retrieve information from a data store, which is not really the same as receiving that information in a message. Also, unlike a data object, which lives only as long as the process instance is running, a data store represents information that persists beyond the lifetime of the particular process.

BPMN 1.x had no notation for data stores, but BPMN 2.0 provides one. Figure 4-16 illustrates access to customer billing information via a data store. Here the customer does not interact directly with the order process, but has provided information needed by that process to a permanent *Customer Profile* record, represented as a data store.

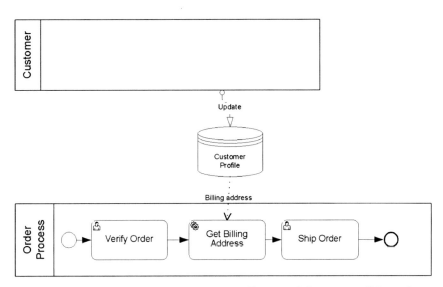

Figure 4-16. Data store represents externally stored data accessible to the process.

Text Annotation

Arbitrary text may be inserted in the diagram and linked to another object with a *text annotation* artifact and *association* connector (Figure 4-17). The text annotation is an enlarged left square bracket symbol. Annotations are *artifacts* and have no defined semantics.

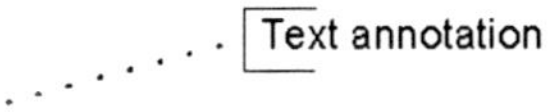

Figure 4-17. Text annotation

Link Event Pair (Off-Page Connector)

A process level that does not fit on one page can be split across two pages using *off-page connectors* (Figure 4-18). Officially called *Link events*, these connectors are not really events but simply connection points for broken sequence flows. If a sequence flow goes from page 1 to page 2, it ends on page 1 with a black ("throwing") Link event, and starts on page 2 with a white ("catching") Link event. The two Link events are paired in the model by referencing a common link ID value; in the diagram it is best to give them identical labels as well.

Figure 4-18. Off-page connector using paired Link events

Link event pairs can be used as *on-page connectors* as well, connecting sequence flows on the same page. Sometimes this simplifies complex drawings with many crossing lines. However, whether on-page or off-page, the link pair cannot be used to connect two points that would be illegal to connect via sequence flow. For example, it cannot be used to cross a pool or subprocess boundary. Therefore care should be taken before using Link events. Best practice is to avoid the need for them by using hierarchical process levels.

CHAPTER 5

BPMN Method: Level 1

The beginning modeler's first instinct is to document a process from the bottom up: "Let's see, first we do this, and then this happens," etc. I recommend instead a top-down approach. You'll get to the end just as quickly and be happier with the end result.

Step 1. Define Process Scope

Top-down process modeling requires first establishing clarity around the process as a whole:

- What constitutes the start of the process? What specifically triggers or initiates a new instance of the process.

- What does an instance of the process represent? If that's hard to answer, fill in the blank: "Each instance of our process represents a different _____." If your "process" can't be described that way, maybe it's not what BPMN means by a process!

- Who is the "customer"? Or is the initiator a participant inside the process?

- What signifies the end of the process? Remember, when the process is over, it's over. If it turns out later that something more needs to be done, that is usually an instance of some other process. For example, an order process typically ends when the goods are shipped and invoiced, or possibly when the invoice is paid. But there are times when the customer might want to return the item for credit after that point. That would be an instance of a different process, credit returns.

It often helps to think about how you measure process performance, such as average time or cost to complete. If you are going to average across all instances, what do you want to consider the start and end points for measuring those key performance indicators (KPIs)?

There is no hard and fast rule about this. When a process is instantiated upon request, usually the start and end are marked by some form of communications with the customer. But the scope of the process is really up to you to define. However, it is critical to come to definitive agreement up front on what constitutes the start and end of your process.

To illustrate the Level 1 method, let's use an example familiar to many from their personal experience – purchasing a new car. Here we'll look at the process from the car dealer's perspective.

> **Scenario: New car sales.** This scenario describes an automobile dealer's sales process.
>
> - The process starts when the customer places an order. Not all orders will result in completed sales.
>
> - The requester, or customer, is the prospective car buyer.
>
> - The normal "happy path" end of the process is signified by closing of the order transaction and delivery of the car.

Step 2. Create the Top Level Diagram for the Happy Path

Once the process scope and customer are understood, we can begin creating the top-level diagram of the *happy path*, the sequence of steps to the normal "success" end state. We want to fit it all on one page using subprocesses. In addition, we want to show all the communications, in the form of message flows, between our process and external participants: the customer, external service providers used by the process, and perhaps any other processes of our own that this process might interact with. We'll represent those other entities and processes as black-box pools. Since they are empty, we draw them as small as possible, as space on the top-level page is usually scarce.

Add Pools

Let's start by inserting a pool in the center of the page to hold our process. Label it with the name of our process, *New Car Sales*.

If there is a customer, add a black-box (empty) pool above the process pool and label it *Customer*. Reduce the pool height as much as possible to save room on the page.

If there are external processes or service providers that communicate with the process, add those as black-box pools below the process pool, and label each with the name of the process or entity. Don't go overboard on this yet. You can always add them later.

Add Lanes to Process Pool (Optional)

We can add lanes to the process pool to represent different roles or organizational units. Lanes usually just make sense for human tasks. Gateways and events can go in whatever lanes you like. In the top-level diagram, we sometimes omit lanes because they can make an already crowded process pool even more so.

Add Happy Path Start and End Event to Process Pool

Inside the process pool at the left we'll put our start event.

- If the process is triggered by a request from Customer, we make it a Message start. Label the event, *Receive X*, where X is whatever message signifies the start, e.g., an order, claim, customer service request, etc. Insert a black-box Customer pool above our process pool and draw a message flow from its border to the Message start event. Label the message flow with the name of the message – probably the same as X in the label for the start event.

- If the process is triggered on some schedule, we make it a Timer start. Label the event to indicate the scheduling, e.g. *Every Monday at 8am*. We may not need an external Customer pool.

- If the process is initiated by an internal participant, we make it a None start; in this case we probably do not have an external Customer pool.

Now at the right end of our pool let's put in an end event for the happy path, the process's success end state. If the process was started on request from Customer, I like to return a final status response to Customer from the end event, such as a confirmation. That should be a Message event, with message flow drawn from the event to the boundary of the Customer pool. (A Message end event that triggers another internal process downstream could have a message flow to that pool instead of to Customer.) As with the start events, it's best practice to label the message flow in addition to the event that sends or receives the message.

Add Major Steps in the Happy Path

We have a little bit of room left to indicate the activities our process performs. Try to break it down to no more than 6 steps. Insert those steps as collapsed subprocesses. You can connect them with sequence flows creating a continuous chain from start event to end event (Figure 5-1). But this flow is preliminary; it will require a bit of adjustment.

Scenario: New car sales (continued)

- We have a pool for our process, labeled *New Car Sales*, and a black-box pool for the buyer, labeled Customer. We label our process pool with the name of the process, and external black-box pools with the name of the role or entity.

- We'll put in lanes for Sales, the Finance department, and the Vehicle Prep team.

- The Message start event represents receipt of an order. The happy path end event represents closing the deal and delivery of the vehicle. We model both of those interactions as message flows.

- We show the following steps as our happy path, each modeled as a collapsed subprocess: *Enter Order, Order Car from Factory, Prepare Car for Delivery, Arrange Financing,* and *Close and Deliver*. We connect these with sequence flows leading from the start event to the happy path Message end event.

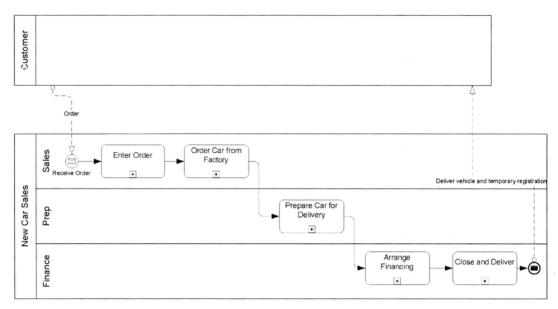

Figure 5-1. New Car Sales process, basic sequence of activities

Reconnect Concurrent and Conditional Steps

To adjust the sequence flows, we want to consider whether any of the steps in our top level diagram are *concurrent* – overlapping in time – with any others, or *conditional*, meaning only performed for some process instances.

If a step runs concurrently with other steps in the flow, it should appear on a parallel sequence flow drawn out of the last step in common before the paths split. In some cases, the parallel paths might emerge directly out of the start event. It is perfectly fine in BPMN to draw two or more sequence flows out of an activity or start event. That means when the activity or event is complete, both sequence flows take place in parallel. In other words, you can omit the AND-split gateway.

When you have parallel paths in the process, all must reach an end event before the process is complete, or you may join them into one flow using an AND-join. If a downstream activity requires activities on both paths to complete before it can start, you should use the AND-join. There is no need to use an AND-join before an end event.

If a step is conditional, you want to insert a gateway before it. If you can, label the gateway with a yes/no question, where the 'yes' answer describes the condition that enables the conditional activity. The 'yes' path out of that gateway leads to the conditional activity, and the 'no' path skips it.

The example and diagram (Figure 5-2) illustrate.

Scenario: New car sales (continued)

- The activity *Arrange Financing* can start as soon as the order is entered. It is concurrent with – runs in parallel with – the sequence *Order Car from Factory* and *Prepare Car for Delivery*. The sequence flow into *Arrange Financing* should come from *Enter Order*, the last activity that must be complete before this activity can start.

- The activity *Close and Deliver* requires both *Arrange Financing* and *Prepare Car for Delivery* to be complete before it can start. Therefore we need to join those paths with an AND-join before *Close and Deliver*.

- *Order Car from Factory* is only needed if the car is not available on the lot. We insert a gateway labeled *Order from factory?* The 'yes' path leads to *Order Car from Factory*; the 'no' path skips that step and goes directly to *Prepare Car for Delivery*.

- After *Order Car from Factory*, we want to go to *Prepare Car for Delivery*, but that activity already has a sequence flow in from the 'no' path of the gateway. That's no problem. Just draw the second sequence flow directly into the activity. No gateway is needed because those two paths are always alternatives, not parallel. One came from the 'yes' path of *Order from Factory?* and the other came from the 'no' path. You can safely merge alternative paths without a gateway in BPMN.

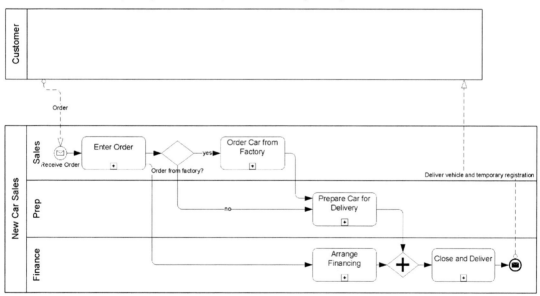

Figure 5-2. Flow refined with conditional and parallel paths

Step 3. Add Top-Level Exception Paths

Not all instances follow the happy path or reach the success end state. In the top-level diagram we often want to identify paths to one or more failed end states representing unsuccessful completion of the process.

Identify Exception End States

Most processes have just one success end state but multiple exception end states representing a "failed" process. By different end state I don't mean just a different reason for failure but a state that you want to distinguish from other end states of the process. There are a few reasons why you might want to distinguish these end states. One is for performance statistics: what percentage of instances ends up in this state versus that one? Another one is that the end state may determine the message that is sent, either to the customer – e.g. order confirmation/invoice versus order rejection notice – or to some chained downstream process.

Insert End Event for Each Distinct End State

If the end state is meant to cancel any parallel paths still running in the process, use a Terminate end event. If a message is returned to the requester, make it a Message end event and draw the message flow. Otherwise, if an end event does not send a message, leave it as a None end event.

Insert Gateways to Define Exception Paths

Now take a look at the exception end states you have identified with its own end event. For each one, think about where the flow splits off the path to that end event. Insert a gateway at that point and label it with a question where the 'yes' answer describes the exception, such as *Fail credit check?* or *Out of stock?*

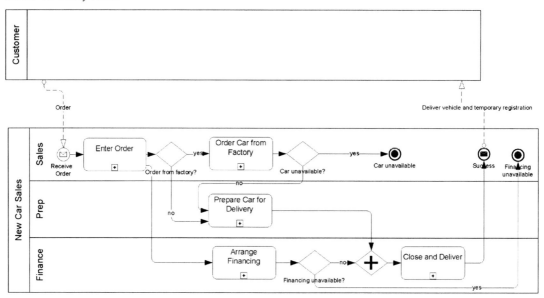

Figure 5-3. Add exception paths to top-level diagram

Again, our scenario and diagram (Figure 5-3) help to illustrate.

Scenario: New car sales (continued)

- We identify two exception end states and provide an end event for each:

    1. If the requested car is not available from the factory – perhaps the availability date is unacceptable to the buyer. In that case we want to cancel the parallel *Arrange Financing* path, so use a Terminate end event and label it *Car Unavailable*.

    2. If financing for the buyer cannot be arranged. In that case we want to cancel the *Factory Order/Prepare Car* path, so again use a Terminate end event and label it *Financing Unavailable*.

- The Car Unavailable end state is detected in *Order Car from Factory*, so we insert a gateway after that activity, with one path leading to the end event and the other to the next activity *Prepare Car for Delivery*.

- The Financing Unavailable end state comes after *Arrange Financing*. Here we put the gateway leading to it before the AND-join, since we don't want to continue *Prepare Car for Delivery* if financing is unavailable.

Once you begin to add exception paths, your process diagram is going to get more crowded and harder to follow. Crossing sequence flows are sometimes unavoidable, particularly with swimlanes. You might find rearranging the lanes makes the diagram a bit neater.

Step 4. Expand Subprocesses to Show Detail at Child Level

The top-level diagram, as represented by Figure 5-3, shows the high-level steps in the process, their sequential, concurrent, or conditional arrangement, and their relationship to various end states of the process. But it doesn't say much about the internal details of the activities involved. Those are hidden (for the moment) inside the collapsed subprocesses. The next step in top-down modeling is to expand each subprocess as needed to describe that detail.

BPMN provides a way to expand a subprocess on the same page, which we call inline expansion. Inline expansion expands the size of the rounded rectangle activity shape and lets you draw the subprocess steps as a process flow within it. However, inline expansion does not address the problem of limited available space on the page. Looking at Figure 5-3, we see there really is not room on the page to expand our processes inline, even if we made our pool and lanes bigger.

Instead of expanding inline – really useful just for simple subprocesses – we can describe subprocess detail by expanding it hierarchically, on another page of the model. The flow containing the collapsed subprocess and the flow of the expanded subprocess on the other page have a parent-child relationship. We say the expanded process is at a *child process level*. Inline expansion effectively displays the parent and child levels on the same page. *Hierarchical expansion* (or *child-level expansion*) means displaying the expanded subprocess in a separate diagram, i.e., on a separate page of the model.

BPMN tools vary in the mechanics of child-level expansion. Some make you define and save the subprocess first and then link to it from the collapsed subprocess. Others let you draw a "rubber band" around a set if contiguous steps in a parent-level diagram and convert that to a collapsed subprocess, moving the rubber-banded detail to a hyperlinked child-level page. Neither of those is truly top-down because you need to describe the detailed flow first.

The tool we use in the BPMessentials training, Process Modeler for Visio from ITP Commerce, supports a pure top-down approach. You add the collapsed subprocess first, and you can add the child-level detail later. When you add that detail, the tool automatically creates the child-level diagram – empty at first – and hyperlinks it to the collapsed subprocess shape in the parent-level diagram. This is especially convenient for top-down modeling, but almost any BPMN tool should allow some way to create hierarchical models.

We discussed what a child-level expansion looks like back in Chapter 2. To recap:

- The subprocess expansion MUST start with a None start event.

- The expanded subprocess need not be enclosed by a pool. In fact, in BPMN 2.0 it is illegal to draw a pool unless the diagram contains more than one. If you have message flows to or from the subprocess, you MAY enclose it in a pool, but it MUST be labeled the same as the pool of the parent process.

- The expanded subprocess MAY include lanes to represent roles or entities performing subprocess activities. If no lanes are used, the activities are all placed implicitly in the lane containing the collapsed subprocess in the top-level diagram.

- The expanded subprocess MAY include other collapsed subprocesses, which can be expanded on another child page. Those expansions are effectively grandchildren of the top-level diagram, i.e. two levels down from the top. There is no limit in BPMN how deep the nested hierarchy can go.

Again we go back to our New Car Sales scenario to illustrate. This time we will expand the *Enter Order* subprocess.

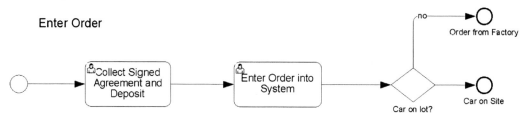

Figure 5-4. Expanded *Enter Order* subprocess

Scenario: New car sales (continued)

- *Enter Order* (Figure 5-4). The salesman collects the signed agreement and deposit from the buyer and enters the order into the computer system.

- The car ordered may be on the car lot or may have to be ordered from the factory. Since this affects the downstream process, we represent those as distinct end states using separate end events. Since they do not send a message, they are None end events. We want one of the end events to match the test indicated by the label of the gateway following the subprocess (Figure 5-3), which is *Order from Factory?*

Step 5. Add Intermediate Message Flows to External Pools (Optional)

Earlier we discussed receiving a request for the process in a Message start event and returning responses from one or more message end events. However, other activities within our process could interact with Customer or other external entities. Using BPMN at Level 1 generally implies you don't want to include too much detail, lest it confuse the audience (and the modeler as well). But, you'll need to show all the message flows at Level 2, so here is how to do it if you'd like to incorporate this in your Level 1 methodology.

Add Black-box pools for External Participants

In the top-level diagram, add black-box pools for any other external participants. Label them with the name of the participant role or entity. I try to draw these pools below the process pool, but sometimes the message flows are less messy if one or more of them share the space above the process pool with Customer.

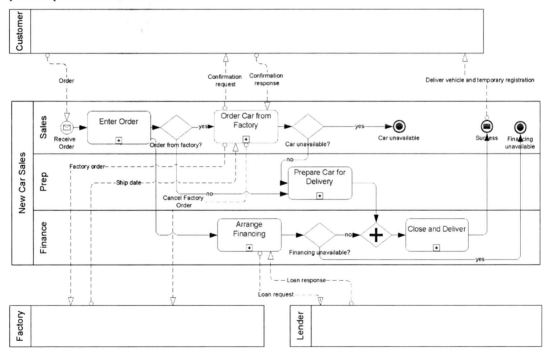

Figure 5-5. Message flows in top-level diagram

Add Top-Level Message Flows

Draw message flows between these pools and subprocesses they interact with in the top-level diagram. They will attach to the external pool boundary and to activities or events in the top-level process (Figure 5-5).

Scenario: New car sales (continued)

- We have two other external participants: the factory and the financing provider, or Lender. Add black-box pools for them below the process pool (Figure 5-5).

- *Order Car from Factory*: If the car must be ordered from the factory, the car dealer places the factory order, and the factory responds with a tentative ship date. The dealer estimates the time in transit plus the prep time and sends the customer a promised date when the car will be ready for delivery, requesting confirmation. If that date is unacceptable, the customer may cancel the order. In that case, the dealer cancels the factory order.

- *Arrange Financing*: The Lender receives the buyer's credit application from the finance department, and responds with either a confirmation or rejection of the requested financing.

Add Message Flows to Child-Level Diagrams

In the top-level diagram, the message flows were drawn attached to the collapsed subprocess boundary. In the child-level expansion, they attach directly to the activities that send or receive them. We don't draw a pool around the subprocess, as that is inherited from the parent level, but we should draw the black-box pools for the message flows that exchange message flows with this subprocess.

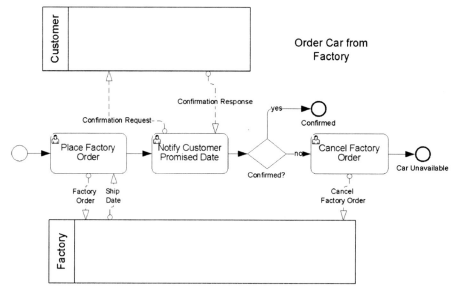

Figure 5-6. Message flows in child-level diagram

- - *Order Car from Factory*: The dealer places the factory order and receives the ship date in the response. Then the dealer calculates the promised date and requests confirmation from the customer.

- - If the customer confirms, the subprocess ends in "Confirmed" end state. Otherwise, the dealer cancels the factory order and the subprocess ends in the "Car Unavailable" end state. We want to match the name of one of the end events with the label of the gateway that follows the subprocess. That gateway tests which end event the process instance reached.

What About Data?

You may have noticed one thing absent from our Level 1 BPMN models: *data flow*. Representation of data plays a significant role in some other process modeling notations, but not so in BPMN, at least in BPMN 1.x. The closest we've come to it so far is the label on message flows, which you might think of as a proxy for some packet of information communicated to or from the process.

It's best to think of the flow of process data in BPMN as *implicit*. If some document or data element is either *received* by the process in a message flow or *retrieved, created,* or *updated* by a process activity, then that document or data is assumed to be available for use by any downstream activity, gateway, or event in the BPMN model.

But some modelers like to see explicit representation of data on the page. As discussed in the previous chapter, BPMN provides shapes for a *data object,* representing a variable inside the process, a *data store,* representing persistent data outside the process but accessible to it, and a *message,* representing the data content of a message flow. Data flow is indicated in the diagram by a dotted line connector called a *data association.* (In BPMN 1.x, it was just a regular association, still used to link artifacts like text annotations to some flow element.) Data association and regular association look identical. To distinguish them from message flow, associations have no circle on its tail and their arrowhead, if they are directional, is V-shaped not triangular.

I don't use data objects very often, but it is a matter of personal style. For Level 1 modeling, if you want to use them, I recommend reserving them for information details or packaging (such as a particular form or business document) that is not obviously implied by the orchestration itself.

Figure 5-7 illustrates two data objects and a message added to our car dealer process. A message linked to the message flow from the lender indicates it contains the Loan Agreement. The Loan Documents package is shown as a data object flowing from *Arrange Financing* to *Close and Deliver,* with another data object representing the executed state of those documents, an output of the process. The state of the data object, such as "executed", is put in square brackets.

For Level 1 modeling, it is perfectly all right to ignore BPMN 2.0's technical rules about data flow modeling and continue the interpretation of data objects as simply annotations of the diagram.

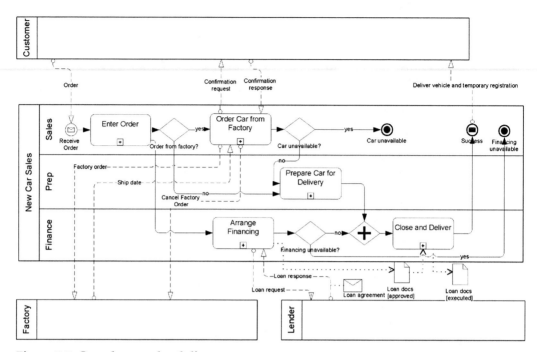

Figure 5-7. Complete top-level diagram

CHAPTER 6

Elements of BPMN Style: Level 1

Principles of Composition

1. *Make the process logic clear from the printed diagram.*

This principle is the central tenet of BPMN style and applies at every level of use. BPMN provides ways to specify all kinds of process details that are not visible in the process diagram. You can see them only by using the BPMN tool or through the package of process documentation generated from the tool. But that is not the way to maximize shared understanding. The process logic – the sequence of activity flow, which paths are concurrent or conditional, the various end states, etc. – all should be clear from the printed diagram itself. That means you should label essentially everything – subprocesses, events, gateways, message flows – using naming conventions that make the flow logic apparent from the diagram. Beginners frequently are stingy with labels, but labels are the key to understandable diagrams.

In the XML representation of BPMN 2.0, the label of a diagram shape is by convention the *name* attribute of the corresponding semantic element.

2. *Make models hierarchical, fitting each process level on one page.*

The top-level diagram should both capture the end-to-end process on one page and show its interactions with external participants: the process requester, service providers, and other entities. Each subprocess in the top level is expanded in a separate child-level diagram, and this nesting can go on as deep as you'd like. As more detail is added at deeper child levels, no change is needed to the parent level diagrams. Most BPMN tools let you navigate up and down the hierarchy by hyperlinking.

Hierarchical modeling is admittedly a personal preference. Some people like "flat" models, effectively all at one process level, using off-page connectors to hold it all together, or simply taping all the pages together on a large wall space. But hierarchical is better, for several reasons. It allows different users to view different levels of detail, while preserving the integrity of a single semantic model. You can zoom in and out. You can visualize the entire end-to-end process on one page, including its connections to external participants. And you can manage process components – subprocesses – as independent reusable units much more easily than in flat models. If you are used to stickies-on-the-wall flowcharting, you may find the hierarchical style jarring at first, but you will quickly come to appreciate its benefits.

3. Use black-box pools to represent external participants.

A common beginner mistake is to insert activities in the Customer or other requester pool (Figure 6-1, left). It's a mistake because you don't know the beginning or the end of the Customer's process... nor the middle, for that matter. Submitting the order is not the end of the interaction. Other messages are exchanged downstream – ship notice, invoice, perhaps other notifications and requests. If you try to anticipate the Customer's internal process for all of that in a white-box pool... well, good luck.

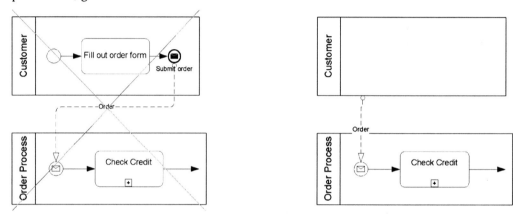

Figure 6-1. Customer and other external participants should be modeled as black-box pools (right)

The right way to do it is in the right-hand diagram. Just make it a black-box pool. Usually no real information is lost. You have enough to worry about describing your own process; let the Customer fend for himself.

4. Begin customer-facing processes with a Message start event receiving a message flow from the Customer pool.

Figure 6-1 illustrates another best practice. A process that is initiated by request should be modeled with a Message start event that receives a message flow from the requester pool.

5. Model internal process participants (activity performers) as lanes within a single process pool, not as separate pools. Label lanes with the role or organizational unit that performs (or is responsible for) its contained activities.

There are a few occasions when your internal business process should be modeled as multiple pools chained by message flows, but most of the time it is best to model it as a single BPMN process, i.e., contain it in a single pool. Representing various organizational units that perform process activities as separate pools (Figure 6-2, left) is usually incorrect. This implies each unit's process is independent of the others, and can stand alone. If these activities are actually related, part of a single business process, make them subprocesses within a single pool, using lanes to indicate the organizational units (Figure 6-2, right).

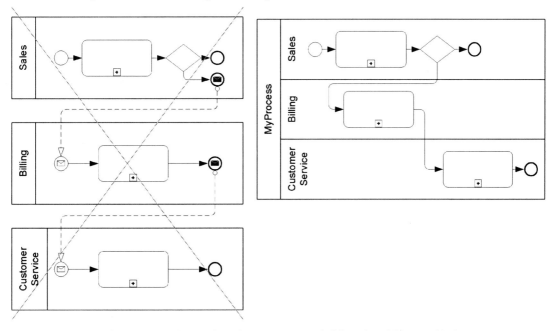

Figure 6-2. Organizational units performing process activities should normally be represented as lanes within a single pool, not separate pools

6. *Label white-box pools with the name of a process; label black-box pools with a participant role or business entity.*

It is not uncommon to see pools labeled with a name like Seller, Manufacturer, or Lender, indicating a role or business entity. Such names are good practice for black-box (empty) pools, but for white-box pools representing internal processes it is better to label them with the name of the process. For one thing, this is typically the only place in the diagram to place the process name. For another, if you label it with the name of your business entity, all of your internal pools will have the same name, making it harder to interconnect them.

7. *Show message flows between the process and all external pools in top-level diagram, and show message flows consistently in parent and child-level diagrams.*

Our *New Car Sales* scenario provides a good example. Figure 6-3 shows the top-level diagram, in which the internal process, shown as a white-box pool, communicates with the Customer and two external service providers using message flows. Figure 6-4 shows the expansion of *Order Car from Factory* in a child-level diagram. Both the collapsed subprocess in Figure 6-3 and the expansion in Figure 6-4 contain the same set of message flows, three outgoing and two incoming, labeled consistently on the two pages. Most tools will not enforce this consistency automatically, so you need to do it yourself. Remember the parent and child diagrams are two views of a single semantic model, not two separate models.

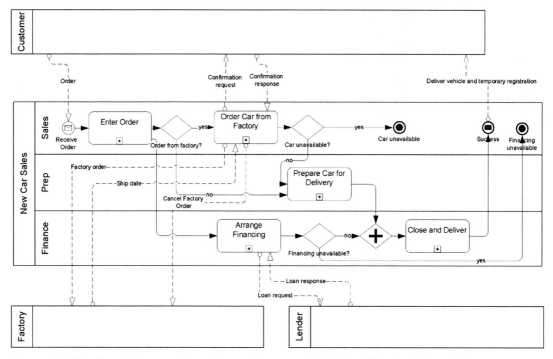

Figure 6-3. Top-level diagram shows internal process linked to all external pools by message flows.

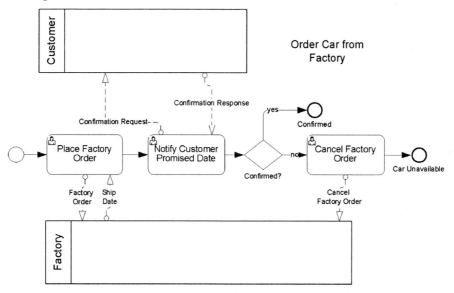

Figure 6-4. Expansion of *Order Car from Factory*. Make message flows consistent in expanded and collapsed views of a subprocess.

8. Label activities VERB-NOUN.

Activities, including subprocesses, represent *work* or *actions* performed in the process, not functions or states. Therefore you should give them names of the form VERB-NOUN. For example:

- *Check credit* (action), not *Credit check* (function) or *Credit OK* (state)

- *Approve loan* (action), not *Loan approval* (function) or *Loan rejected* (state)

- *Receive report* (action), not *Report received* (state)

9. If possible, label exclusive decision gateways with a yes/no question, and label the outgoing sequence flows yes and no.

An exclusive decision gateway (no marker inside) means any instance follows just one of the outgoing sequence flows, depending on a data condition. If there are two outgoing paths, and the data condition could be framed as a boolean (true/false) expression, label the gateway as a yes or no question, and label the outgoing sequence flows *yes* and *no*, respectively.

10. Label Message start events "Receive X," where X is the object triggering the process.

A Message start event indicates a new process instance is triggered upon receipt of a message. Label the start event to indicate the object received, such as *Receive loan application, Receive order,* or *Receive customer service request.*

11. Label Timer start events to indicate the process schedule.

A Timer start event indicates a new process instance is triggered upon some predetermined schedule. Label the start event to indicate the schedule, such as *Monday 8am, January 1,* or *Monthly.*

12. Indicate success and failed end states of a process with separate end events, and label them to indicate the end state. If multiple paths lead to the same effective end state, route them all to a single end event.

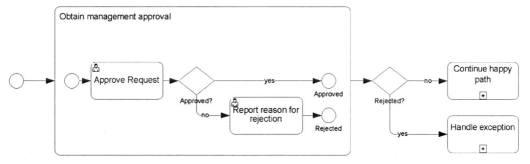

Figure 6-5. Success and failed subprocess end states represented as separate end events.

BPMN diagrams are easier to understand if distinct end states of a process or subprocess lead to separate labeled end events. It is common to test the end state of a subprocess in a gateway immediately following it in order to route failed end state instances to an exception path (Figure

6-5). If there is an end event representing the failed end state, label the gateway with the name of the failed end event, plus a question mark, e.g., *Rejected?* as in Figure 6-5.

Use as many end events in the subprocess as the number of end states you want to distinguish. If two end states are technically distinct but have no different effect on the downstream process, it may be better to combine them into a single end event representing a single effective end state. For example, if there are different reasons a request is not approved but all disapprovals are handled the same way following the subprocess, you can combine them in a single end event of the subprocess, as illustrated in Figure 6-6.

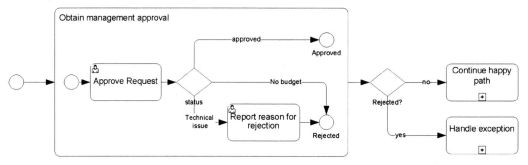

Figure 6-6. Technically distinct end states should be combined in a single end event if the difference has no effect on subsequent flow.

13. *Label message flows with the name of the message. Use a message linked to the message flow to indicate additional detail, if necessary.*

Even if implied by the label of the sending or receiving Message event, best practice is to label message flows with the name of the message. Names like *X Request* and *X Response* are good for request and response messages. It is best not to link a data object (or message) to an unlabeled message flow (Figure 6-7, left). Instead label the message flow directly. If you need to display additional information about the message content, you can optionally add that in a message symbol overlaid on the message flow (Figure 6-7, right).

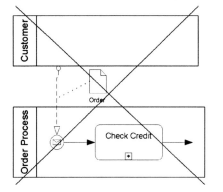
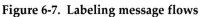
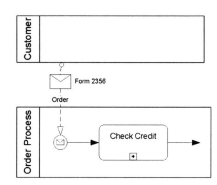

Figure 6-7. Labeling message flows

Elementary Rules of Usage

14. *Use one start event in a process or subprocess. Use an end event to represent the end of each path of a process or subprocess.*

Technically, the spec says under certain circumstances you can omit start events, or have more than one. Also, sometimes it is legal to omit an end event. But few people understand those circumstances, so best to get into the habit of always using *exactly one* start event in each process or expanded subprocess, and ending *every* path in an end event.

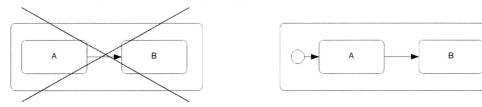

Figure 6-8. Subprocess drawn without start and end events (left) is sometimes technically allowed, but showing start and end events (right) is preferable.

15. *All activities, gateways, and events must be connected via a continuous chain of sequence flows leading from a start event to an end event.*

All flow objects (activities, gateways, and events) must be part of the orchestration. They cannot be "floating" in the diagram. For example, the left diagram in Figure 6-9 is incorrect. If you want to say that the process has steps A and B, and sometimes also C, you cannot do it this way. The diagram on the right is correct. It says you always do C along with A and B. There are other ways to indicate doing C "sometimes" – based on an explicit condition, based on an event, based on the action of the performer of A or B – but these are beyond the scope of the Level 1 palette. To stay within Level 1, better to use the diagram on the right, as it is valid BPMN, and indicate further details in a text annotation.

Figure 6-9. Activities cannot be "floating" in the diagram.

16. *Sequence flow (or equivalent Link event pair) must not cross a pool boundary. Use message flow to link pools.*

A sequence flow must start and end within a single process. It cannot go from one pool to another. Suppose you want Process 2 to start when Process 1 finishes. You cannot do that by connecting the end event of Process 1 to the start event of Process 2 using sequence flow (Figure 6-10, left) or by the equivalent link pair (Figure 6-10, center). The way to communicate between pools is with a message flow, as shown in the diagram on the right.

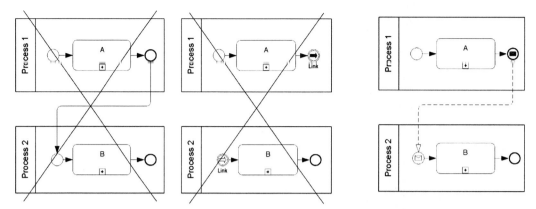

Figure 6-10. Sequence flow cannot cross pool boundary.

17. *Sequence flow (or equivalent Link event pair) must not cross subprocess boundary, i.e., from child level to parent level.*

You cannot connect a child-level element to a parent-level using sequence flow. Instead you must end the child-level process (subprocess) and continue the flow out of it at the parent level. A common use case is when an exception inside a subprocess means you cannot continue the parent level process. For example (Figure 6-11), a *Fulfill Order* subprocess first picks the order items from inventory and then packs them for shipment. But if the picking step detects the item is out of stock, the process cannot continue.

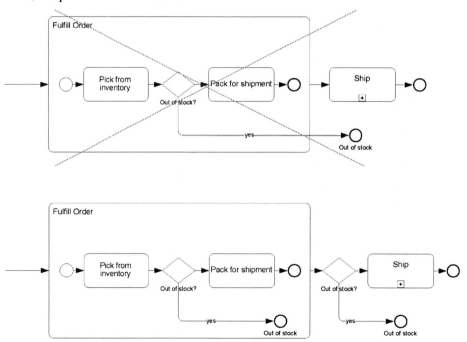

Figure 6-11. Sequence flow cannot cross subprocess boundary

The top diagram tries to end the process with a sequence flow from the gateway inside the subprocess to an end event at the parent level, but this is illegal. Instead you need to do it as in the bottom diagram: End the subprocess first, and test its end state afterward to see if the process should end.

   18. *Message flow cannot connect points in the same pool.*

A message flow represents a signal exchanged between the process and an outside entity. It cannot be used to mean communication between lanes within the same pool. For example (Figure 6-12), in a budget process the Employee prepares a budget and the Manager reviews it. If the Manager needs the employee to revise and resubmit it, that request cannot be represented as a message flow (top diagram), since both Employee and Manager in this case are lanes in the same pool. Instead that "request" is sent back to the Employee via sequence flow (bottom diagram).

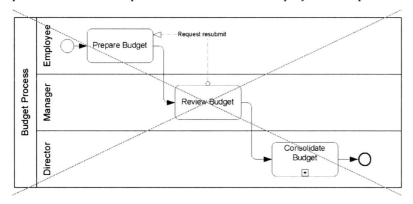

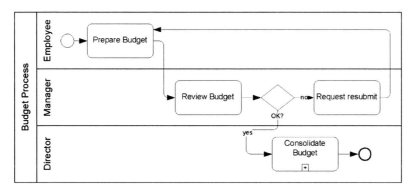

Figure 6-12. Message flow cannot be used within a pool.

   19. *Message flow cannot connect to a gateway.*

A message can only be sent or received by an activity or an event, so a message flow cannot come out of or go into a gateway. For example (Figure 6-13), in an insurance claim process, if additional information is needed to process the claim, a message flow to the claimant requesting the information is appropriate. But that message flow cannot come from the gateway that tests whether the claim is complete (top diagram). It must come from an activity or event issuing the request (bottom diagram).

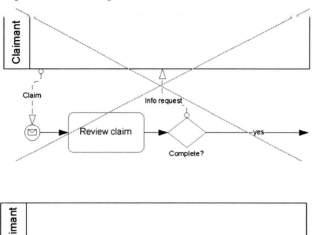

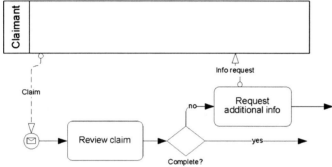

Figure 6-13. Message flow cannot connect to a gateway

PART III.
LEVEL 2: ANALYTICAL BPMN

CHAPTER 7

BPMN's Deeper Meanings

Stepping Up To BPMN Level 2

Level 1 modeling is an adaptation of familiar flowcharting concepts to the notation and terminology of BPMN. It may not show every step in the flow, and may ignore exceptions that come "out of the blue": the customer calls to change or cancel the order, the report is late and must be moved to a "fast track" process variant, etc. If such exceptions are infrequent, this is perfectly appropriate. Even if they are frequent, capturing them may not be the modeler's objective. This is all to say that Level 1 BPMN modeling is a perfectly good solution for certain aspects of a BPM program.

But there are certain things you cannot do with Level 1 BPMN models. You cannot use them to project quantitative performance improvement using simulation analysis, and you cannot use them to underpin executable processes. Those require precisely defined flow semantics – exactly what happens when, under what conditions – as if the model were actually controlling execution by some automated program.

BPMN provides those precise execution semantics, including those describing out-of-the-blue exceptions and how they affect the process. And those more precise semantics can be applied to non-executable processes as well as executable ones. This is what we call Level 2 modeling. It means applying the strict meaning of the shapes and symbols as described in the specification, even for processes that will never be "executed" on a process automation engine.

The problem for students of BPMN is that these deeper meanings are never explained in the spec. Instead, they are buried beneath unstated assumptions. Stepping up to BPMN Level 2 thus begins with understanding BPMN's deeper meanings.

Starting and Completing

We said previously that the major question BPMN tries to answer about a process is *when* things happen: when they start and what happens next when they complete. Thus the notions of starting and completing have profound importance in BPMN, but they are rarely discussed. In fact, one of the biggest changes from Level 1 to Level 2 modeling is coming to terms with the "process engine interpretation" of starting and completing versus the traditional flowcharting interpretation.

Starting

In traditional flowcharting, an arrow from one activity to the next means simply that the second activity occurs sometime after the first one, and it is fine to maintain that loose interpretation in Level 1 BPMN modeling. At Level 2, the interpretation is somewhat different. At Level 2, when the first activity completes, the second one starts immediately.[13]

But what does "starting" mean? Here we need to say more about BPMN's hidden assumptions. Recall that BPMN originated as a graphical design language for executable processes: not just any kind of executable processes, but processes in which automated tasks are implemented as *services*. (You may remember that BPMN's technical name for an automated task is a *Service task*.)

In today's IT world of *service oriented architecture* (SOA), a *service* is a business function that is executed or "invoked" automatically upon receipt of a request. Service requests are based on universal Internet standards and delivered over the network. This endows services with qualities frequently missing from activities in the real world: immediate availability upon request and accessibility to any authorized requester with access to the Internet.

In BPMN, a *Service task* is assumed to invoke the service – issue the request – *immediately* as soon as the sequence flow into it arrives, and the service provider is assumed to begin performing the business function immediately upon invocation. So in BPMN Level 2, a *Service task* is performed immediately when the preceding node in the diagram completes. When the business function provided by the service is done, the *Service task* is complete, and the process continues to the next step.

Human tasks work differently. BPMN's hidden assumption is that a human task – technically called a *User task* – is presented to its assigned performer in bit of software called a *worklist*. This is the way BPM Suites work. When a process instance reaches a User task, an entry (sometimes called a *work item*) is created immediately in the performer's worklist. The performer may be notified in addition (e.g., via email), and the task becomes immediately available to be performed.

Even though the performer has not begun work on it yet, technically the activity has been "started." For example, your model can specify that some new exception flow should be triggered if a message flow arrives after the activity is started but before it completes. Even if the assigned performer has not yet even looked at the worklist, the exception flow would be triggered.

---

[13] A late change in the BPMN 2.0 specification provides a boolean *isImmediate* attribute to sequence flow. What I call the Level 2 interpretation corresponds to an isImmediate value of true, the normal value. While you could set isImmediate to false, meaning simply time-ordering not control flow, there is no distinguishing notation for it in the diagram. So while it is technically possible to avoid the implication of immediacy in this way, it violates the general principle that modeling conventions should be employed to make the semantics unambiguous from the diagram alone.

Similarly, a Timer event attached to the activity boundary specifies some exception activity triggered if the activity is not completed within a specified interval after the activity starts. That starting time is, by convention, when the sequence flow arrives at the activity, not when the performer begins work on it.

So, to summarize, even when there is no actual process engine, *Service tasks* in a Level 2 model are assumed to be performed *immediately*, but User tasks are assumed to *wait* for some time in the assigned performer's worklist before task performance begins. From the perspective of events attached to the task boundary, however, Service and User tasks are equivalent: The event is "enabled" as soon as the sequence flow to it arrives, and is disabled when the task completes. We'll talk a lot more about such boundary events later.

A subprocess starts as soon as the sequence flow into it arrives. That means that the flow beginning with the subprocess's start event – remember, it must be a None start – is triggered immediately upon the arrival of the sequence flow into the subprocess.

Start events, end events (even those that throw a result signal), and gateways are not performed by a resource. You can think of them as control logic performed by the process engine itself. Even when there is no actual process engine, their behavior is assumed to occur immediately and instantaneously.

Completing

The thing that triggers a sequence flow out of an activity is "completion" of that activity. As discussed previously, subprocess is complete when all its parallel paths have reached an end event. Actually, that just describes *normal completion*. A process or subprocess can also be *interrupted* by various exception conditions, such as a timeout, received message, or error. In that case the process or subprocess is aborted immediately and is said to have *completed abnormally*.

Like a subprocess, a task can complete either normally or abnormally. Unlike a subprocess, however, a task's internal state while running is invisible to BPMN. The logic within each task that decides when it is complete is hidden, at least for normal completion. Events attached to the boundary of a task, just like a subprocess, can be used to model abnormal completion based on timeout, message, error, or other exception condition.

When an activity – task or subprocess – completes normally, the sequence flow out of the activity happens immediately, starting the next node in the orchestration. Similarly, when an activity completes abnormally, the *exception flow* – the sequence flow out of the boundary event that represents the interrupting exception – happens immediately, triggering the next node downstream. The sequence flow out of the activity itself, called the *normal flow*, does not get executed in this case.

Sending and Receiving

BPMN's strict interpretation of *sending* and *receiving* is narrower than beginning modelers realize. Those terms refer specifically to sending and receiving *messages*, which are represented in the diagram by *message flows*. Recall that a message means any communication between the process and an outside entity – a customer or service provider, another internal process, or possibly even an IT system. That communication could take any form. It does not have to be a SOAP or JMS message as assumed by SOA middleware. It could take some human-centric form, such as a fax or phone call. The term message simply means communication between a process activity or event and some entity outside the process.

Sending

The term "send" in BPMN implies a message, represented in the diagram by a message flow. In the Level 1 palette, a number of node types can send a message: a User or Service task, a subprocess, or a Message end event. At Level 2, using the full BPMN palette, you can also send a message from a *Send task* or a *throwing Message intermediate event* (Figure 7-1). Intermediate events are events in the middle of a process, after the start and before the end. They are drawn as circles with a double border. Message intermediate events that *throw* a signal have a black envelope icon, to distinguish them from Message intermediate events that *catch* a signal, which have a white envelope icon.

Figure 7-1. Send task (left) is same as Throwing Message intermediate event (right)

A node in the diagram that does nothing but send a message would be modeled either as a throwing Message event or as a Send task, which is the same thing. Thus communication between lanes of a single pool, which cannot use message flow, is technically not "sending," even if what you are trying to describe is packaging up a report and forwarding it via email. Because it is intra-pool, it cannot be represented by a throwing Message event or a Send task. Those node types do only one thing: send a message flow.

But here you see how, at Level 2, BPMN secretly changes the rules. A throwing Message event, remember, has no performer. It does not "do work." Since a Send task is the same as a throwing Message intermediate event, it technically has no performer either. The Send is assumed to occur *immediately* when the Message event or Send task is enabled. All this makes perfect sense with the kind of messages used in SOA middleware or a BPMS, such as SOAP or JMS messages. It doesn't necessarily make sense with human-centric communications like telephone, email, or fax, which require a performer to be available and do "work" to compose and send the communications. The BPMN spec is silent on this point.

Thus we are forced into the domain of method and style. Here is how I resolve the issue.

1. If a message flow represents some human form of communication – mail/fax, email, phone – send it from a *User task*, not from a Send task or throwing Message event. That implies, for one thing, that the Send is not immediate upon enablement of the task.

2. If a message flow represents machine-to-machine communication, such as SOAP or JMS, send it from a *Send task* or *throwing Message event*. Since those node types mean the same

thing, either will do, but you should try to be consistent, and choose either one or the other.

3. One exception to the above rules applies if the message flow represents a terminating response, such as confirmation or rejection message, from a process that was triggered by a request. In that case, I prefer to send it from a *Message end event*, even if the response is delivered via phone, email, or some other human-centric form. This suggests the process represents some type of *business service*, and aligns the process model with the way such services are conceived in SOA, using a contract defined by request and response messages. Admittedly, this convention is not entirely consistent with the others.

We still have not answered the question how to model communications *within* a pool. It is not a message, so you cannot use a Message event or Send task. Again the BPMN spec is silent, making it a matter of method and style.

There are two typical scenarios for intra-pool communications:

Sending information to a downstream task performer is the most common use case. Here beginners frequently make the mistake of using a Message event or Send task. The solution actually requires no sending activity or event at all, since that "send" is implied within the sequence flow itself. This is part of BPMN's hidden assumption of a process execution environment – a BPMS – handling intra-process communications.

By itself, a sequence flow to a human activity *implies* the following:

*   Creation of a work item in the performer's worklist

*   Notification of the performer that a new work item has been assigned

*   Delivery of process data and document attachments needed to perform the task. This assumes that the data and documents have either been created by upstream process activities or received from outside.

Therefore these actions do not need to be explicitly modeled in the diagram. You can simply *assume* they occur. If you want a way to show the particular data or documents delivered, BPMN provides a way to do that using *data objects*. A data object can be either linked to the sequence flow using an *data association*, or can be represented using directional associations linking the sending and receiving tasks.

Notifying a participant within the pool without creating a work item is another common use case. What separates this from the previous one is the information is not received in the context of a task to perform. It is simply a notification. In fact, the recipient may not even be represented by a lane in the diagram.

This is a case where BPMN provides no good solution. I recommend adding a *User task* labeled something like *Notify Manager*. In the task name, use the keyword *Notify* rather than *Send,* which suggests a Send task, i.e., a message.

For either of these intra-pool use cases, it is *not* appropriate to use a Signal event. Even though technically Signal can communicate within a pool, it requires a catching Signal event as well, and that catching event can only do certain things: start a process, resume a waiting process, interrupt a running activity, or start a parallel flow from a running activity. If those actions are triggered upon receipt of the information, then Signal is appropriate. Otherwise it is incorrect.

Receiving

Receiving is closely related to sending. Again, the term technically applies only to *messages*, communications from external pools. In Level 1 we saw we could receive a message using a Message start event. A User or Service task can also receive a message. At Level 2 we can also model receiving with a *catching Message intermediate event* or a *Receive task* (Figure 7-2), which means the same thing. Actually, the catching Message event must be *in sequence flow*, drawn with sequence flows in and out, not attached to an activity boundary. In the latter case, the event is "listening" for a message, but this is not what BPMN means by "receiving." That is because receiving really means *waiting for a message*.

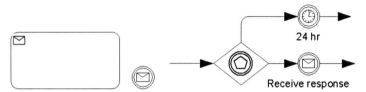

Figure 7-2. Receive task (left) is same as Catching Message intermediate event (center). Use event gateway (right) to model a timeout for the wait.

What if the message does not arrive? You may want to wait only so long before doing something else. BPMN provides a nice way to handle this using an *event gateway* (Figure 7-2, right). The gateway diamond has an intermediate event inside and intermediate events on each gateway output. A Timer intermediate event determines the deadline. A Message intermediate event waits for the message. If the message arrives before the deadline, you take the path out of the Message event; if not, you take the path out of the Timer event.

Receiving always implies waiting, whether the message is a human-centric type or machine-to-machine, so it is not necessary to reserve Message events and Receive tasks for machine-to-machine messages only. You can use them to show that the process must pause and wait for receipt of any kind of message. If a task has other actions to perform beyond waiting for the message, you should use a User or Service task instead of Receive.

Automated Tasks

In Level 1, we model all automated tasks as Service tasks. Full BPMN offers three ways to model automated tasks.

Script Task

A *Script task* (Figure 7-3) means that the task is code – a *script* – executed on the process engine itself. Usually a process engine's main function is to automate the orchestration, or process flow logic, not to perform tasks within the process, so Script tasks are typically used only for simple utility functions. If you don't have an actual process engine executing the process, you should have no need for Script tasks at all.

Figure 7-3. Script task

Service Task

Much more common is a *Service task* (Figure 7-4). A Service task means an automated task performed by something other than the process engine. Technically, BPMN assumes (or pretends) the task *invokes a service*. A *service* is SOA's term for exposing a business function to be *performed upon request*, usually with a response back to the requester upon completion. Much of today's IT investment involves transformation of business systems into collections of services.

Figure 7-4. Service task

I recommend using a Service task when the service is *synchronous*. That means the task completes when the service returns its completion response. In other words, the process *waits* at the Service task until the requested service is done. In an executable process, the process engine's service call waits for the reply. Automated systems like this do not like to wait very long – a few seconds, maybe – so synchronous services are typically used for functions that can be performed very quickly, such as a database query, not for functions performed by people or automated functions that may take minutes, hours, or days to return a response.

Asynchronous Request

Synchronous invocation is not the only way to perform a service. You can also do it *asynchronously*. That means the process issues the request but does not stop to wait for the response. It can do other things and get the response later, waiting for it downstream or in a parallel path. Long-running services, those that take more than a few seconds to complete, are typically modeled as asynchronous.

If we want to reserve Service task for synchronous calls, how should we model asynchronous service calls? One good way is to model the service provider as an external entity, a black-box pool, and represent the invocation as a request message. Instead of a Service task, the process invokes the service using a *Send task* or *throwing Message intermediate event*. It can wait downstream for the response in a *Receive task* or *catching Message event*. If more than one response message (or a timeout) is possible, the process can wait for the response using an *event gateway*.

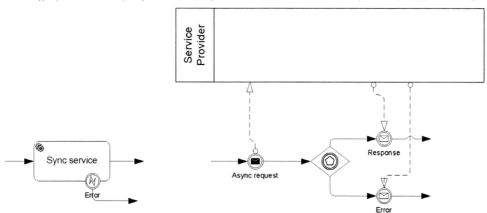

Figure 7-5. Synchronous and asynchronous service calls

You often see diagrams where the service request (message throw) is followed immediately by a node that waits for the response, such as an event gateway. Since the process has nothing else to do between the request and the response, why not model it as synchronous? From an orchestration logic standpoint, there is actually no difference. It is more a matter of convention. It also describes how an executable implementation of the process would likely work. Even if you have no immediate plans to execute your process, it doesn't hurt to get into the habit of modeling short-running automated activities as Service tasks and long-running ones as separate Send and Receive tasks (or their Message event equivalents).

Decisions and Rules

There is widespread misunderstanding, even within the BPM community, about the relationship between process models and business rules, and BPMN provides little help in sorting it out. Process and rules should not be considered alternative ways of describing the business, but complementary. While implementing one without the other can provide benefit, it is much better to use them together.

By a *business rule*, we mean here a named set of related conditions and results. Within the business rule community, such a thing is sometimes called a *decision* or *ruleset*, with the term *business rule* meaning a single condition and result. While the result could be specified as an action – *reject the request* – in BPM it more often simply sets the value of a data element – *customerType is Gold*. Any "action" required by the business rule is modeled as a process activity conditional on the rule result value.

A key attribute of business rules is that they are defined *independently* of the processes that use them. They may represent *business policies* applicable across any process. Typically they are maintained in a central location and can change independently of the process definition. A process instance executing a particular business rule thus uses the latest definition of the rule, not the definition at the time the process model was created or even when the process instance was started. This allows business rules to enhance the agility of business processes.

In BPMN, the condition expressions on sequence flows out of a gateway are also "rules" or a sort, but they are not "business rules" as the term is generally understood. A better term would be *routing rules*. Routing rules are hard-coded in the process model, so they lack the agility of real business rules. If the same conditional logic is used in multiple gateways within the process model, or in other process models, the process definition must be updated in each location whenever the rule changes. Also, gateway expressions can only reference data "known" to the process, meaning data either received in a message or created through a process activity. That assumption does not apply to business rules, which can reference data unknown to the process, such as the customer's purchasing history.

BPMN provides two constructs related to business rules: the *Business Rule task* and the *Conditional event*, formerly known as the *Rule event*.

The *Business Rule task* (Figure 7-6) is brand new in BPMN 2.0. You can think of it as a special type of *Service task* that evaluates a business rule – or, more accurately, a *decision service* – at a particular point in the process. The *Business Rule task* provides the input data needed to evaluate the rule, and receives the result in an output variable. A gateway following the *Business Rule task* can test the variable and route the process to perform any actions required by the business rule.

Figure 7-6. Business Rule task

The *Conditional event* (Figure 7-7) is used when a business rule engine continuously monitors some boolean data condition and publishes an event when the condition becomes true. You could call it a special type of Message or Signal event, considering the rule engine to be an external system. The Conditional event can be used as a start event, catching intermediate event in sequence flow, or boundary event. There is no throwing form of the event.

Not many BPMN tools currently support the Conditional event. One use case is to monitor conditions of the BPM system as a whole, such as if a queue length exceeds some threshold or a service level agreement is not being met. Another might be to signal between processes or parallel segments of a single process, as we have seen with the Signal event. One process activity effectively sets the condition to true, and the Conditional event detects it, triggering some action.

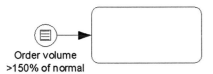
Order volume
>150% of normal

Figure 7-7. Process triggered by Conditional event

CHAPTER 8

Using Subprocesses

The Value of Subprocesses

One of the most powerful features of BPMN is one of the least appreciated, by modelers and tool vendors alike. I'm talking about subprocesses. Most of the process models I see in my BPMessentials training would be much improved if subprocesses were used more liberally, and more effectively.

In BPMN, a subprocess is simultaneously a single activity, within the context of a process, and a process unto itself. This dual nature is reflected in the notation, which allows you to draw the subprocess both *collapsed*, as a single rectangle with a + symbol inside, and *expanded* as a process diagram. Both representations refer to the same semantic element. They just show different levels of detail, and tools usually let you navigate back and forth between those views with a single click. Moreover, in BPMN 2.0 those views cannot get out of sync – at least in a valid diagram – because they reference the same XML in the semantic model.

This notion of a subprocess gives BPMN significant advantages over traditional modeling notations:

1. Unifies "end-to-end" process models

BPM as a management discipline is based on managing and monitoring your business from the perspective of "end-to-end" processes, core customer-facing flows that cut across traditional organizational and system boundaries. That means conceptualizing the end-to-end process as a *single entity*, not multiple related things. By collapsing visible detail without losing the integrity of a single semantic model for the process, subprocesses let you visualize your process end-to-end on a single page.

Subprocesses make BPMN inherently *hierarchical*, since the collapsed view of a subprocess at a parent level is a "container" for the expanded view of the subprocess at a child level, and this nesting can be continued as many levels deep as you like. The top level expresses a global view of the end-to-end process.

This global view of the process is not a separate "artist's conception," disconnected from the "actual" model, but expandable to reveal actual detail at any level. The simple idea that any process fragment can be displayed either collapsed or expanded allows the end-to-end process to be visualized at multiple levels of detail, all within the context of a single semantic model.

Hierarchical modeling is admittedly just a style. It is not mandated by the BPMN specification. In fact, it represents a change for traditional practitioners of process improvement, who often capture the workings of the as-is process in flat models stretching out over thirty feet of wall space. But flat models make it difficult to comprehend the end-to-end process as a single entity, since you cannot visually consume it all at once. The traditional solution, creating high-level views and detailed views as separate models, has the problem of keeping those models in sync. BPMN's hierarchical style does not have this problem because collapsed and expanded subprocesses are simply different views of the same semantic model.

The hierarchical style I recommend starts with a top-level view in which the whole end-to-end process fits on one page, using very coarse-grained subprocesses. Then you can expand any of those top-level subprocesses in a child-level diagram. All of these second-level diagrams should be hyperlinked to the top-level diagram. The second-level diagrams may contain subprocesses as well, and you can repeat this nesting to drill down to any level of detail while maintaining the integrity of a single semantic model end-to-end.

2. Defines reusable business services

A related benefit of subprocesses is they encourage "top-down" process modeling, giving business a greater voice in defining reusable *business services*. This is important in the relationship of BPM to Service Oriented Architecture (SOA). SOA is an IT-driven initiative that seeks to improve agility by optimizing reuse of IT assets. Historically, business services have been defined by IT architects and presented to business after the fact as the building blocks of to-be business processes.

BPMN allows an alternative to this IT-driven bottom-up approach. A subprocess can serve as a placeholder for a not-yet-defined business service. For example, a process activity could be modeled as a collapsed subprocess with the expansion of that subprocess left undefined. Even without detailing its internals, the subprocess can be incorporated in various end-to-end models, providing important business input to the scope and use of reusable business services in SOA.

3. Defines governance boundaries

A third benefit is that subprocesses support distributed process ownership and governance. End-to-end processes are rarely "owned" by a single person, but instead cross organizational boundaries within the enterprise. Each segment of the process may be defined and governed by a different organization.

Subprocesses provide clear demarcation of those governance boundaries without disturbing end-to-end model integrity. If the top-level diagram accurately describes the interaction between those parts, including the exception paths, then each part can be modeled and maintained independently. This can be enforced by a model repository and its associated authorization and governance features.

4. Defines event-handling scope

A fourth benefit of subprocesses quite powerful but unfamiliar to most process modelers. In BPMN, a subprocess can be used to define the *scope* of an *event*, meaning the portion of the process in which some signal – a timeout, error, or external event – is handled in a particular way. An *intermediate event* attached to the boundary of any activity – task or subprocess – defines that activity as the scope of the event. If the event signal occurs while that activity is running, the sequence flow out of the event describes the triggered behavior, called *event handling*. That behavior could include aborting the activity and redirecting flow along an exception flow, or initiating a parallel exception path without aborting the activity. This is described in full detail in Chapter 10 and Chapter 12.

In fact, modelers may wrap a fragment of the process in a subprocess for the sole purpose of defining the scope of a particular event handler. The association of the event handler with the subprocess is defined either by placing an intermediate event on the subprocess boundary or – something new in BPMN 2.0 – defining an *event subprocess* (see Chapter 12). If the event occurs while that subprocess is running, the defined event handling is triggered. If the event occurs after that subprocess has completed, the event handling is not triggered. If the same event occurring later in the process is handled differently, another event handler may be added to that part of the process.

Thus, a subprocess in the BPMN diagram may have no business significance other than describing when a deadline Timer starts and ends, or where a particular error or message results in a particular action. In order to precisely describe exception handling, process analysts using BPMN need to understand the use of subprocesses to define event scope.

Subprocess Types

Subprocess vs. Call Activity

BPMN 2.0 distinguishes a regular *Subprocess* node, formerly called *embedded subprocess*, from a *Call Activity*, formerly called *reusable subprocess*. This distinction has to do with whether the subprocess is defined within the end-to-end process definition or externally, so it could be reused in multiple processes. Level 1 modelers – and many Level 2 modelers, as well – have little interest in this distinction, but it is good to know about.

In BPMN 1.x, there is no visual difference, but in BPMN 2.0, a regular Subprocess is drawn with a normal thin border and a Call Activity is drawn with a thick border (Figure 8-1). A Call Activity represents invocation of either a reusable *global task* or a *process*. Call Activity represents the calling element, and the global task or process represents the called element. The process containing the calling activities typically *imports* its referenced global tasks or processes, usually stored in separate files.

Figure 8-1. Subprocess and Call Activity

With a regular subprocess, the collapsed and expanded views represent the same semantic element, not a call from one element to another. With Call Activity, the collapsed shape represents the calling activity and the expanded view represents the called global task or process. Data must be explicitly passed from the Call Activity to the global task or called process. While this distinction is important for process execution, many business-oriented process modelers may ignore it.

Inline vs. Hierarchical Expansion

The hierarchical modeling style that I recommend implies subprocess expansion on a separate hyperlinked page. Expanding a subprocess this way does not require re-drawing the model, and lets the viewer zoom in and out to any level of detail. You won't find the term *hierarchical expansion* in the BPMN specification. In fact, the spec discusses expanded subprocesses only in their *inline* representation, in which the parent-level and child-level activities are drawn together on the same page.

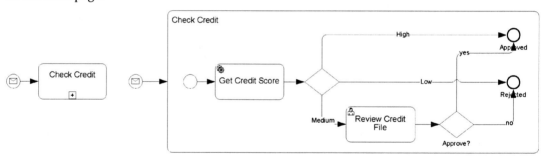

Figure 8-2. Collapsed (left) and expanded inline (right) views of Check Credit subprocess

With inline expansion (Figure 8-2), the rounded rectangle activity shape is enlarged and the child-level activities are drawn within it. With hierarchical expansion (Figure 8-3), the rounded rectangle activity shape is omitted; only the child-level activities are drawn. Intermediate events on the subprocess boundary (see Chapter 10) would appear on the parent-level page, not on the page showing the expansion.

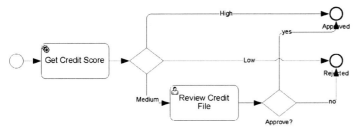

Figure 8-3. Hierarchical expansion of Check Credit subprocess.

Some have interpreted the BPMN 1.x specification as requiring inline expansion for an embedded (i.e., regular) subprocess. This, however, is incorrect, and BPMN 2.0 explicitly allows hierarchical expansion, which is generally better for modeling complex real-world processes. I recommend using it. Inline expansion is best used with simple subprocesses where the value of rendering parent and child levels on one page is greater than the benefits of hierarchical modeling described at the beginning of this chapter.

Ad-Hoc Subprocess

An *ad-hoc subprocess*, denoted with a tilde marker (Figure 8-4), is a special type of subprocess. Its expansion does not contain sequence flows specifying the defined order of activities,[14] but merely a list of activities that *could* be performed. Their order of execution is not specified, and it is not necessary to complete all of the activities in order to complete the ad-hoc subprocess. The selection and order of activities are the choice of the performer, not specified by the process model.

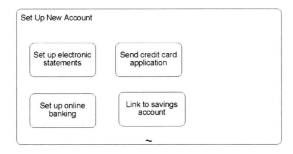

Figure 8-4. Ad-hoc subprocess

The primary value of ad-hoc subprocesses is to enumerate a menu of possible functions that could possibly be performed at a particular step of the process, without requiring a particular order or completion requirement in the model. In BPMN 1.x, ad-hoc subprocesses were inherently non-executable, but BPMN 2.0 attempts to give them execution-related attributes, such as an expression that specifies when the subprocess is complete, and whether the activities may be performed in parallel.

---

[14] Sequence flows in ad-hoc subprocesses are allowed in BPMN 2.0.

Transactional Subprocess

A *transactional subprocess*, denoted with a double border (Figure 8-5), signifies an activity modeled as a single *business transaction*. If the transactional subprocess does not complete successfully, then a consistent state of the system, equivalent to the state before the start of the subprocess, must be restored before the process can continue. Recovery of failed transactions using rollback and compensation is part of BPMN, and is discussed more fully in Chapter 14.

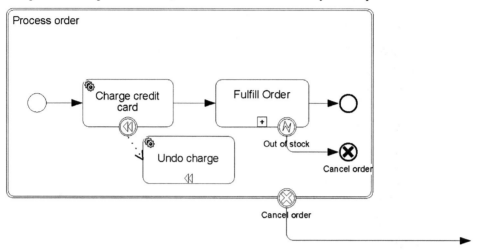

Figure 8-5. Transactional subprocess

CHAPTER 9

Start and End Events

Start Events

In Part I we introduced the concept of start events for processes and subprocesses, and we included None, Message, and Timer start events in the Level 1 palette. Here we take a more complete look at BPMN start events.

A start event indicates where (in the diagram) and how a process starts. In a top-level process, how it starts is specified by the *trigger type*, such as Message or Timer, representing the signal that creates a new process instance. In a subprocess, the trigger *must* be None (no icon inside), since what triggers the start of the subprocess is actually the sequence flow into it, not an event signal. A start event can only *catch* a signal, never throw one, so it cannot have an outgoing message flow.

Message Start Event

Message start (Figure 9-1) means the process is triggered by an external signal, a message. Typically this represents a *request* from the Customer, or equivalent. It is good practice to show the requester as a black-box pool with a message flow to the Message start event.

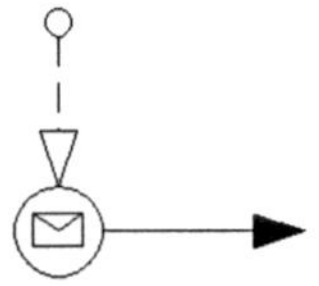

Receive order

Figure 9-1. Message start event

Timer Start Event

Timer start (Figure 9-2) signifies a scheduled process, typically a recurring one. It could be used, for example, to indicate that a process starts every Monday at 8am, or on April 15 every year, or at midnight every weekday.

Mondays, 8am

Figure 9-2. Timer start event

Signal Start Event

Signal start (Figure 9-3), like Message, signifies triggering by an external signal. Unlike Message, which is addressed to a specific process, Signal is broadcast to *any* listening process. The broadcaster or *publisher* may not be aware that this process is listening for, or *subscribing to*, the Signal. For example, the ERP system might publish a Signal indicating that a new customer has been added to the system, and various processes could be triggered by that event. Because Signal has no defined target, you cannot show the communication graphically in the diagram using message flow.

New customer

Figure 9-3. Signal start event

Conditional Start Event

Conditional start (Figure 9-4) signifies triggering by a watched data condition, similar to a database trigger. The condition is a boolean expression, and the Conditional event implies it is continuously monitored. When the expression becomes true, a process is triggered. For example, a watched condition might be *item.inventoryCount < 10*.

Low inventory

Figure 9-4. Conditional start event

Multiple Start Event

Multiple start (Figure 9-5) signifies triggering by *any* one of multiple signals representing the simple start event types just described. For example, if two different pools could invoke the process with a request message, technically that should be modeled as a Multiple start, not a Message start. BPMN 2.0 adds another type of Multiple start event called *Parallel start*, in which *all* of the signals must be received (in any order) before the process can start.

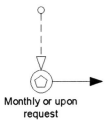

Monthly or upon
request

Figure 9-5. Multiple start event

How Many Start Events Can You Use?

Since BPMN describes business processes primarily from the perspective of *when* things happen, one would think that start event semantics would be intuitive and non-controversial. Surprisingly, that is not the case. In fact, some aspects of start events remained contentious within the BPMN 2.0 technical team right up to the end.

One such issue concerns how many start events you can have in a process or subprocess, and what it means if you have some number other than one.

It is allowed, in certain situations, to model a process or subprocess with *no start events* at all! In that case, any activity, gateway, or intermediate event (with a few exceptions) that has no incoming sequence flow is by default a *start node* for the process or subprocess, equivalent to a None start event immediately preceding it in the orchestration. However, you can only omit a start event if there are also *no end events* modeled for that process or subprocess.

Figure 9-6 shows an example of this, sometimes called a *parallel box*, in which a subprocess encloses multiple activities without sequence flows. This merely signifies that when the subprocess starts, the enclosed activities are enabled in parallel, meaning there is no prescribed order of execution, although both must complete in order for the subprocess to complete.

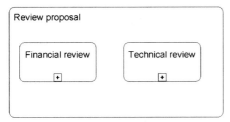

Figure 9-6. Parallel box

It is allowed to omit start and end events from more complex processes as well, but I do not recommend it. As the diagram gets more complex it is likely that an extraneous start or end event will be added and this will make the implied start nodes illegal. Also, I favor consistency across all process levels in the diagram to simplify shared understanding. The only good reason to omit start and end events is to save critically needed space on the page.

More Than One Start Event

The case of more than one start event is more troublesome and was debated within the BPMN 2.0 team for long time. While I advise using one and only one start event in a subprocess, it is technically allowable to have more than one. In that case, each represents an *exclusive alternative* start point, but you can't really tell from the diagram which one is enabled. (This is hidden in the *targetRef* attribute of the sequence flow.) I strongly recommend you use only one start event in a subprocess.

In a top-level process, multiple start events are sometimes a good idea. In fact, we use them in our Level 2 method. Each start event represents an alternative trigger for the process. Once triggered, the process or subprocess instance will *ignore a signal subsequently received by any other start event.* (In other words, such a signal would initiate a *new* process instance.)

A common use case for this is *channel-dependent start*. For example, a process triggered by customer request may require different initial step if the request arrives via the call center versus web or fax, but has the same backend processing regardless of the contact channel. One way to model this is with multiple Message start events, each representing an alternative start point for the process (Figure 9-7).

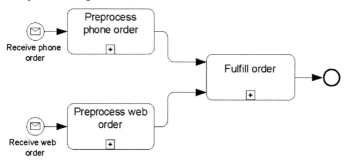

Figure 9-7. Channel-dependent start

An alternative notation for this use case based on an event gateway (Figure 12-13) is discussed in Chapter 12.

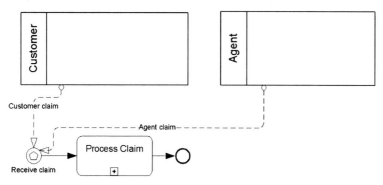

Figure 9-8. Multiple start event

Note that this is *not* the same semantics as a *Multiple* start event (Figure 9-8). You would use Multiple start if any of the triggers initiates the *same* flow. You would use more than one start event if each trigger initiates a *different* path.

End Events

An end event signifies the end of a path in a process or subprocess. In contrast to start events, where using only one is generally best, it is good practice to use *more than one* end event, specifically one for each distinct end state of the process or subprocess. The issues around combining or separating end events were discussed previously in the section on Level 1 modeling style.

In a process or subprocess containing parallel paths, each parallel path must reach an end event in order for the process or subprocess to complete *normally*. Certain special end event types – Terminate, Error, or Cancel – have the effect of completing a process or subprocess *abnormally*, that is, immediately, even if other parallel paths have not reached their end event.

It is not necessary, and in fact bad style, to use a gateway to join parallel paths immediately preceding an end event. A merge is always implied when multiple sequence flows connect into the same end event, whether they are alternative or parallel.

End events may propagate a signal, called a *result*, when they are reached. Each result type is represented in the notation by a different *throwing* event, denoted by a black-filled icon. (An end event may never *catch* an event signal or receive an incoming message flow.) Unlike subprocess start events, which must not have a trigger, subprocess end events may throw a result, and this is a frequent occurrence.

Message End Event

A *Message* end event (Figure 9-9) sends a message to an external participant. When a top-level process is initiated by a request message, it is best practice to represent distinct end states of the process with Message end events that report final status (e.g., confirmation, rejection notice, etc.) to the requester.

Figure 9-9. Message end event

Signal End Event

A *Signal* end event (Figure 9-10) broadcasts or *publishes* a result signal that can be caught either externally or by a paired catching Signal event within the process model. Unlike Message, the Signal result is not addressed to a particular process, and in fact the thrower need not even be aware of the other processes or activities that are listening for it. Thus it is useful for modeling a mode of loosely coupled interactions known as *publish-subscribe integration*. Because of this loose coupling, there is no connector in the diagram equivalent to message flow, linking the throw and the catch. Instead they are linked by reference to a common Signal definition. The use of Signal events is discussed more fully in Chapter 10 and Chapter 12.

Figure 9-10. Signal end event

Error End Event

Reaching an *Error* end event (Figure 9-11) in a process or subprocess immediately ends that process level, even if there are parallel paths still active. The event propagates an error result signal from the child level of a process to its parent level. This result can only be caught by an *intermediate Error event* attached to the subprocess boundary.[15] Technically, the BPMN spec says the signal is caught by the nearest enclosing parent level – e.g., it could be the grandparent level – but it is definitely best practice to propagate errors one level at a time.

The throwing and catching Error events are linked by referencing the same error definition[16]. (If the catching event lacks such a reference, it will catch any error thrown from the child level.)

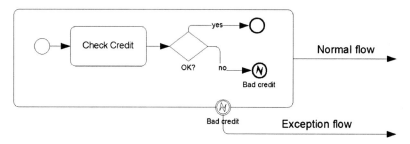

Figure 9-11. Error throw-catch pattern

This *Error throw-catch* pattern is a staple of Level 2 modeling. Its main purpose is to propagate an exception in a subprocess to the parent level process. In Figure 9-11, any instances reaching the Error end event *Bad credit* continue on the sequence flow out of the paired boundary event, called the *exception flow*. Instances following the happy path to the None end event continue on the sequence flow out of the activity, called the *normal flow*. This is discussed in detail in Chapter 10 and Chapter 12.

Escalation End Event

The *Escalation* end event (Figure 9-12) is new in BPMN 2.0. Its throw-catch semantics are similar to Error, except that the process or subprocess is not aborted if there are parallel paths still active.

---

[15] In BPMN 2.0, the error may also be caught by an event subprocess instead of a boundary event. More on this in Chapter 12.

[16] In BPMN 1.x, both reference the same ErrorCode attribute.

This non-interrupting behavior is signified by the dashed border style of the catching Escalation boundary event.

An Escalation end event signifies that some *additional* activity is required in parallel with the current normal process. Upon reaching an Escalation end event, an escalation result signal is propagated from child level to parent level, initiating a new parallel thread on the exception flow. However, unlike Error throw-catch, the normal flow out of the activity also continues as usual.

In the example of Figure 9-12, the Escalation end event labeled *Customer service request* triggers the exception flow to *Update Account Info*, which occurs *in parallel with* the normal flow to the next activity after *Take Order*.

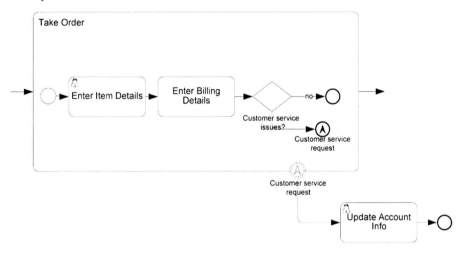

Figure 9-12. Escalation throw-catch pattern

Cancel End Event

A *Cancel* end event (Figure 9-13) is another special form of Error event. It is used only in transactional subprocesses, denoted with a double border, and like Error, it is always interrupting. Throw-catch semantics are identical to Error, except that before commencing the exception flow out of the catching event, transaction recovery via rollback and compensation is implicitly invoked. Transactions are discussed in detail in Chapter 14.

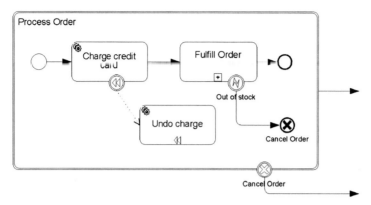

Figure 9-13. Cancel end event is only used in transactional subprocesses

Terminate

Terminate (Figure 9-14) is a special type of end event. Reaching a Terminate event in a process or subprocess immediately ends that process level, even if parallel paths are still active. In that sense it is like Error, but it does not propagate a result signal to the parent level. Following Terminate in a subprocess, the process continues on the *normal flow* out of the activity. For example, in Figure 9-14, if the *Financial Review* step results in disapproval of the project, Terminate aborts *Technical Review* if it has not yet completed. Then the process continues on the normal flow out of the *Project Review* activity.

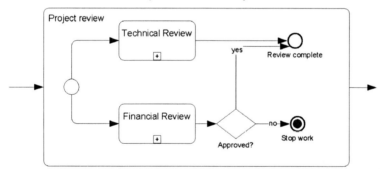

Figure 9-14. Terminate end event

Beginning modelers frequently make the mistake of assuming Terminate in a subprocess ends the parent-level process. That is incorrect. Reaching Terminate in a subprocess only ends that subprocess. Then the next activity begins.

In BPMN 1.1, Terminate was valuable for modeling a "workaround" to the absence of non-interrupting boundary events in BPMN. Now that non-interrupting events have been introduced in BPMN 2.0, the workaround is unnecessary, but if your tool does not yet support them, you should be aware of it. See Chapter 10 for details.

Intermediate Events

The most obvious difference between BPMN diagrams at Level 1 and Level 2 is the use of *intermediate events*. As the name implies, an intermediate event represents a signal that something happened *during* a process or subprocess, i.e., after its start event and before an end event.

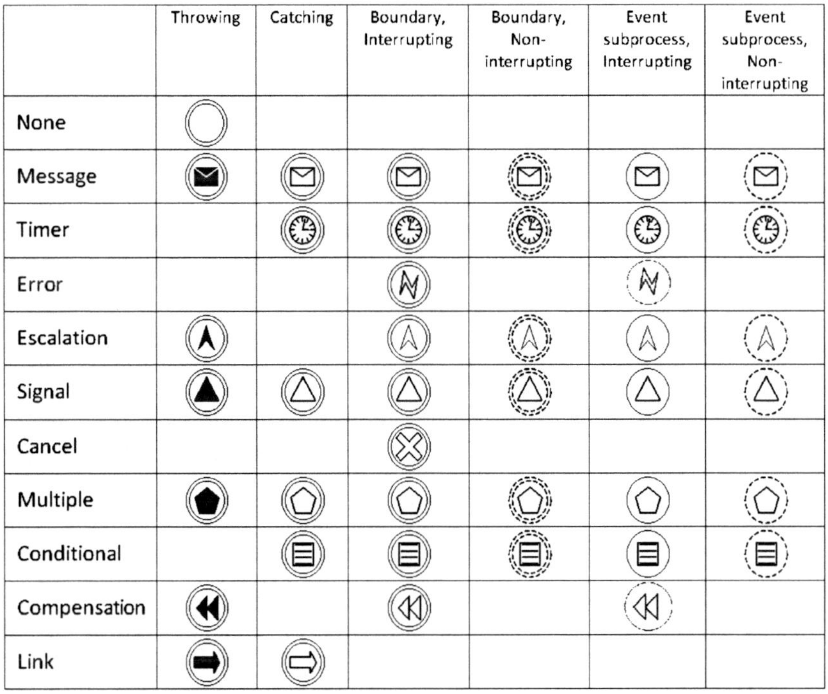

	Throwing	Catching	Boundary, Interrupting	Boundary, Non-interrupting	Event subprocess, Interrupting	Event subprocess, Non-interrupting
None	○					
Message	⊠	⊡	⊡	⊡	⊡	⊡
Timer		⊕	⊕	⊕	⊕	⊕
Error			Ⓝ		Ⓝ	
Escalation	⒜		⒜	⒜	⒜	⒜
Signal	▲	△	△	△	△	△
Cancel			⊗			
Multiple	⬟	⬠	⬠	⬠	⬠	⬠
Conditional		☰	☰	☰	☰	☰
Compensation	◀◀		◀◀		◀◀	
Link	➡	⇨				

Figure 10-1. Complete set of intermediate events

BPMN provides a wide variety of intermediate event types, distinguished by border style, symbol inside, and placement in the diagram, either in sequence flow or attached to an activity boundary (Figure 10-1). In addition, BPMN 2.0 introduces a new construct, the *event subprocess*. It is effectively a type of intermediate event and associated handler, although it uses a different notation. Like the boundary event, it comes in interrupting and non-interrupting varieties.

Classifying Intermediate Events

Drawn as a circle with a double border, an intermediate event can be used to model many different types of process behavior. The behavior is precisely expressed in the diagram based on the combination of the trigger or result symbol inside the event, the event's border style (solid or dashed), and its placement in the diagram. Figure 10-1 catalogs the complete set of intermediate event types. We will focus on the three most important: Message, Timer, and Error. The others are convenient in certain circumstances, but Message, Timer, and Error are the intermediate event types you really need to know.

Throwing vs. Catching

The first thing you notice about Figure 10-1 is that in the throwing column the symbols are black (filled) and in the other three columns the symbols are white (unfilled). We've seen that before. End events, which can only throw a signal, have black symbols, and start events, which can only catch signals, have white symbols. Some intermediate events can do both, so the color of the symbol[17] indicates whether it is throwing or catching.

The modeled process behavior depends on how the event is placed in the diagram. There are two basic arrangements.

Drawn *in sequence flow* (Figure 10-2) – that is, with a sequence flow in and a sequence flow out – a catching event means the process *waits* at the event until the trigger signal occurs. A throwing event means the process throws the event signal immediately and continues.[18]

Figure 10-2. Catching (left) and throwing (right) Message events in sequence flow

A catching intermediate event can also be drawn *attached to the boundary* of an activity, either a task or subprocess. In that case it has no sequence flow in, and exactly one sequence flow out. That arrangement is called an *attached event* or *boundary event*.

---

[17] In BPMN 1.1 and later

[18] The BPMN spec uses the term *in normal flow* rather than *in sequence flow*, but that is confusing because *normal flow* refers to the sequence flow out of an activity, as opposed to *exception flow* out of an attached event. So I use the term "in sequence flow" to describe this intermediate event pattern.

Boundary Events

All boundary events are catching types. They signify that while the attached-to activity is running, the event is *listening* for the trigger signal. *If* that signal occurs – in most instances it does not – then some new behavior is triggered.

In BPMN 1.1 that behavior was limited to *interrupting* the activity – aborting it in flight – and proceeding on the sequence flow drawn out of the event, called the *exception flow* (Figure 10-3). If the activity completes without the occurrence of the trigger signal, the process continues on the flow out of the activity itself, called the *normal flow*.

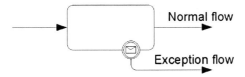

Figure 10-3. Interrupting message boundary event

BPMN 2.0 adds an important new behavior, triggering a new parallel path without interrupting the activity. Such *non-interrupting boundary events* are distinguished from interrupting types by their border style. Non-interrupting events have a dashed border (Figure 10-4), while interrupting events have a solid border.

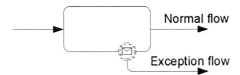

Figure 10-4. Non-interrupting message boundary event

Here is an example to illustrate the use of interrupting vs. non-interrupting boundary events. Consider an order process. After the order is placed but before it is shipped, the customer may cancel it without penalty. During the subprocess *Prepare to Ship Order*, we indicate that the process is listening for the Customer cancel message with an interrupting boundary event. If that message occurs before *Prepare to Ship Order* is complete, we interrupt that activity and proceed on the exception flow, as illustrated in Figure 10-5.

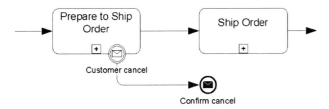

Figure 10-5. Interrupting message boundary event example

In this case, the exception flow simply ends the process with a cancellation confirmation message back to the customer. (A more complete diagram would also show a message flow into the boundary event and a message flow out of the end event.) Note that if the *Customer Cancel* event occurs, the *Ship Order* activity – on the normal flow – does not. This is exactly what we want! With interrupting boundary events, the normal flow (to *Ship Order*) and the exception flow (to the end event) are always *exclusive alternatives*. Any process instance takes either one path or the other; it cannot take both.

What happens if the customer's cancel message arrives after *Prepare to Ship Order* is complete? Absolutely nothing, at least as modeled by Figure 10-5! Boundary events stop listening for the signal once the activity they are attached to is complete, so the message is ignored. This illustrates that messages are simply *requests*; they do not directly *control* process execution. An event able to receive the message must be active in order for it to be acted upon.

Now consider the case where a different message is received from the customer during *Prepare to Ship Order*, not to cancel the order but merely to update the shipping address. In that case we do not want to interrupt the order, but we want to perform an additional task, in this case to update the order details. Prior to BPMN 2.0, this required a complicated diagram pattern, but with non-interrupting boundary events it is now much simpler.

This is illustrated in Figure 10-6. The dashed border of the event indicates it is non-interrupting. That means the normal flow and the exception flow are not exclusive alternatives but parallel paths. If the event occurs, *Prepare to Ship Order* completes normally and continues to *Ship Order* on the normal flow. *Update Order* is triggered in parallel with this on the exception flow, which then ends in an end event. Remember that the process does not end until all parallel threads reach their end event, so the main thread of the process continues even after the end event following *Update Order*.

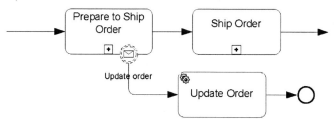

Figure 10-6. Non-interrupting message boundary event example

Event Subprocess Start Events

In addition to boundary events, BPMN 2.0 introduces a second way to respond to event signals caught in the context of a running activity: *event subprocesses*. An event subprocess is an event handler that runs *inside* of a regular subprocess if the event signal occurs. The event subprocess start event performs a function similar to a boundary event: It listens for the event signal while the regular subprocess is running, and triggers the handler if and when that signal occurs. That is why it is classified as a sort of intermediate event in Figure 10-1.

Event subprocess start events come in both interrupting and non-interrupting variants, with single solid thin and dashed border styles, respectively, as indicated in Figure 10-1. An interrupting event subprocess aborts the regular subprocess when the event signal occurs, and then executes the event subprocess (the handler). If the handler ends in a None end event, processing continues on the normal flow out of the regular subprocess. The event subprocess could also end in an Error or Escalation end event, which rethrows the exception to a paired boundary event. In that case, processing continues on the exception flow out of the boundary event.

The semantics of event subprocesses are discussed at more length later in this chapter.

Listening vs. Waiting

It is worth reiterating an important difference between a catching event in sequence flow (Figure 10-2) and a boundary event or event subprocess. With a catching event in sequence flow, the process *pauses and waits* for the trigger signal. It stops at that point, and does not continue until the signal arrives. If the signal never arrives, the process instance is stuck there.

A boundary event or event subprocess just *listens* for the trigger signal. Nothing stops while it is listening. After an activity completes, its boundary events and event subprocesses become inactive. They stop listening. That is what occurs in most instances, because these events typically represent *exceptions*, not the normal path of execution.

Timer Intermediate Events

A Timer intermediate event listens or waits for a signal from the process's own internal clock. BPMN has no throwing Timer event, only catching.

Timer event In Sequence Flow

Drawn in sequence flow, a Timer intermediate event represents a *delay*. It means either *wait for [specified duration]* or *wait until [specified date/time]*. That is all it can mean. For example, you might want to wait for a short while before retrying an activity, such as polling for data (Figure 10-7). Or, to model a batch job run overnight, you could use a Timer event in sequence flow to mean "wait until 8am."

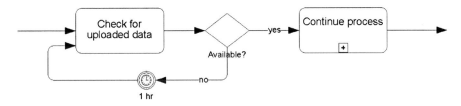

Figure 10-7. Delay using Timer event

A Timer event in sequence flow does NOT mean wait for something to occur, such as a response to a request. That would typically be a Message event.

BPMN provides attributes for the Timer event to specify the duration or date/time, but typically these are not directly visible in the diagram. Therefore it is best practice to always label a Timer event with the duration or date/time parameter.

Timer Boundary Event

As a boundary event, a Timer event acts like a combination stopwatch and alarm clock. The stopwatch always starts when the attached-to activity starts. As discussed previously, for a User task that means when the sequence flow into that activity arrives, not when the performer decides to begin work on it. The alarm sounds either after the specified time interval (relative to the start time) or at the specified date/time.

What happens when the alarm sounds depends on whether the event is interrupting or non-interrupting. An interrupting Timer event aborts the activity, and the process continues on the exception flow. A non-interrupting Timer event triggers a parallel thread of execution on the exception flow without aborting the activity or the normal flow out of it.

For example (Figure 10-8), you could use an interrupting Timer event in a hiring process to indicate that if a search for internal candidates does not complete within two weeks, you want to abandon it and engage an external search firm. Note that because the exception flow and normal flow are exclusive alternatives, they can be merged at *Screen resumes* without a gateway.

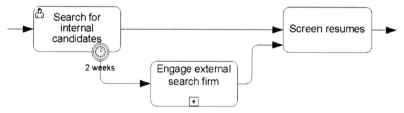

Figure 10-8. Interrupting timer boundary event

For timeout handling, the non-interrupting Timer event may be more useful. You could use it, for instance, to send a reminder or notification if a service level agreement is in danger of being violated. In Figure 10-9, the event does not abort the activity, so *Perform service* continues while *Notify manager* is executed.

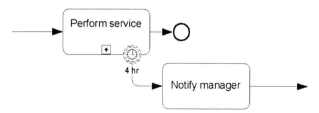

Figure 10-9. Non-interrupting timer boundary event

Message Intermediate Events

A Message intermediate event either sends or receives a message, meaning a signal between the process and some external entity.

Throwing Message Event

A throwing Message event sends a message. It is virtually identical to a Send task. It can only be drawn in sequence flow, never as a boundary event. One typical use case is to request something from the customer or external service provider. Another is to send a notification to an external entity without ending the process. Many beginners mistakenly use a throwing Message event to send a notification to participant within the process. A message can only be sent to someone *outside* the process. You should get into the habit of drawing message flows attached to any Message event. If you can't represent the target of the message as an external pool, maybe it's not really a message!

After the message is sent, the process continues. It does not wait at the throwing event for a response.

Catching Message Event in Sequence Flow

A catching Message event in sequence flow waits for a message. It is virtually identical to a Receive task. Typically it is used to receive a response to a prior request message. For example (Figure 10-10), if an application for credit is incomplete, the bank may request additional information. The request is issued in a throwing Message event and the process waits for the response in a catching Message event.

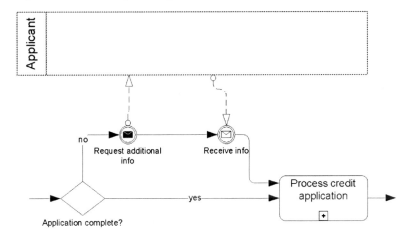

Figure 10-10. Throwing and catching Message events

The process is not just listening for the message, it is waiting. Even if the external entity is "required" to respond, there is always the possibility the respondent will ignore the request, or the process may be prevented from receiving the response because of some communications problem. For that reason, it is best practice to specify what should happen if the response is not received within a reasonable period of time.

Event Gateway

A good way to do this is using an *event gateway*. An event gateway is like a regular exclusive gateway, except that the choice of outputs is not based on a data condition. Instead it is based on which event occurs first. The most common use of event gateway is to wait for one or more messages in combination with a timeout (Figure 10-11).

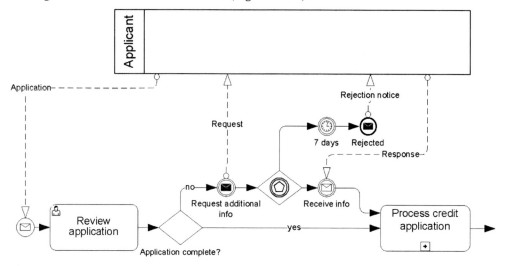

Figure 10-11. Message exchange using event gateway

In an event gateway, the diamond shape has an intermediate event symbol inside (technically it is the Multiple intermediate event) and a catching intermediate event on each sequence flow out of the gateway, typically Message or Timer. The event that occurs first determines the path enabled out of the gateway. Any trigger signals arriving after that are ignored.

Figure 10-11 represents an improved version of the request for additional information in Figure 10-10. Instead of waiting for the response in a bare catching Message event, we wait for it in an event gateway. This says if the response is not received within 7 days, the credit application will be rejected and the process will end. If the response is received within 7 days (measured with respect to the sequence flow into the event gateway), then the flow continues to *Process credit application*.

Message Boundary Event

We have already discussed the basics of the Message boundary event in both interrupting (Figure 10-5) and non-interrupting (Figure 10-6) flavors.

The activity the event is attached to determines the *scope* of the event, meaning the portion of the process during which that message will trigger a particular exception flow. If the same message triggers some different behavior if it occurs at a different point in the process, a second Message event attached to a different activity downstream can be used to model this.

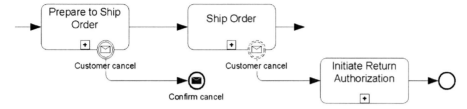

Figure 10-12. Multiple handlers for the same message

For example, in Figure 10-5 we said the customer could cancel the order without penalty before the activity *Prepare to Ship Order* is complete, but after that it would be too late. If the message arrived after that it would be ignored by the process.

A better approach from a customer service perspective might be to notify the customer that the ordered goods were in process of being shipped, something that cannot be stopped, and send the customer the forms needed to return the goods for credit. In this case (Figure 10-12), a second event representing the same *Customer cancel* message is inserted, this one attached to the boundary of *Ship Order*. In fact, since we cannot abort shipment once it has started – this is our company's policy, nothing to do with BPMN – we make it a non-interrupting event. The key point here is that the same trigger signal – the *Customer cancel* message – has a different effect depending on the state of the process when it is received, as modeled by separate message boundary events.

Error Intermediate Events

The last of the three major event types is *Error*. An error is an exception signal generated within the process. The only type of Error intermediate event allowed is the interrupting boundary event. You cannot have a non-interrupting Error event.[19] Also, you can only throw an Error signal from an end event, not from a throwing intermediate event, and you cannot wait for an Error signal in a catching event in sequence flow or in an event gateway.

Error Boundary Event on a Task

Because a task in BPMN is opaque – you cannot look inside it – you cannot explicitly show in the diagram the specific source of an Error event on a task boundary. In the diagram, the source is simply implied by the event label.

While the BPMN spec does not require it, you can make your diagrams more expressive by applying the following interpretations to an Error event on a task boundary:

---

[19] BPMN 2.0 adds a non-interrupting event with similarities to Error, called *Escalation*; we'll talk about that later.

- An Error event on a *Service task* boundary indicates a *fault*. A fault is a technical term meaning the service could not complete normally. The system providing it may be unavailable, or the communication link to it may be down, or maybe you have just provided invalid data in your invocation of it. Thus a fault is a *technical exception*, as distinct from a *business exception*. For example, if I try to withdraw $100 from an ATM machine and the ATM cannot read my card, that is a fault. If the withdrawal fails because I only have $50 in my account, that is a business exception.

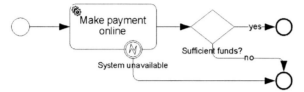

Figure 10-13. Error boundary event on *Service task* indicates a fault

- An Error event on a *User task* boundary indicates a *user-declared exception*. For example, the task user interface allows the performer to declare this instance has some kind of problem, diverting it from the happy path onto an exception path. Previously in the BPMessentials training I advised use of Error events on tasks only for Service task faults, and use of a gateway following the User task to model all business exceptions. That is still good practice, but some may prefer using attached Error instead, and I think that is OK. It takes up less space on the page. For example, Figure 10-14 shows Figure 10-11 redrawn using a user-declared Error instead of the gateway.

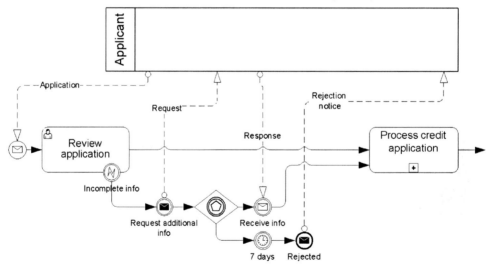

Figure 10-14. Error boundary event on User task indicates user-declared exception

Error Throw-Catch

When an Error event is attached to a subprocess, you can generally assume that the source of the error is indicated by an Error end event in the subprocess expansion. The error signal thrown by the end event is caught by the boundary event. We call this *error throw-catch*.

Since there can be more than one possible error, thrower and catcher are linked by reference to a common Error event definition.[20] This information does not print in the diagram, however, so you should use matching labels as well.

When an error throw-catch occurs, it means that the subprocess has completed abnormally. The process continues on the exception flow out of the boundary event instead of the normal flow out of the subprocess. Note that error throw-catch is not anywhere-to-anywhere. It is very limited. The error signal can *only* be sent from an end event of a subprocess to a boundary event of the same subprocess.[21] This effectively propagates the exception from a child level to its parent level in the process model hierarchy.

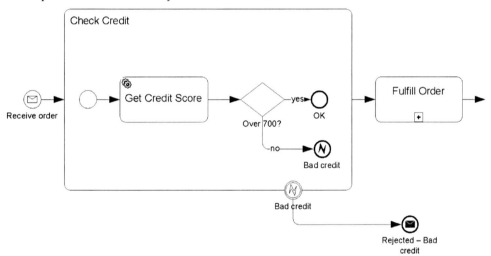

Figure 10-15. Error throw-catch

Figure 10-15 illustrates error throw-catch in an order process. Here we have used the expanded-inline representation of the *Check Credit* subprocess to show both the thrower and catch on the same page. If we had expanded *Check Credit* on a child page, we would see just the Error boundary event in the top-level page, and just the Error end event in the child-level page. Even though *Check Credit* is actually complete once it reaches the end event, the Error result means it

---

[20] In BPMN 1.x, by matching ErrorCode values

[21] Technically BPMN 2.0 says it is caught by the nearest enclosing parent of the thrower, but if there is no Error boundary event on the direct parent – i.e. the subprocess boundary itself – the diagram is going to be very confusing.

completed abnormally. The throw-catch diverts the flow to the *Rejected-Bad credit* end event, so the instance does not proceed to *Fulfill Order*.

Escalation Intermediate Events

BPMN 2.0 introduces a variant of the Error event called *Escalation*. Escalation events support the same throw-catch behavior but with three important differences:

- The boundary event is by default *non-interrupting*, with a dashed border. (You may, however, specify an Escalation boundary event to be interrupting, with a solid border.)

- Escalation does not imply an error, just some additional processing triggered during a process activity.

- Escalation can be thrown from either an end event or a throwing intermediate event. Like Error, however, you cannot pause the process to wait for an *Escalation* signal in a catching event or event gateway. You can only catch it in a boundary event or event subprocess.

Escalation is brand new, so it has no history of common usage. However, as with Error, you can enhance your diagrams' expressiveness by applying the following interpretations to Escalation event patterns.

Escalation Boundary Event on a Task

Escalation attached to a User task boundary is a valuable addition to the Level 2 palette.[22] It can be interpreted as optional additional processing initiated by the task performer. This additional processing, drawn on the exception flow out of the boundary event, runs in parallel with the User task and the normal flow out of it.

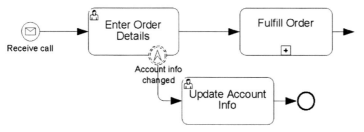

Figure 10-16. Escalation boundary event on User task

For example, a call center rep taking telephone orders might be asked to correct certain information about the customer's account. This additional activity, performed by a customer service rep, can be modeled using Escalation (Figure 10-16). It does not interrupt the entry of

---

[22] There is no rule that Escalation cannot be attached to a Service task, but I can't think of a use case for it.

order information or the normal flow to order fulfillment, but represents a parallel path of the process.

If the User task is inside a subprocess, the path out of the Escalation event must complete before the subprocess is complete. For example, in Figure 10-17, *Fulfill Order* cannot start until *Update Account Info* is complete. If that potential delay presents a problem, you can always make *Update Account Info* an independent process, i.e. separate pool, triggered from a message in the Escalation exception flow (Figure 10-18). The subtle difference between Figure 10-17 and Figure 10-18 illustrates the attention required in Level 2 modeling to exactly when activities start and complete.

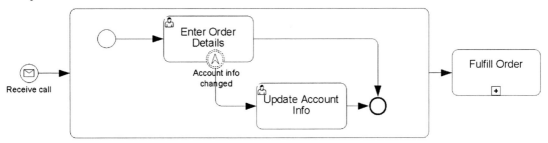

Figure 10-17. *Fulfill Order* **cannot start until** *Update Account Info* **is complete.**

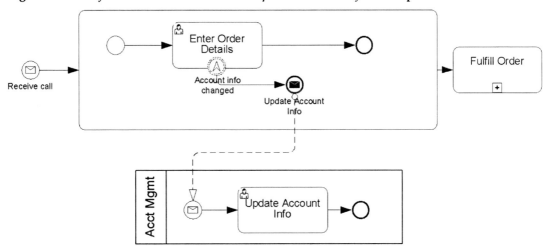

Figure 10-18. *Fulfill Order* **can be concurrent with** *Update Account Info***.**

Escalation Throw-Catch

As with Error, Escalation attached to a subprocess boundary implies that the source of the exception can be found in a throwing Escalation event in the subprocess expansion. (Unlike Error, the throw can come from an intermediate event as well as from an end event.)

Figure 10-19 illustrates how this works. Suppose your model details the flow of the call center order-taking subprocess. At some point in the subprocess – it doesn't have to be at the end – a gateway or exception flow within the subprocess leads to an event that throws the escalation signal. As with error, it is caught by an Escalation event attached to the subprocess boundary. Here *Update Account Info* occurs in parallel with the main process, so *Fulfill Order* is not delayed until it completes, but it has the advantage over Figure 10-18 of all being contained in a single pool. In BPMN, simpler is almost always better.

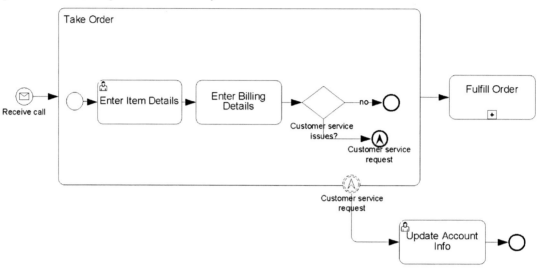

Figure 10-19. Escalation throw-catch

Signal Events

You may have noticed that while Message, Error, and Escalation events all support throw-catch signaling, each only works within a limited domain:

- Message throw-catch only works between pools; it cannot be used to communicate within a pool. Moreover, the target of a Message must be identified, for example, by a message flow drawn to a particular pool or process node. That means the sender of the Message must know who the target is.

- With Error throw-catch, the signal can only be sent from an end event of a subprocess to a boundary event on that same subprocess. The Error boundary event is always interrupting. Error cannot be caught by a start event or event gateway. And, of course, Error always implies a problem, so it is not optimum for general-purpose signaling.

- Escalation throw-catch is only slightly more flexible than Error, in that you can throw the signal from an intermediate or end event, but it can still only be caught by a boundary event on the same subprocess. Escalation cannot be caught by a start event or event gateway. By default Escalation is non-interrupting, although you can use interrupting Escalation events. But Escalation throw-catch is still not general-purpose.

In BPMN 1.1 a new event type, *Signal*, was introduced to provide a general-purpose form of throw-catch signaling:

- Signal can communicate both within a pool and across pools.

- Unlike Error or Escalation, Signal can be caught by a start event to trigger a new process instance.

- Signal can be caught either by a boundary event or an intermediate event in sequence flow (including event gateway). In other words, a process node can either listen for the signal or wait for it.

- Unlike Message, a Signal throw is not targeted to a specific pool, but broadcast or *published* so that any listening Signal event can *subscribe* to it. This more loosely coupled communications means the thrower does not need to know which other processes or activities are listening for the signal.

Because Signal is not necessarily directed at a particular target, the throw-catch conversion cannot be represented graphically like a message flow. Throwing and catching events are linked by referencing a common Signal event definition. Since this is not displayed, you should use matching labels in the diagram.

I recommend using Signal throw-catch only when one of the other throw-catch event types – Message, Error, or Escalation – cannot represent the intended behavior. The reason is that Signal is generally more difficult to follow in the diagram, since the event definition reference on a throwing Signal event gives no hint of the location of the catching event. (The thrower does not need to even know who is subscribing to the event!)

The following examples illustrate some use cases for Signal throw-catch.

Milestone Pattern

The milestone pattern refers to synchronization of some process step with an *intermediate state* or *milestone* of a concurrent (i.e., parallel) activity. Gateway joins are the normal way to synchronize parallel paths based on *completion* of activities, but until Signal was introduced, BPMN had no way to synchronize with some internal milestone, or state of *partial completion*.

For example, to initiate a new employee's 401K retirement account, there is an IT activity *Setup 401K Account* and an employee activity *First-Time Login* to initialize access. The *First-Time Login* step actually should not have to wait until the account is fully set up, i.e., until *Setup 401K Account* is complete, which could take two weeks. It can start as soon as the account is created, which is an internal *milestone* of the that activity (Figure 10-20).

The milestone-triggered behavior is modeled by expanding *Setup 401K account* and inserting a throwing Signal event after *Create new account*. The signal is caught by a paired catching Signal event before *First-time login* in the Employee lane. A catching event in sequence flow waits for the signal before proceeding, so *First-time login* is not enabled until *Create new account* is complete.

In Figure 10-20, the throw-catch is easy to read from the diagram. But what if the subprocess is shown collapsed, as in Figure 10-21? There the throw is hidden inside the subprocess, invisible unless you drill down to the child level. This is why Signal should not be your first option if a standard throw-catch is available.

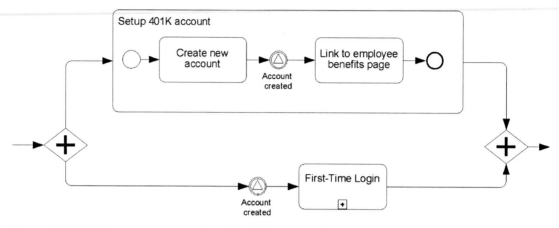

Figure 10-20. Milestone pattern using Signal throw-catch

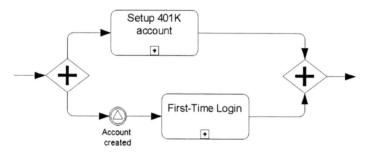

Figure 10-21. Source of Signal may be hidden

You might ask why not just erase the subprocess enclosing *Setup 401K Account*? Then you could just use sequence flows and joins the normal way (Figure 10-22).

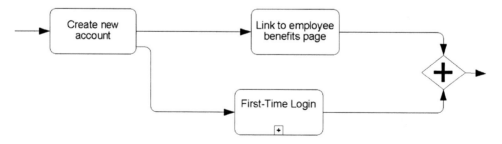

Figure 10-22. Erasing the subprocess boundary allows simpler synchronization

Admittedly, this is much simpler, and if you can do it this way, by all means do so. But it might not be possible. The subprocess may be a reusable service defined and governed externally to your process, so you can't assume you can break it apart. Or the subprocess might have a boundary event attached to it, which would not allow you to simply erase the boundary. With Signal used in the milestone pattern, you don't have to.

Communicating Exceptions Between Parallel Paths

Another use of Signal throw-catch is to communicate exceptions between parallel paths in a process. Remember Error and Escalation can only communicate between child and parent levels, not across parallel paths.

For example, in a large project bid it is common to begin developing specifications prior to contract signing if final agreement is expected. In Figure 10-23, this is indicated by modeling *Negotiate with client* and *Develop specifications* as parallel subprocesses. Should a problem arise in the negotiations that results in withdrawing the bid, we want to abort the *Develop specifications* activity. We do this by throwing a Signal, *Withdraw bid*, in the exception flow of an Error boundary event on *Negotiate with client*. The thrown *Withdraw bid* Signal is caught by an interrupting Signal boundary event on *Develop specifications*, which aborts that activity. [23]

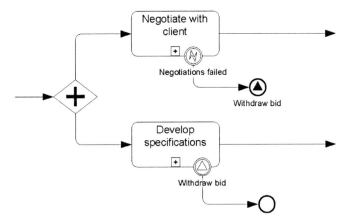

Figure 10-23. Exception handling using Signal throw-catch

A different type of exception might be caught by a non-interrupting Signal boundary event on Develop specifications, which would create another parallel path. For example, while the negotiations are underway, the client might request additional features. In that case (Figure 10-24), an Escalation boundary event on *Negotiate with client* could throw a Signal from the exception flow that is caught by a non-interrupting Signal event on *Develop specifications*. The exception flow for that event initiates *Develop spec for additions* without aborting the original activity.

---

[23] Here we could simply Terminate instead of throw the Signal, but Signal throw-catch allows cancellation of specific activities without ending the whole process.

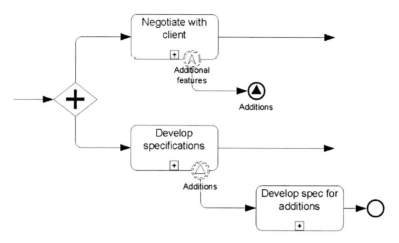

Figure 10-24. Signal catch may be non-interrupting

Subscribing to an External Event

A third use case for Signal throw-catch is *subscribing to an external event*. In the IT world, *publish/subscribe* refers to a loosely coupled form of integration in which the thrower or *publisher* of an event does not need to know what other activities are listening for that event. On the web, if you subscribe to a blog's feed you receive an event whenever a new post is added, but the blog publisher may be unaware of your subscription. This makes it easy for subscribers to register interest in an event without affecting the publisher.

A common application of this in BPM is instrumenting a business system to publish an event whenever some specific piece of data changes. For example, you could publish an event whenever a new customer is added to the CRM system, or whenever a new employee is hired, or whenever a fax arrives. If there is one particular process that is initiated when that event occurs, you could model that with a Message event. But actually there may be multiple processes that are interested in that event, including new ones added over time. With Signal, the system publishing the event does not even need to be aware of who they are.

While it is theoretically possible for the subscription to interrupt a running activity via a Signal boundary event, it is more common to trigger a new process instance with a Signal start event. The Signal throw typically would not be shown. You could represent it as a black-box pool, but without something like message flow there would be little point. You just need to indicate the source in the label of the Signal start event.

Event Subprocesses

As an alternative to boundary events, BPMN 2.0 introduces a new event-handling mechanism called an *event subprocess* (also called an *inline event handler*). An event subprocesses runs in the context of the activity that contains it, which must be a subprocess, not a task. Like a boundary event, an event subprocess listens for its trigger signal only while the containing activity is running. When that activity is complete, the event subprocess stops listening. However, unlike a boundary event, event handling is not performed on an exception flow external to the containing activity but internally, within the context of that activity. If a given subprocess contains both a boundary event and event subprocess with the same trigger definition, the event subprocess takes precedence.

Event subprocesses were introduced to align event handling between BPMN and BPEL and solve other data access issues in Level 3 modeling (executable BPMN), but they are a useful addition to the Level 2 palette, as well. In the process diagram, the event subprocess is drawn "floating" within the expanded view of the regular subprocess, that is, detached from its main flow. The event subprocess shape is distinguished from a regular subprocess by a dotted border, its trigger denoted by the start event type. Like a regular subprocess, a event subprocess can be rendered either as collapsed or expanded. Unlike a boundary event, presence of an event subprocess is invisible in the collapsed view of the containing subprocess.

As with boundary events, event subprocesses may be either interrupting or non-interrupting. You can define multiple event subprocesses within the same regular subprocess. Triggering of an event subprocess is similar to triggering of a boundary event, but the event subprocess executes entirely within the context of the regular subprocess, while the exception flow from a boundary event is external to it.

Non-Interrupting Event Subprocess

Non-interrupting event subprocesses are indicated by a non-interrupting start event. A particular non-interrupting event subprocess may be triggered multiple times. The regular subprocess must wait for any running event subprocess to complete before it is complete itself. The event subprocess can either complete normally, in which case the regular subprocess exits on the normal flow, or it can rethrow an Error to a boundary event on the regular subprocess, triggering the exception flow.

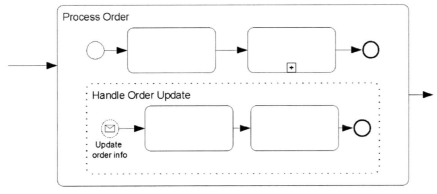

Figure 10-25. Non-interrupting event subprocess, shown expanded

When the event subprocess is rendered expanded, as in Figure 10-25, its trigger is indicated by the start event, which can be either interrupting (solid border) or non-interrupting (dashed border). When the event subprocess is rendered collapsed, as in Figure 10-26, the trigger is indicated by an icon equivalent to the start event symbol in the upper left corner.

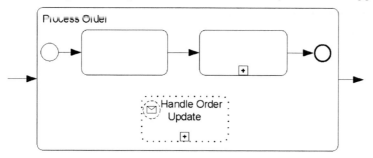

Figure 10-26. Non-interrupting event subprocess, shown collapsed

For example, in these figures, while *Process Order* is active, any *Update Order Info* events received will be handled by the event subprocess *Handle Update Order*, without aborting *Process Order*. When *Process Order* and any running event subprocess instances are complete, the process continues on the normal flow out of *Process Order*.

An event subprocess can *rethrow the exception* to the boundary of the containing activity. Figure 10-27 illustrates rethrow of an Error from the event subprocess to a boundary event on *Process Order*. If the event subprocess reaches the None end event, flow continues out of *Process Order* on the normal flow. If the event subprocess reaches the Error end event, the exception is rethrown to the boundary. This aborts *Process Order* if it is still running, and continues on the exception flow in the usual way.

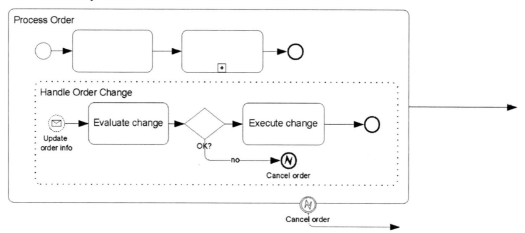

Figure 10-27. Non-interrupting event subprocess, rethrowing an error to a boundary event

Interrupting Event Subprocess

Interrupting event subprocesses are indicated by an interrupting start event, denoted by a solid thin border. A regular subprocess may define multiple interrupting event subprocesses, but only one may be executed in any process instance. When an interrupting event subprocess is triggered, the regular subprocess is aborted and the event subprocess is executed. If the event subprocess ends in a None end event, flow then continues out of the normal flow from the regular subprocess. The event subprocess may optionally rethrow the exception to the regular subprocess boundary via an Error end event. In that case, the process continues out of the exception flow from the boundary event.

For example, Figure 10-8, which shows an interrupting Timer boundary event, could be alternatively modeled using an interrupting event subprocess (Figure 10-28). A task cannot have an event subprocess, so here we wrap the task in a subprocess, and add the event subprocess inside the wrapper.

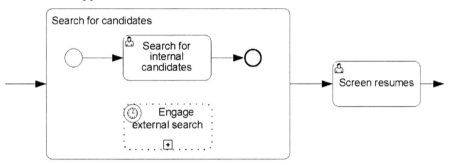

Figure 10-28. Interrupting event subprocess

A common use of interrupting event subprocess is an alternative form of Error throw-catch in which processing continues on the normal flow out of the activity instead of on a separate exception flow. This is closer to the way fault handling works in BPEL, and is a good choice for BPMN modelers anticipating implementation in a BPEL engine.

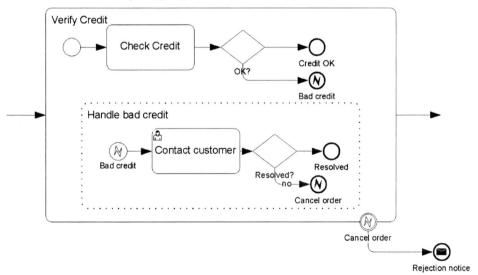

Figure 10-29. Error throw-catch using event subprocess

Figure 10-29 illustrates both Error throw-catch to an event subprocess and rethrow to the boundary. The initial Error throw, labeled *Bad credit*, is caught by the event subprocess *Handle bad credit*. The handler can end either in a good end state, represented by the None end event *Resolved*, or a bad end state, represented by the Error end event *Cancel order*. If *Resolved*, processing continues out of the normal exit from *Verify Credit*. If *Cancel order*, the error is rethrown to the *Cancel order* boundary event, which ends the order on the exception flow.

Non-Interrupting Events in BPMN 1.x

Non-interrupting events may be BPMN 2.0's most useful addition to the Level 2 modeler's palette. But what if your BPMN tool is still version 1.x? There is a way to model something equivalent there, too, but it is a little complicated and confusing to many beginning modelers. For that reason, I call it a workaround.

In BPMN 1.x, all boundary events are interrupting. The way to model a non-interrupting boundary event on a subprocess is to remove the event from the subprocess boundary and instead place it in a parallel path out of the subprocess's start event. Thus, in addition to the main path of your subprocess, a parallel path is paused *waiting* for the event. If the main thread completes before the event occurs, you need to end it with a Terminate event. Otherwise the subprocess will keep waiting for the path containing the event to reach completion. If the event occurs before the main path completes, the handling of that event is modeled on the parallel path, i.e., the one containing the event.[24]

There are two ways to model this event handling. The difference between them is roughly equivalent to the difference between a non-interrupting event subprocess and a non-interrupting boundary event. Recall that with a non-interrupting event subprocess, flow does not continue to the next activity until both the regular subprocess and the event subprocess complete. Thus, if the event handling is relatively quick, like sending a notification or reminder, this is usually what you want. But if the event handling could be long-running, and you want it to run in parallel with the main process but not hold up its continuation, you would use a non-interrupting boundary event instead.

Consider first the case of the short-running event handler. An example might be sending a reminder if a task is overdue. We don't want to abort the overdue task, just send a reminder if it is not completed by the deadline. Instead of modeling a Timer boundary event, which in BPMN 1.x is always interrupting, we use a Timer intermediate event on a parallel path, and follow the task with a Terminate (Figure 10-30). Because the event handling just sending the reminder is quick, we model it inside the subprocess, following the Timer event.

Figure 10-30 is the BPMN 1.x workaround equivalent to BPMN 2.0's simpler non-interrupting event subprocess notation shown in Figure 10-31. Note that Terminate is not required with the event subprocess, since if *Perform task* completes before four hours, the subprocess is complete.

---

[24] And what about non-interrupting events on a *task*? As with event subprocesses, you need to first wrap the task in a subprocess, as we did in Figure 10-28.

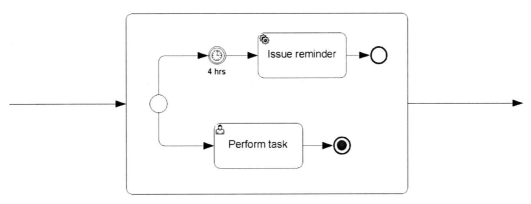

Figure 10-30. BPMN 1.x workaround for non-interrupting event with short-running handler

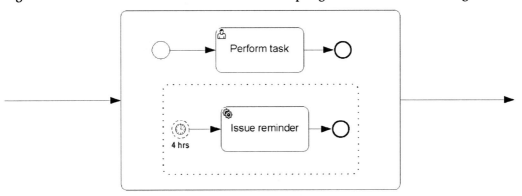

Figure 10-31. BPMN 2.0 event subprocess equivalent to Figure 10-30

Now consider the case where handling the non-interrupting event is long-running, and we do not want it to delay continuation of the main process. Figure 10-32 repeats a previous example illustrating how BPMN 2.0 models a non-interrupting Message event. Once an order is packed, a *Customer Cancel* message can no longer abort the shipment. Instead it triggers a return authorization activity. It is long-running and, as modeled in Figure 10-32, does not delay the start of the activity following *Ship Order*.

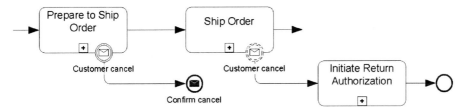

Figure 10-32. BPMN 2.0 non-interrupting boundary event allows long-running handlers

This can be described in BPMN 1.x as well using the workaround. If your tool does not provide non-interrupting events, you can use the method shown in Figure 10-33. Instead of modeling the handler on the parallel path of the subprocess, we invoke it as a separate process via a message flow. *Initiate Return Authorization* is no longer a subprocess on a parallel thread but a separate pool. This is the only way to model independent event-triggered parallel flows in BPMN 1.x.

Notice that this provides the desired behavior, equivalent to Figure 10-32. If *Ship Order* completes without a *Customer Cancel* message, it proceeds normally to the next activity. If *Customer Cancel* occurs while *Ship Order* is running, return authorization is initiated without interrupting *Ship Order* and without delaying start of the next activity when *Ship Order* is complete.

In this example, there is no synchronization with the main process required when the return authorization process completes. If such synchronization is necessary, you can model it with a return message flow caught by a Message intermediate event in the main process.

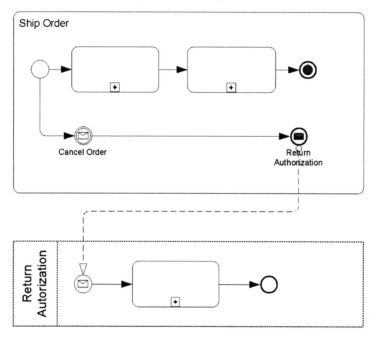

Figure 10-33. BPMN 1.x workaround for non-interrupting events with long-running handlers

CHAPTER 11

Branching and Merging Patterns

We have already been introduced to BPMN's most commonly used branching and merging patterns:

- Exclusive decision using a data-based gateway

- Exclusive decision using an event gateway

- Exclusive merge without a gateway

- Parallel split with or without a gateway

- Parallel join using a gateway

In this chapter we take a brief but more systematic look at all of BPMN's sequence flow branching and merging patterns.

Exclusive Branch

When an activity completes, all of the sequence flows leading out of it directly are enabled. Usually there is only one, but if there are three sequence flows out, all three execute in parallel. If the intent is that *just one* of the paths is taken by any instance, you use an exclusive gateway.

XOR Gateway

Drawn with either no symbol inside or an X inside – there is no difference between them – the technical name for this flow element is *exclusive data-based gateway*, because the condition that enables each sequence flow, or *gate*, out of it is based on a boolean data condition. It is also commonly called an *XOR gateway*.

BPMN lets you define the boolean data condition for each gate, but I think of those data conditions as part of the executable Level 3 model. For Level 2 modeling, I recommend instead labeling both the gateway and all sequence flows out. If the data condition can be framed as a yes/no question, that question should be the gateway label and the sequence flows should be labeled yes and no. But in any case, try to label both the gateway and the sequence flows out.

Even though it is called a "decision" gateway, a gateway is purely conditional logic. It does not have a performer, so a gateway cannot "make" a decision such as approving or rejecting a request. You should use a User task for *making* the approval decision; the gateway merely routes the flow this way or that based on the decision that was made.

Event Gateway

The *event gateway* is another form of exclusive gateway, except that the choice is not determined by a boolean expression of process data. Instead it is based on the *event* that occurs first. The event gateway is drawn with a Multiple intermediate event inside the diamond, and an intermediate event (or Receive task, which is the same as a Message intermediate event) drawn as the first node on each gate.

Common use cases for event gateway are:

- Response timeout. When a request message sent to another pool expects a response, the event gateway provides a way to say what should happen if the response does not arrive by a certain time. The event gateway is drawn with a Message event to receive the response and a Timer event representing the timeout (Figure 11-1). If the response message is received before the timeout, the path out of the Message event is taken. If not, the path out of the Timer event is taken.

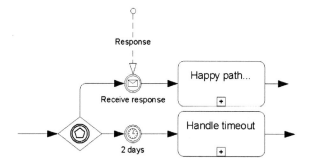

Figure 11-1. Event gateway branches to exception path if no message is received by deadline

- Handling exception response. In SOA, particularly, it is common to model normal and exception responses to a request as separate messages rather than a single message with different values. To distinguish handling of the normal happy path response from one or more exception responses, you can use an event gateway (Figure 11-2). The gateway can also account for a timeout, as in the previous use case.

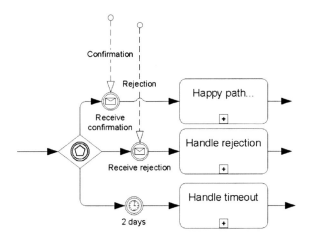

Figure 11-2. Event gateway branches to exception path if exception message is received

Parallel Split

From the earlier section on Level 1 modeling, recall that the *parallel gateway*, or *AND-gateway*, can be used to split an incoming sequence flow into two or more parallel paths. Those paths execute concurrently, overlapping in time. We have also seen previously that two or more sequence flows out of an activity also **are** executed in parallel when the activity is complete.

In other words, the two **diagrams** shown in Figure 11-3 mean *exactly* the same thing. In both cases the parallel flow is *unconditional*, meaning it applies to every instance of the process.

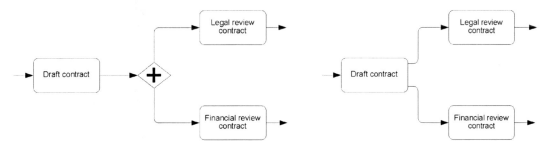

Figure 11-3. Parallel split using either AND-gateway (left) or uncontrolled sequence flow (right). Both diagrams have the same meaning.

Since the two diagrams are equivalent, which one should you use? It's really a matter of preference. I prefer the one on the right, the *implicit parallel split*, without a gateway. It occupies less space on the page, and the BPMN 2.0 spec advises a preference for it as well. However, some BPMN tools may only support parallel split using the AND-gateway. Also, some flowcharting conventions use a notation **similar** to the one on the right to mean exclusive choice, not parallel split. That's not illogical **but** it's not BPMN. If your organization is used to diagrams in which multiple outputs from **an** activity meant exclusive choice, you might find using the AND-gateway to signify parallel split less confusing to users.

Also, remember that implicit parallel split only works out of an activity or start event. You should not draw multiple sequence flows out of an intermediate event. So to signify a parallel split following an intermediate event or another gateway, use the AND-gateway. While it is allowed, you should try to avoid multiple sequence flows out of a gateway that has multiple sequence flows into it. If you use such a pattern, the gateway symbol should refer to the branching semantics, and the merging sequence flows should always be exclusive alternatives.

Conditional Split

There is a third type of splitting behavior that seems absolutely befuddling to some people. Here one or more paths may be taken in parallel based on a condition applied to each, so I call it *conditional split*. Unlike exclusive choice, here the conditions are independent, so more than one of them could be true for a single instance. Thus the flow paths out of a conditional split are neither exclusive alternatives nor unconditionally parallel. They are "conditionally parallel." In any instance, *at least one* of the path conditions must be true, but it could be more than one.

For example, in a banking process, in addition to a standard reporting activity performed for all deposits, cash deposits over $10,000 require an additional compliance reporting step, and deposits from foreign banks require a second additional compliance step. There is no sequential order for these reporting steps; they would be modeled as parallel activities.

BPMN provides two ways to model this behavior.

OR-Gateway

The first way uses an *inclusive decision gateway*, commonly called an *OR-gateway*. The gateway diamond has an O symbol inside. Drawn with one sequence flow in and multiple sequence flows out, it means that the conditions on the gates are independent, so more than one can be true. The pattern is sometimes called an *OR-split*.

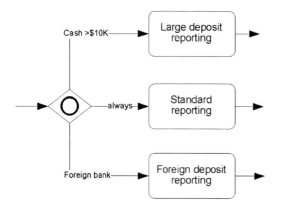

Figure 11-4. OR-gateway signifies conditionally parallel flow based on independent conditions

The banking scenario described above is modeled in Figure 11-4 using the *OR-gateway*. As with the XOR gateway, BPMN provides attributes to hold the gate conditions, but in Level 2 modeling it is more useful to indicate the conditions by labeling the gates. Note that in this example, one of the gates is labeled *always*, meaning its condition is always true, so Standard reporting is performed for every process instance. The three conditions are independent. If one of them is true, it does not imply the others are false. All paths with conditions evaluating to true are taken in parallel.

Unconditional flow, such as the path marked "always" in Figure 11-4, is *not* the same as *default flow*. This is also confusing to many people. Default sequence flow, denoted by a tickmark (Figure 11-5), means "otherwise," i.e., *if no other path conditions evaluate to true*. Thus Figure 11-5 does not mean the same thing as Figure 11-4. Figure 11-5 says perform *Standard reporting* only if the deposit is neither cash over $10,000 nor from a foreign bank. Just remember, unconditional means "always," and default means "otherwise."

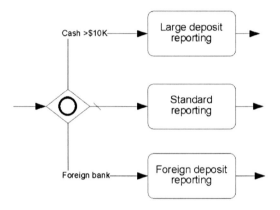

Figure 11-5. Default flow (tickmark) signifies "otherwise", not "always"

Conditional Sequence Flow

As if the OR-gateway were not confusing enough, BPMN provides an alternative way to represent the same semantics. It's called *conditional sequence flow* and is only allowed for sequence flows out of activities, not out of gateways or events. A conditional sequence flow is drawn with a little diamond on the tail, signifying a data condition. As before, a sequence flow out of an activity with a tickmark signifies *default flow*, meaning "otherwise," i.e., enabled if no other sequence flow has a "true" condition. A sequence flow out of an activity without either a diamond on the tail or a tickmark means it is *unconditional*, or "always." Thus the two diagrams below, equivalent to Figure 11-4 and Figure 11-5, respectively, do *not* mean the same thing.

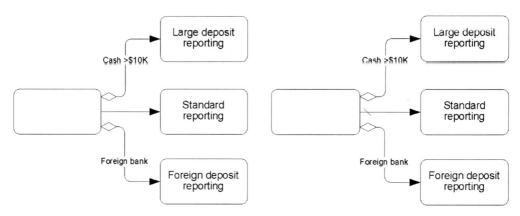

Figure 11-6. Conditional sequence flow representations equivalent to Figure 11-4 (left) and Figure 11-5 (right). They do NOT mean the same thing.

Why not use conditional sequence flow to represent an exclusive choice between two outputs, as in the left diagram of Figure 11-7? Some tools do this, usually those provided by BPM Suites where routing decisions are made within the tasks. It is technically legal but I think bad BPMN style. It only works for two outputs, not more than two. (You could say that with more than two, the diagram is ambiguous. Is it meant to signify exclusive choice or not?) Also, to me it implies a tool that does not fully support basic BPMN conventions. To model exclusive choice between *A* and *B*, as in Figure 11-7, just use the notation on the right.

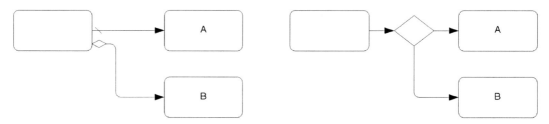

Figure 11-7. Conditional and default flow (left) can sometimes signify exclusive choice, but XOR gateway (right) is preferred

Merging and Joining

When any process instance can follow only one of two or more paths, we call those paths *exclusive alternatives*. Otherwise those paths are either *unconditionally parallel* or *conditionally parallel*. Whether a given set of paths represents exclusive alternatives, unconditionally parallel flows, or conditionally parallel flows determines how they are merged downstream.

It is not necessary to merge paths in a BPMN diagram. Each can proceed to its own end event, and the process or subprocess instance completes normally when all parallel paths have reached their end event. But you frequently want to merge alternative or parallel paths into a common downstream portion of the process. Even though there is rarely confusion about the modeler's intent, BPMN unfortunately requires a different type of gateway to be used to merge exclusive alternatives, unconditionally parallel paths, and conditionally parallel paths.

Merging Alternative Paths

Two paths are known to be exclusive alternatives if, for example, they were originally split by an XOR gateway or event gateway, or if one represents the normal flow out of an activity and the other the exception flow out of an interrupting boundary event on that activity. In Figure 11-8, *A* and *B* are exclusive alternatives in all three diagrams.

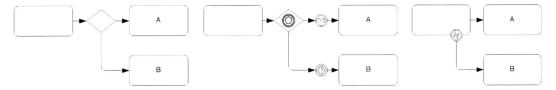

Figure 11-8. A and B are exclusive alternatives

To merge exclusive alternatives, you do not need a gateway at all, at least leading into an activity. Just drawing the sequence flows directly into the activity, called *implicit merge*, is sufficient, and this is the notation I typically use. Alternatively, you may want to insert an XOR gateway to merge the sequence flows. Also, use the XOR gateway to merge alternative flows into another gateway. The two representations in Figure 11-9 mean exactly the same thing.

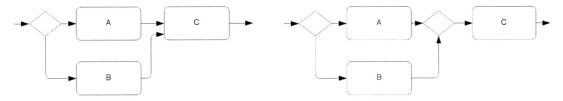

Figure 11-9. Merging alternative flows can use uncontrolled merge (left) or XOR gateway (right)

Loopback is a special case of merging alternatives. In this pattern, an exclusive gateway or boundary event loops back to a previous step in the flow, typically used for rework in the case of an exception. BPMN treats this the same as exclusive alternatives, allowing either implicit merge or merge with an XOR gateway (Figure 11-10).

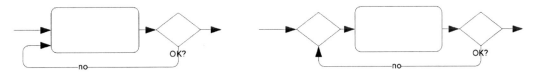

Figure 11-10. Loopback from XOR gateway is merged like exclusive alternative

Merging Parallel Paths

If two paths are unconditionally parallel, they are typically merged with an *AND-gateway* in what is known as a *join*. A join is a merge that waits for all its inputs to be "complete" before continuing. A *parallel join* or *AND-join* waits for all of its incoming sequence flows to arrive before executing the outgoing sequence flow. Because it requires all parallel activities into it to be complete before continuing, the join "synchronizes" them. An AND-join is thus a type of *synchronizing join* in BPMN.

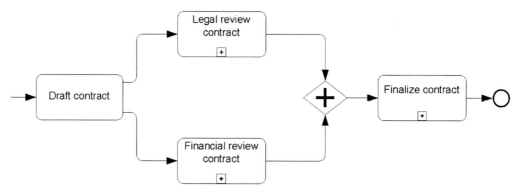

Figure 11-11. Parallel join must use AND-gateway

Figure 11-11 illustrates an AND-join. Even though an AND-split can be implicit – represented without a gateway – an AND-join cannot. The join gateway is absolutely *required*.

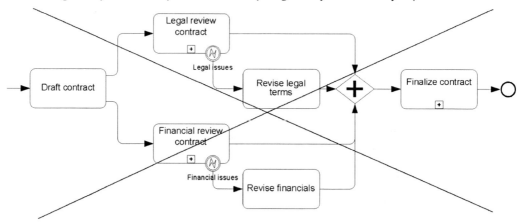

Figure 11-12. If *all* sequence flows in are not enabled in every instance, AND-join is not allowed

All of the sequence flows drawn into the AND-gateway must arrive before the join is complete. This sounds simple enough, but exception handling can make it tricky. For example, Figure 11-12 is *not correct*, because the normal flow and exception flow out of the parallel activities are alternatives. Thus in any process instance only *some* of the sequence flows into the AND-join will arrive. From the perspective of the join, the incoming sequence flows are neither parallel nor alternative. There is a way to join them, but it does not use the AND-join.

On the other hand, there is nothing wrong with the AND-join in Figure 11-13. Instead of going to the join, the exception flows loop back. In this diagram both the sequence flows into the AND-join can always arrive. Now Figure 11-12 and Figure 11-13 don't say the same thing. *Legal review contract* and *Financial review contract* are performed once in Figure 11-12 and possibly more than once in Figure 11-13. The point is just that one is valid BPMN and the other is not.

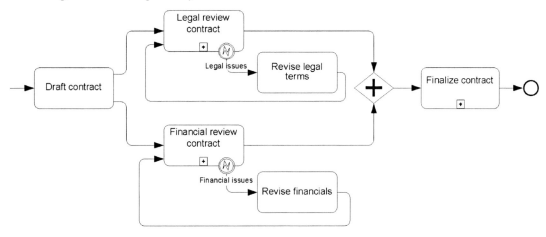

Figure 11-13. Modified flow allows the AND-join

Merging Conditionally Parallel Paths

There is a way to do the join of Figure 11-12 and other cases where the incoming sequence flows are neither alternative nor unconditionally parallel. These include the conditionally parallel paths resulting from an OR-split or conditional sequence flow.

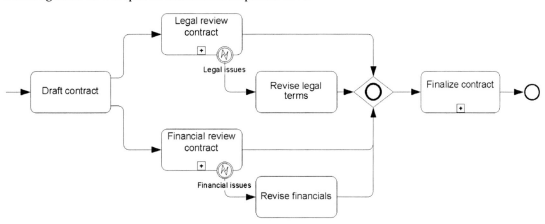

Figure 11-14. OR-join waits for all enabled paths in conditionally parallel flow

The join uses an *OR-gateway*, the one with the O inside, and is called an *OR-join*. An OR-join means the gateway waits for all *enabled* incoming sequence flows to arrive before completing the join. In Figure 11-12, in any process instance *either* the normal flow or exception flow out of *Legal review contract* and *Financial review contract* is enabled, not both, so the join waits for whichever one was enabled for that instance. Figure 11-14 is valid BPMN.

Similarly, following a conditional split the join waits only for the *enabled* paths to complete, as illustrated in Figure 11-15.

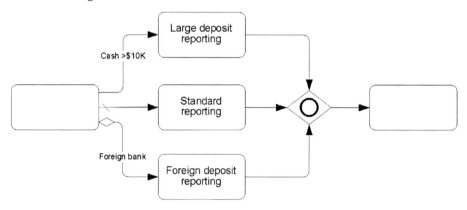

Figure 11-15. Use OR-join to merge after conditional split

Conditional Split/Join Workaround

A few tools do not support the notion of conditional split and join. To model this behavior, those tools use a combination of exclusive and parallel gateways. It is clumsy, and for that reason I call it a workaround. To model the behavior of Figure 11-15 without conditional splits or joins, for example, you could do something like Figure 11-16. Enough said.

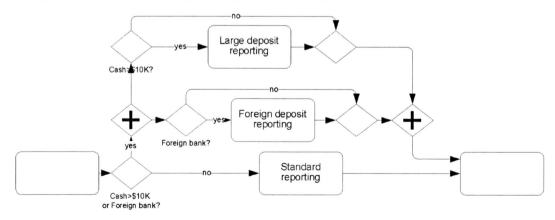

Figure 11-16. Workaround equivalent to Figure 11-15

Implicit OR-Join at End Events

Something important but rarely discussed is the implied OR-join of all end events in a process or subprocess. In other words, the process or subprocess is complete when all of the enabled paths reach an end event. As a practical matter, this means you should not use a gateway to merge paths into an end event. Just draw the sequence flows directly to the end event; the OR-join is implied.

Merging Flow from Non-Interrupting Boundary Events

Non-interrupting boundary events are new in BPMN 2.0. The spec does not give clear guidance on how to merge the exception flows out of them with other parts of the process, warning it might be best to end each of them in its own end event. However, such an exception flow should be viewed as no different than any other conditional sequence flow. If you need to merge it with the happy path flow downstream, just use an OR-join.

Other Branch and Merge Patterns

With parallel or conditionally parallel flow, join is the typical merging behavior, but not the only one allowed by BPMN.

Discriminator and Voting Patterns

It is possible to merge N parallel paths without waiting for all N to complete. The *Discriminator workflow pattern* passes the first path to complete and discards the others. For example, referring back to the contract review scenario of Figure 11-11, suppose we wanted to start *Top management review* when either *Financial review contract* or *Legal review contract* is complete, whichever comes first. All three reviews must be complete in order to perform *Finalize contract*. This requires both a Discriminator merge and an AND-join (Figure 11-17).

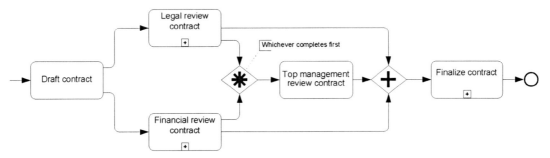

Figure 11-17. Discriminator pattern uses Complex gateway to pass first path to complete

The *Discriminator pattern* in BPMN uses the *complex gateway*, with an asterisk icon inside. The complex gateway is a catch-all. It is used for any split or merge semantics not handled by the standard gateway types. There is no really good use case for the complex split, but Discriminator is a useful merge pattern. The problem with the complex gateway is that the semantics are not unambiguous from the diagram without an explanation, such as via text annotation.

The *Voting pattern* is similar. It also uses the complex gateway, and requires M out of N incoming sequence flows to arrive before the join is complete. It also requires text annotation to explain the intended semantics in the diagram. It is probably less useful than the Discriminator pattern, because each voter's activity flow must be described explicitly with its own path in the diagram. The more common implementation of voting in BPMN would use the completion condition of a Multi-instance activity (see Chapter 13).

Multi-Merge Pattern

The *Multi-merge pattern* is technically legal, but I advise you not to use it. Except in very special cases, it will "break" any simulation engine or runtime process engine, and it will certainly confuse anyone looking at your model. In the Multi-merge pattern, parallel path instances are merged by simply passing each of them through as they arrive, so activities downstream of the merge are executed multiple times. This is not usually what you want.

Multi-merge of parallel or conditionally parallel paths is modeled either with uncontrolled merge – sequence flows drawn directly into an activity, without a gateway – or with an exclusive gateway, which for merge simply passes through any incoming sequence flow. Thus, in Figure 11-18, activity C is executed twice, as are all activities downstream of C.

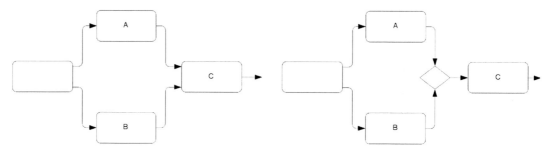

Figure 11-18. Multi-merge modeled with uncontrolled merge (left) and exclusive gateway (right)

CHAPTER 12

Exception Handling Patterns

To this point we have focused on the meaning and usage of BPMN's various gateway and event types. The essence of BPMN Level 2, however, is the ability to describe all the significant paths from process start to end – most notably the exception paths – in a way that is both semantically precise and clear from the diagram itself. That requires going beyond simple shape semantics to matters of method and style.

The BPMN spec allows considerable latitude in the business-level interpretation of its shapes and symbols. It is mostly concerned with their operational semantics in a process execution engine. However, for most process modelers the important thing is not execution semantics but unambiguous interpretation of the diagram in a business context. That means equating a particular business-oriented meaning with each commonly used *exception handling pattern* in the diagram. Ideally, that meaning should depend only on the BPMN shape and its placement in the diagram, not on text in a label or annotation.

In this chapter, we provide both a simple set of rules for categorizing exceptions and the recommended diagram patterns to use for each. These rules and patterns are not part of the BPMN spec, but part of the method and style. The meaning assigned to each diagram pattern is consistent with the BPMN spec, but typically represents just one of a range of possible interpretations. Conversely, the pattern recommended for a particular category of exceptions is just one of multiple ways it could be diagrammed.

While you might argue this limits your creative expression, individual creativity is not the overarching goal of process modeling. Shared understanding is. By associating a specific interpretation to each pattern, you can express extremely subtle behavior, such as exception handling, in your BPMN models, and others will understand exactly what you mean – just by looking at the diagram.

Categorizing Exceptions

By *exception* we mean anything that causes a process instance to divert from the happy path. It does not necessarily imply an error or problem. Here we classify exceptions based on their original *source,* rather than how they are propagated to ultimately triggered actions. We have seen, for example, how Error, Escalation, and Signal events can be used to propagate exceptions from an error source to trigger actions in another part of the same process.

Our framework considers the following types of exceptions, based on their source:

- Internal business exception
- User action
- Fault
- Timeout
- Unsolicited external exception
- Solicited response exception

Each type of exception is represented by a distinctive diagram pattern that indicates where it is first detected or received, and its immediately triggered actions or *handling.* In addition, any type of exception, regardless of its original source, can be *propagated* for additional handling in the parent process level, in a parallel path, or in an external process.

Internal Business Exception

The majority of exceptions occurring in process models can be classified as *internal business exceptions.* That means that the exception is detected or declared by a process activity that *completes normally.* Normal completion signifies an activity that is not aborted by an interrupting event, and that continues upon completion along the sequence flow out of the activity, the *normal flow.*

An internal business exception is commonly a human judgment or decision: *This request is not approved.* It could be an exception reported by a business rule engine: *This is a Premier customer.* (Not all exceptions indicate problems, just special behavior.)

Figure 12-1. Internal business exception in a user or Service task

The occurrence of an internal business exception means the activity, while completing normally, ends in some *exception end state.* In a task, this end state is implied by the business context. Because tasks are opaque, you cannot look inside to see the source. That is not the case for a subprocess. Within the subprocess, different end states should be represented by distinctly labeled end events. Because the activity completes normally, the exception is handled by testing the end state in an exclusive gateway following the activity, diverting internal business exception instances to an exception path (Figure 12-2).

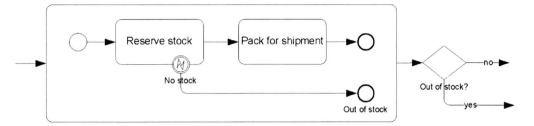

Figure 12-2. Gateway tests exception end state in a subprocess

We have seen this pattern countless times already, and it is by far the most common exception handling pattern in BPMN. It is good to get into the habit of labeling the gateway with the name of the exception end event, followed by a question mark, such as *Out of stock?* The *yes* path out of the gateway in this case is the exception path.

The exception path can lead anywhere as long as it follows the basic rules of sequence flow, meaning it cannot cross the boundary of a subprocess or pool. It can ultimately loop back to a previous step in the process, merge with the happy path at some point downstream, or lead immediately to an end event. It can trigger additional behavior in the model by throwing event signals from an intermediate or end event on the path. BPMN, unlike some other process languages, allows complete flexibility here.

User Action

A variant of internal business exception is *user action*, signified by an *Escalation boundary event on a User task*. It is new in BPMN 2.0. While the normal internal business exception is based on the *end state* of an activity that completes normally, user action signifies an exception detected or declared *during* the performance of a User task, not after the end.

Typically the user action does not abort the task, so the *non-interrupting Escalation boundary event* is used. This initiates a parallel exception flow, while the User task continues to completion and exits on the normal flow.

Figure 12-3. Escalation event on a User task indicates non-aborting User Action

In some circumstances, the modeler's intent might be for the user action to abort the User task. In that case the *Error boundary event* (or *interrupting Escalation boundary event*) could be used. However, aborting user actions not be used for exceptions that represent normal end states of the task, such as *Rejected* in a task that reviews and approves a request. For those, use the regular internal business exception pattern.

Figure 12-4. Error event on a User task indicates aborting User Action

Fault

A *fault* is an exception on an automated task that does not allow the task to complete normally. The reason could be invalid parameters to the task, a problem communicating with the system performing the task, or a problem within that system. It should not be used to represent normal completion of the task, but with a bad business result. For example, if I try to withdraw $100 from an automated teller machine but I only have $50 in my bank account, that is an internal business exception. If the ATM cannot read my card, that is a fault. A fault is indicated by an *Error boundary event on an automated task type, such as Service.*

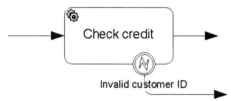

Figure 12-5. Error event on a Service task indicates a Fault

Timeout

A *timeout exception* is triggered when an activity is not completed within a specified interval after starting or by a specified date/time. It can be modeled using either a *Timer boundary event* or a *Timer event subprocess.* Both can be used in either interrupting or non-interrupting form.

When the timeout is specified as a time interval, the interval by convention is measured from the instant when the sequence flow arrives at the activity. For a User task, this marks the start of the "ready" state, when it appears in queue or worklist, not the instant when the performer begins work on it. A standard boundary event[25] has no standard way to distinguish between a task instance that is ready but not yet active and one that is 99% complete. Both trigger the *Timer event* in exactly the same way if the activity is not complete by the timeout.

Use an *interrupting Timer boundary event* (Figure 12-6) to cancel the activity and divert the process to an exception flow. For example, the exception flow can end the overall process or divert to an expedited process flow.

---

[25] This would be a nice future enhancement.

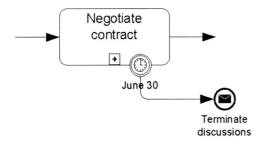

Figure 12-6. Timer event on any activity indicates a timeout

Use an *interrupting Timer event subprocess* (Figure 12-7) to cancel a subprocess activity, perform simple or short-running handler actions, and then continue on the normal flow out of the activity. It could be used, for example, to cancel a standard subprocess if it is not completed by a deadline and instead perform an expedited variant of that subprocess. Following completion, processing continues on the normal flow out of the subprocess.

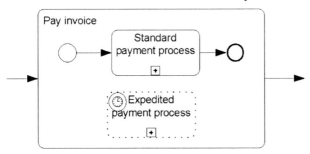

Figure 12-7. Timer event subprocess

Use a *non-interrupting Timer boundary event on a task* (Figure 12-8, left) to initiate any kind of deadline-triggered actions without aborting the task. A common use case is to send a reminder to the performer or notification to a supervisor. If the event handler is short-running, such as a reminder, you could alternatively wrap the task in a subprocess and use a non-interrupting Timer event subprocess (Figure 12-8, right) instead.

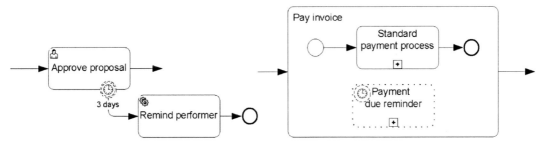

Figure 12-8. Non-interrupting timeout using boundary event (left) or event subprocess (right)

Use a *non-interrupting Timer boundary event on a subprocess* (Figure 12-9) to initiate complex or long-running flows without interrupting the subprocess itself. If the triggered action is quick, such as a simple reminder or notification, use a *non-interrupting Timer event subprocess* instead.

The reason is with non-interrupting event subprocesses, the activity following the normal flow exit must wait until the event subprocess is complete.

For example (Figure 12-9), a subprocess that reviews and approves a proposal has a 2-week time limit. If not completed within two weeks, an extension must be obtained. Because the extension can take time to secure, the non-interrupting boundary event allows the process to continue in parallel before *Obtain extension* completes.

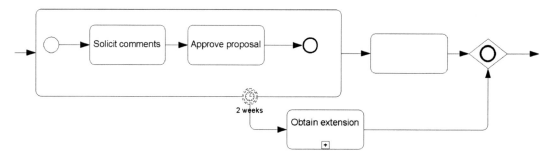

Figure 12-9. Merging exception flow from non-interrupting boundary event

A similar subprocess could have a deadline in which the only triggered action is a notification to the manager. Since this is quick, it is simpler to model this as an event subprocess (Figure 12-10). Downstream actions will not be delayed waiting for the event subprocess to complete.

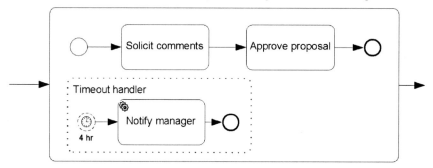

Figure 12-10. Notifications and reminders modeled using event subprocess

Unsolicited External Exception

An *unsolicited external exception* means a signal from an external participant that is not a response to a previous request. Exception handling can do one of three basic things:

- Start a process
- Abort a running process activity
- Start a parallel thread in a running process

The last two of these can be modeled either with boundary events or event subprocesses. Also, depending on whether the signal is addressed directly to the process or is simply published to the world at large, it could be modeled with either a Message or Signal event type. This gives rise to a variety of diagram patterns.

Start a Process

Handling an exception by starting a new process is quite common. Most often it is modeled using a *Message start event* with a message flow from another pool. That pool typically represents either the Customer (e.g., refund request), an IT system (e.g. item out of stock), or another internal process. In the first two cases, the external entity is typically represented as a black-box pool. When the message comes from another internal process, known as *process chaining*, the message flow typically comes from a message end event of a white-box pool.

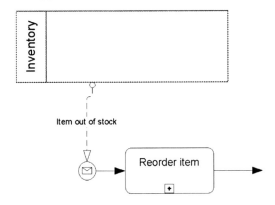

Figure 12-11. Starting an exception process via Message event

It is possible that two or more messages could trigger the same process. Modeling this correctly depends on whether both messages are handled by exactly the same sequence of steps or there is some minor difference, typically in the initial step. If exactly, then technically BPMN says to use the *Multiple start event*. Some tools don't support it, and many users don't know what it is, so using a Message start with multiple message flows in would not be a grave error.

Channel-Dependent Start

As discussed in Chapter 9, the start of a process may depend on the channel of contact but the bulk of the process is channel-independent. For example, a process triggered by customer request may require different initial step if the request arrives via the call center versus the web or fax, but has the same backend processing regardless of the contact channel.

The most straightforward way to model this is with multiple Message start events (Figure 12-12). An alternative way is to start the process with a *"bootstrapped" event gateway* (Figure 12-13). The event gateway can be drawn either with no sequence flow in, as in Figure 12-13 – I find this jarring myself – or with a None start leading directly into the gateway. The events on each gate *must* be Message events; Timer is not allowed. Even though they are intermediate events, in this configuration they "bootstrap" instantiation of the process, meaning they act like start events for the process. The difference between this and the Multiple start is that here each Message event leads to a different activity flow. Since the gates are exclusive alternatives, these paths can be freely merged downstream. Otherwise it would be difficult to characterize it as a single process.

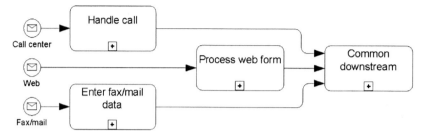

Figure 12-12. Channel-dependent process start using multiple start events

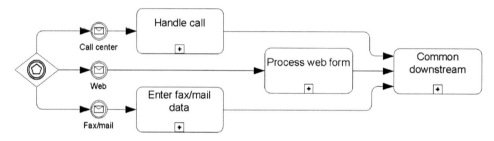

Figure 12-13. Channel-dependent process start alternative, using event gateway "bootstrap"

When the exception source is an IT system, or possibly another internal system, it is possible to use a *Signal start event* instead of Message. Unlike Message, Signal has no visual representation linking the source and target of the request, so Message is preferable unless you specifically want to indicate that the system generating the signal is simply *publishing*, i.e., announcing, the event, not making a request to start a specific process.

By *subscribing* to that event, Signal start triggers the new process without a request from the publisher. In SOA, the IT infrastructure may be set up to publish many business events that services – including processes – may freely subscribe to. For example, when an employee is terminated, an event published by the HR system could trigger any number of processes (Figure 12-14). In the chained process example, we have already seen the Milestone pattern (see Chapter 7), which could be used to signal exceptions.

Figure 12-14. Signal event start indicates publish-subscribe integration

Abort a Running Activity

Aborting a running activity uses either an *interrupting boundary event* or *interrupting event subprocess*. As discussed previously, use Message if the signal is specifically directed to the process (Figure 12-15) and Signal if the process is subscribing to a published event or the throw-catch is to a parallel path of the same process. Use an *interrupting Message event subprocess* (Figure 12-16) only when the process continues on the same normal flow out of the activity as if the exception did not occur. Otherwise use the interrupting boundary event.

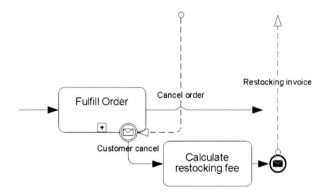

Figure 12-15. Aborting external exception using Message boundary event

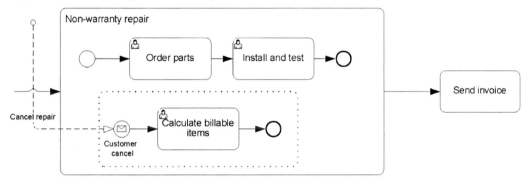

Figure 12-16. Aborting external exception using event subprocess

Start a Parallel Process Thread

An external exception received while a process activity is running can initiate a parallel process thread. Use a *non-interrupting boundary event* on the process activity to initiate a thread *in parallel* with that activity. The event can be either Message or Signal, as discussed above. That thread, on the exception flow out of the event, can lead to its own end event or be merged downstream with the main path using an OR-join (Figure 12-17).

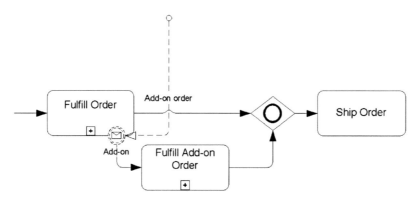

Figure 12-17. Non-interrupting external exception using Message boundary event

If the activity is a subprocess, you can use a *non-interrupting event subprocess* to initiate a parallel thread *within* the activity. Both the regular activity and event subprocess must complete before the process continues on the normal flow out of the activity.

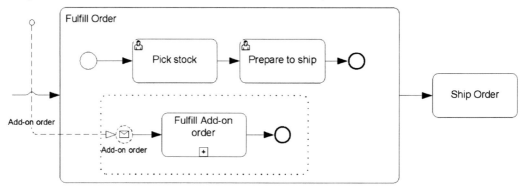

Figure 12-18. Non-aborting external exception using event subprocess

Using Subprocesses to Scope the Event Handler

If a particular exception can occur anytime during a particular segment of the process without changing the way it is handled, the best way to model it is by enclosing that segment in a subprocess (if it is not already a subprocess). Then you can either use a boundary event on the subprocess or an event subprocess to model the handler. If another segment of the process handles the same exception in a different way, you can enclose that segment in another subprocess, with another boundary event or event subprocess.

For example (Figure 12-19), in an order process you may allow the Customer to cancel the order without penalty during the *Check Credit* or *Fulfill Order* steps, or to cancel the order with a restocking fee during the *Ship Order* step. We can draw a new subprocess enclosing *Check Credit* and *Fulfill Order* and attach a Message boundary event to it. The same Message boundary event attached to *Ship Order* has a different handler flow.

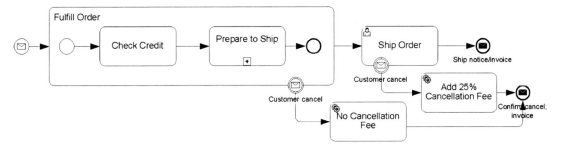

Figure 12-19. Using subprocess to scope process fragment with common exception handler

Solicited Response Exception

A *solicited response exception* means the process has made a request but does not receive the expected response. Because the response was solicited, the process pauses at some point to *wait* for it. Most of the time that will – we hope – be the happy path response, a *confirmation* or *approval* message. But it could be an exception response, a *rejection* or *disapproval* message. Or you might get no response at all.

BPMN provides a neat solution to this: the *event gateway*. An event gateway is the preferred pattern used to wait for a response, because it allows the model to describe not only the subsequent flow when the expected response finally arrives, but what to do if an exception response arrives or if no response arrives by a specified deadline. Remember, the event gateway does not issue the request. That has to come from a task or throwing Message event earlier in the flow.

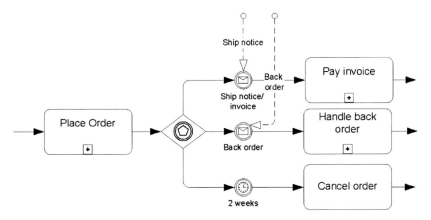

Figure 12-20. Solicited response exception using event gateway

Responses, both the expected or normal response and the exception response, are modeled as *Message intermediate events* on gates of the event gateway. You can have as many as you like. If there is no chance of an exception response, you may have just one. It is still best to use an event gateway instead of a simple catching event in sequence flow since a response may not arrive at all. The timeout is modeled by a *Timer intermediate event* on one output of the gateway. If a duration is specified for the timer, it is measured from the time the instance reaches the event gateway.

Each Message event on the gateway should have an incoming message flow from an external pool. If you cannot draw one, maybe it's not really an external event!

An important thing to remember about using this pattern is that the normal and exception responses are *different messages*. That is technically not the same thing as a *single message* with different possible values, even though there may be no business-meaningful difference. Figure 12-21 and Figure 12-22 illustrate the distinction.

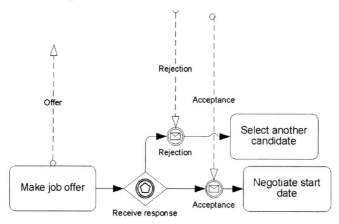

Figure 12-21. Modeling acceptance and rejection as separate messages

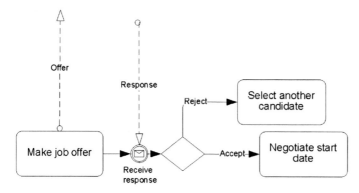

Figure 12-22. Modeling acceptance and rejection as alternative values of a single message

In Figure 12-21, *Acceptance* and *Rejection* are separate messages. Their content is implied by their names. In Figure 12-22, a single *Response* message can contain a data value of either *Accept* or *Reject*. The process waits for *Response* in a single Message event, and then tests the data value using a regular XOR gateway. To consider the possibility of no response before the deadline, you could also use the *Response* Message event in an event gateway with a Timer event.

Rethrowing Exceptions

Our classification of exceptions has focused on their source or detection and their immediate handling. But it is also common in BPMN that following some handling activity local to the point of detection, the exception is forwarded to some other part of the process for further handling. For example, this is how an exception detected in a subprocess can redirect the flow of its parent. It is called *rethrowing* the exception, and it involves some type of *throw-catch pattern*. The most common example is the familiar Error throw-catch, but Escalation, Signal, and Message throw-catch patterns can also be used to rethrow exceptions.

Error Throw-Catch

When you see an *Error boundary event on a subprocess* you should assume that the source of the exception is further specified in the subprocess expansion, specifically in the path leading to an *Error end event* rethrowing the exception. For that reason, it is not recommended to use an Error boundary event on a subprocess without modeling the associated child-level Error end event.

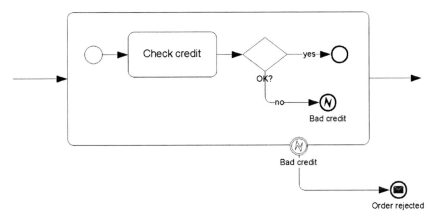

Figure 12-23. Error throw-catch to a boundary event

The presence of an Error boundary event on a subprocess does not reveal the nature of the original exception. At the child level, the source of the exception may be *any* of the types discussed here. For example, in Figure 12-23 it is an internal business exception.

An *Error event subprocess* can be used instead of an Error boundary event, or together with it. If a subprocess includes both, the event subprocess takes precedence, meaning the throw from the Error end event is first caught by the Error event subprocess. Upon completion, an Error end event of the event subprocess should rethrow the error to the Error boundary event (Figure 12-24). If the event subprocess does not rethrow the error, upon completion processing continues on the normal flow out of the activity.

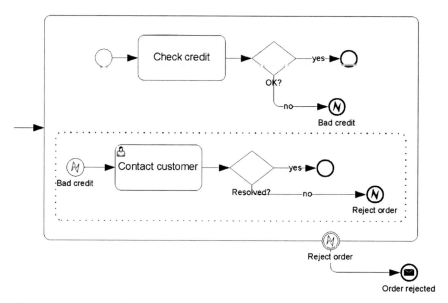

Figure 12-24. Error throw catch to an event subprocess, with rethrow to boundary event

Any type of event subprocess, such as a Message or Timer event subprocess, *even a non-interrupting event subprocess*, can rethrow an exception to an Error boundary event (Figure 12-25).

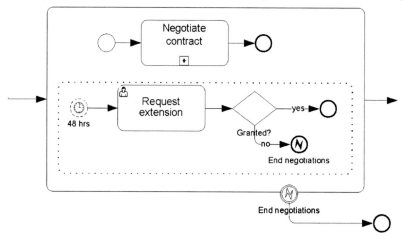

Figure 12-25. Any event subprocess type can rethrow Error to boundary

Error throw-catch to a boundary event – whether from an Error end event in the original subprocess or from an Error end event in an event subprocess – does two things. First, it aborts the original subprocess, if it is not already complete. Second, it propagates the exception from a child level of the process to its parent level. In the parent level, flow continues on the sequence flow out of the boundary event, the exception flow.

Escalation Throw-Catch

An *Escalation event subprocess* in an activity is used to describe a thread of exception handling initiated in parallel with that activity, triggered by some source exception within that activity. As in the previous example, the original exception could be of any type, including internal business exception, fault, or timeout, interrupting or non-interrupting. The handling of that original exception, whether by exception flow or event subprocess, includes a throwing Escalation event that triggers the event subprocess. If the event subprocess does not further rethrow the exception to a boundary event, once all running event subprocesses and the original activity are complete, processing continues on the normal flow out of the activity.

For example, in Figure 12-26 some required action after *Assess problem* represents an internal business exception. In the exception path, while the problem is being fixed the financial impact of that action is studied via escalation throw-catch to an event subprocess. The event subprocess performs a *Quick study* of the problem; if that activity is not complete within 24 hours, a Timer event aborts it and rethrows an escalation to a boundary event. The boundary event is non-interrupting, so *Perform full study*, on the exception flow, can happen concurrently with *Fix problem*. The *Next normal activity* following *Fix problem* cannot start until *Quick study* is complete, but it does not need to wait for *Perform full study* to complete.

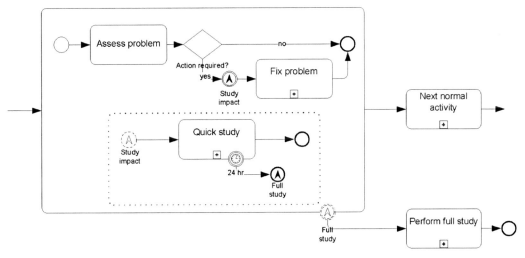

Figure 12-26. Escalation throw-catch to event subprocess, with rethrow to boundary

In most cases, the behavior of escalation throw-catch to an event subprocess is exactly the same as a sequence flow connection, possibly using an AND-gateway. Because it is simpler and more readily understood, the sequence flow connection would be preferred in that situation. For example, Figure 12-27 and Figure 12-26 mean exactly the same thing.

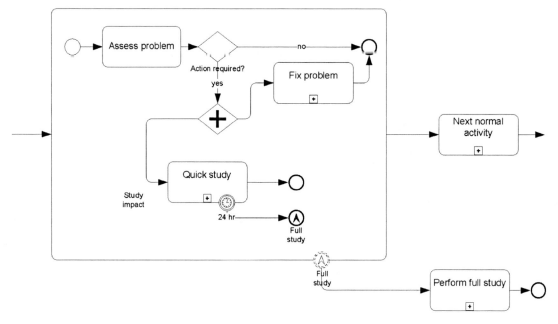

Figure 12-27. Escalation event subprocess can usually be replaced by AND-split

Message Throw-Catch

Message throw-catch implies communications between separate pools, not within a pool. When used to represent exception propagation, often we are talking about two white-box pools, meaning two internal processes linked in some nested or chained fashion. The original exception could have come from any source, including internal business exception, fault, or timeout. The throw is represented by a *Message end event* or *Message intermediate event* on an exception path of the first process.

Throw-catch to a *Message start event* (possibly implied by message flow to a black-box pool boundary) is used to handle exceptions by starting a new process (Figure 12-28).

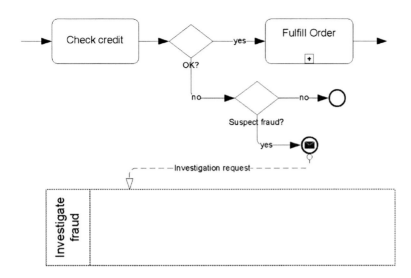

Figure 12-28. Starting an exception process using Message throw-catch

Throw-catch to a *Message boundary event* or Message event subprocess, either interrupting or non-interrupting, is used to handle exceptions by modifying a running process activity in a separate pool. For example, following an error, a requested service can be cancelled using Message throw-catch (Figure 12-29).

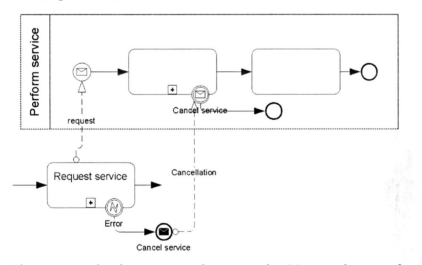

Figure 12-29. Aborting a requested process using Message throw-catch

Signal Throw-Catch

Exception propagation with Signal throw-catch can be used either between white-box pools, like Message throw-catch described earlier, or within a pool, like Escalation or Error throw-catch. For reasons cited previously, Signal should only be used if one of the "standard" patterns cannot express the modeler's intent. Examples of this could include:

- The throw is broadcast to multiple catching events (Figure 12-30). The throw could be caught at multiple points within the business process diagram, or possibly by other unseen processes outside the business process diagram.

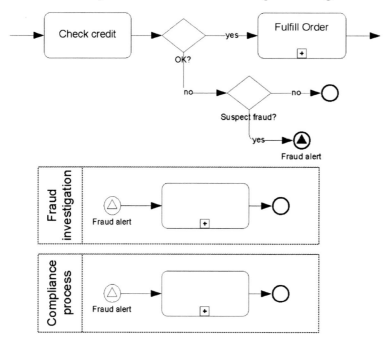

Figure 12-30. Starting multiple exception processes using Signal throw-catch

- The throw and catch lie on parallel segments within a single pool (Figure 12-31). Escalation and Error throw-catch can only be used to communicate from a subprocess to its parent. In this example, the Signal cancels the parallel activities. Terminate would work as well here, but Signal allows selection of specific activities to cancel, whereas Terminate ends all of them.

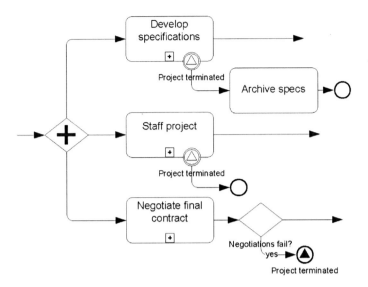

Figure 12-31. Aborting parallel activities using Signal throw-catch

Interpreting Exception Handling Patterns in the Diagram

A good modeling style should allow a user to understand precisely the intended exception handling semantics simply from the diagram pattern. Figure 12-32 summarizes the patterns discussed in this chapter. (As discussed previously, in each case an event subprocess could be substituted for the boundary event if the event handler is short-running.) Patterns shown with a task type icon or subprocess marker apply specifically to that type of activity. Patterns shown with a generic activity shape apply to any type of activity, either task or subprocess.

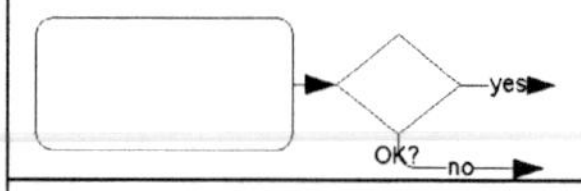	Internal business exception	Exception detected by performer upon completion of task
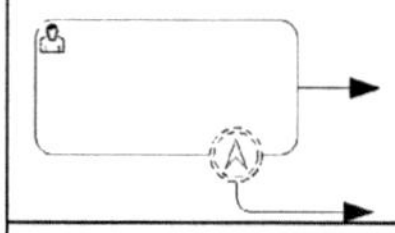	User action	Parallel action triggered manually by performer
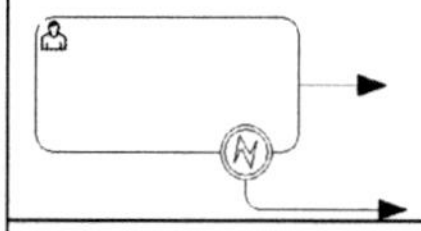	User cancel	Task cancellation prior to completion, triggered manually by performer
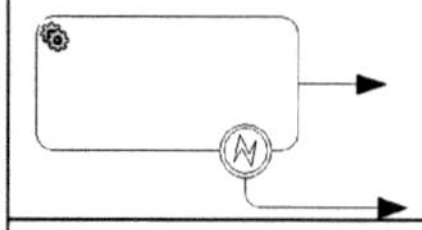	Fault	Automated task cannot complete normally
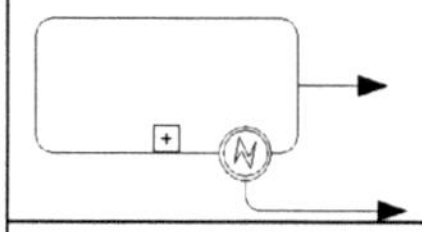	Error throw-catch	Propagation of interrupting exception (any source) from child level to parent level
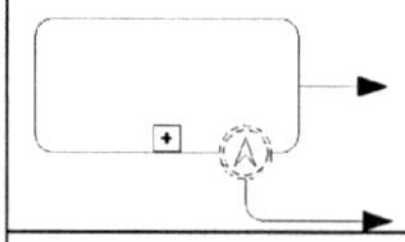	Escalation throw-catch	Propagation of non-interrupting exception (any source) from child level to parent level
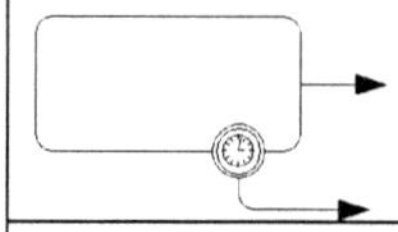	Interrupting timeout	Activity canceled when it does not complete before deadline
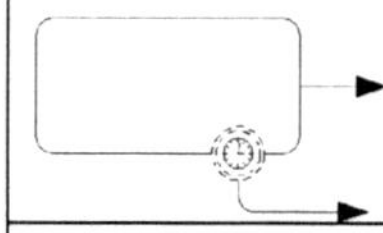	Non-interrupting timeout	Parallel action triggered when activity does not complete before deadline
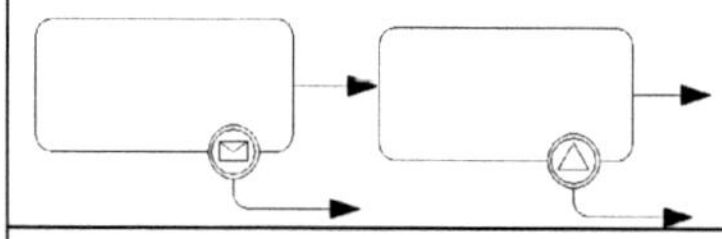	Interrupting unsolicited external exception	Activity canceled on external event.
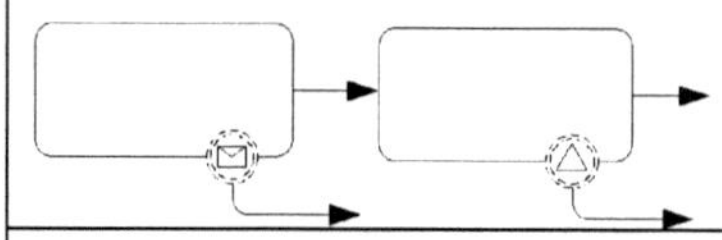	Non-aborting unsolicited external exception	Parallel action triggered on external event.
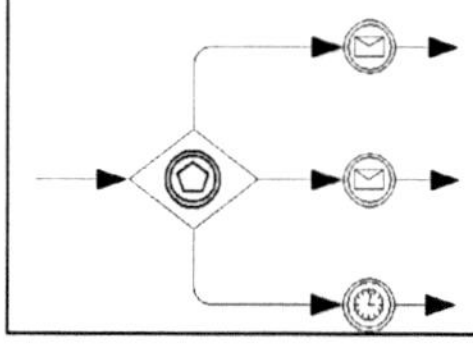	Solicited response exception	Alternative exception path selected upon receipt of exception response or no response by deadline

Figure 12-32. BPMN exception handling patterns

Exception Propagation Patterns

Regardless of its source, the effects of a particular exception may be felt in more than one place within a process: *locally* at the point of origination, and elsewhere in the model following *propagation*. The most common use of propagation is from an child-level subprocess to its parent level process. Occasionally you may also need to propagate exceptions to a parallel path in the process. (You can also propagate the exception to other processes, but here we are concerned with propagation within a process.)

Child-to-Parent Propagation

We have already discussed the three patterns used for child-to-parent level exception propagation. They are:

- Gateway test of labeled end states (Figure 12-33). A labeled *None end event* (or *Terminate end event*) of the child-level process is tested by a gateway following the subprocess at the parent level. This is perhaps the most common, and the only propagation pattern supported at Level 1.

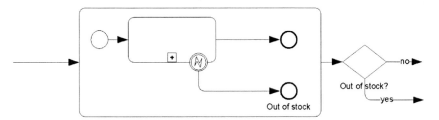

Figure 12-33. Exception propagation using gateway to test child end state

- Error throw-catch (Figure 12-34). A labeled *Error end event* of the child-level process is caught by a matching *Error boundary event* attached to the subprocess at the parent level. The Error end event could occur either in the regular subprocess or in an event subprocess triggered by any source.

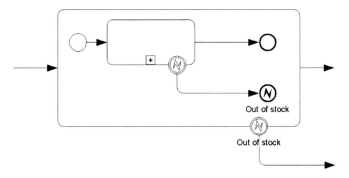

Figure 12-34. Exception propagation using Error throw-catch

- Escalation throw-catch (Figure 12-35). A labeled *Escalation end event* of the child-level process is caught by a matching *Escalation boundary event* (non-interrupting) attached to the subprocess at the parent level. The Escalation end event could occur either in the regular subprocess or in an event subprocess triggered by any source.

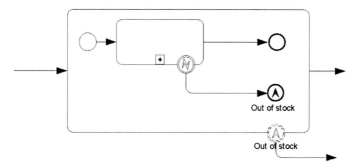

Figure 12-35. Exception propagation using Escalation throw-catch

The gateway pattern can be used to describe semantics equivalent to either the Error throw-catch or Escalation throw-catch. The top and bottom diagrams of Figure 12-36 are equivalent in terms of propagation, as are the top and bottom diagrams of Figure 12-37. However, if the child-level process contains parallel paths, then the two diagrams of Figure 12-36 are not exactly equivalent. The gateway pattern waits for all parallel paths to complete before branching to the exception path, while the Error throw-catch pattern interrupts the child process even if the parallel path is not yet complete.

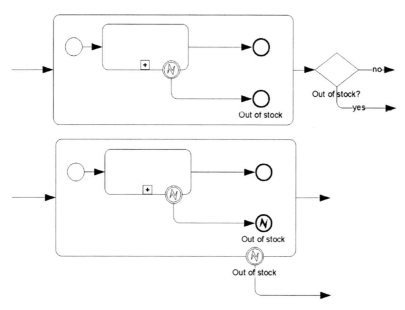

Figure 12-36. End state test (top) and Error throw-catch (bottom) are equivalent if subprocess does not contain parallel paths

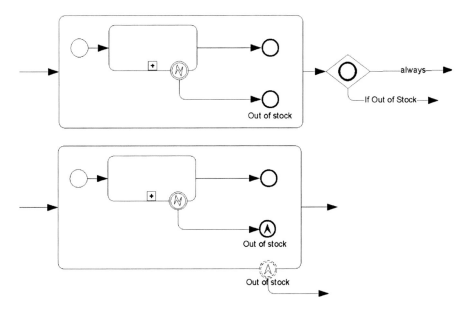

Figure 12-37. End state test with OR-split (top) and Escalation throw-catch (bottom) are equivalent

Parallel Propagation

Sometimes an exception must be propagated to one or more parallel paths. This can be done using Signal throw-catch. There are many patterns possible, depending on the intended effect in the catching path.

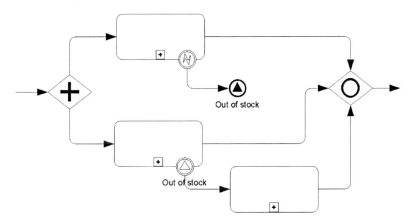

Figure 12-38. Aborting an activity in a parallel path using Signal throw-catch

In Figure 12-38, an activity in the parallel path is aborted upon the catch and diverted to an exception flow. In Figure 12-39, the catch triggers another parallel path joined downstream. In Figure 12-40, the catch alters an activity in the parallel path via an event subprocess but does not change the flow. Other combinations are possible. In Figure 12-38 and Figure 12-39, the Signal throw and catch events are in the same process level, so you can see them together on the page. With Signal, however, this is often not the case, so a viewer of the model may need to hunt through the model to understand the throw-catch.

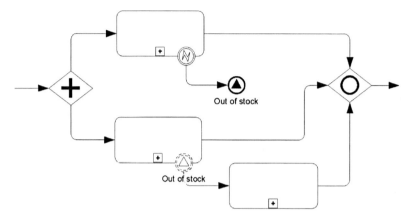

Figure 12-39. Triggering additional action in parallel path using Signal throw-catch

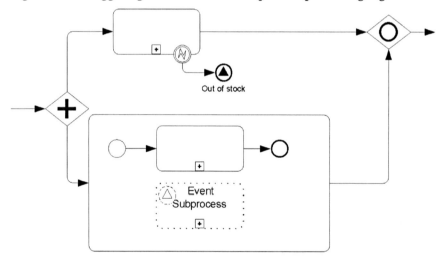

Figure 12-40. Modifying activity in parallel path using Signal throw-catch

Figure 12-41 summarizes six basic patterns for propagation within a process.

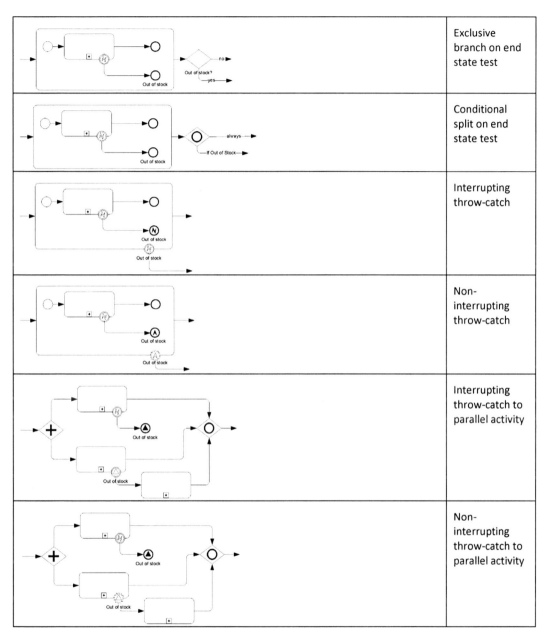

	Exclusive branch on end state test
	Conditional split on end state test
	Interrupting throw-catch
	Non-interrupting throw-catch
	Interrupting throw-catch to parallel activity
	Non-interrupting throw-catch to parallel activity

Figure 12-41. Exception propagation patterns

CHAPTER 13

Repeating Activities and Pools

In my BPMessentials class, one of the certification exercises involves a hiring process. Following the job posting, the process needs to receive and screen job applications, interview candidates, make a job offer to a selected candidate, and possibly negotiate the employment terms. Throughout the exercise, the model must deal with a wide variety of possible exceptions. But the hard part, it turns out, is not the exception handling. It is modeling activities related to multiple candidates within the context of a single hiring process.

A common mistake of beginners is to do something like this:

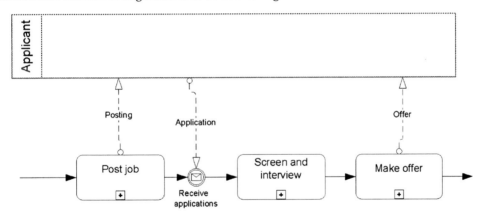

Figure 13-1. Incorrect solution to the hiring process exercise

Do you see the problem? If not, look again.

This hiring process considers just *one applicant*. Sure, more than one can submit an application, represented here by the message flow, but a single instance of the hiring process – a specific job opening – only can receive *one* of them. After that, the instance has moved on past the *Receive applications* Message event. Remember, message flows do not "control" the process. What control the process are the events and activities that receive them.

To do this exercise correctly, we need a way to repeat that Message event within the context of a single instance of the hiring process. BPMN provides a couple alternatives, and they are the subject of this chapter.

Looping Activities

The simplest way to repeat the message catch is with a *loop*. You can model this simply with a gateway and loopback in sequence flow (Figure 13-2). The gateway represents the *loop condition*. If the condition is true, we loop back. If false, we continue ahead.

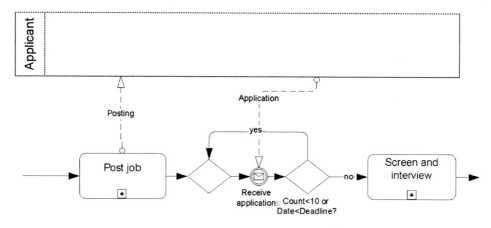

Figure 13-2. Receiving multiple messages using sequence flow looping

Let's say, for example, we want to continue to collect applications until we get 10 or two weeks have elapsed, whichever comes first. That would represent the loop condition. (In Figure 13-2, the merge gateway before the Message event is just there for a technical reason, since the spec says you should not have multiple sequence flows into an intermediate event.)

BPMN provides an alternative way to model looping. An activity can be specified to repeat based on a *condition*. That is called a *looping activity*, shown with a circular arrow marker at bottom center (Figure 13-3). Any kind of activity – task or subprocess – can be modeled as looping. You cannot put a looping marker on an event.

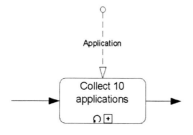

Figure 13-3. Receiving multiple messages using a looping activity

A looping activity is equivalent to a *Do-While structure* in programming. It means perform the activity once, then evaluate a condition, and if the condition is true perform it again. The cycle can continue without end, or you can specify a maximum number of iterations for the loop.

A variant of the loop is equivalent to a *While-Do structure*. It means test the condition first, and if true perform the activity, and repeat this cycle. If the condition is false, do not perform the activity, and continue on. There is no difference in the notation between Do-While and While-Do; you would need to look at the activity's detailed attributes to tell. For that reason, I recommend standardizing on the more common Do-While. You can always explicitly annotate the diagram when you mean While-Do.

Looping activities are a more compact representation than explicit sequence flow loops, but they have one drawback: the loop condition is not obvious from the diagram. For that reason, it is best to suggest the condition either in the name of the looping activity or in a text annotation.

One important aspect of looping activities is that the number of iterations is *unknown*. The loop condition is simply evaluated with each iteration until it is false.

In our hiring exercise, to collect multiple applications we can use a looping Receive task, or we could put a catching Message event inside a looping subprocess. The loop condition would be something like *Count <10 or Date<DeadlineDate*. You could indicate this in the diagram by labeling the subprocess *Loop until 10 or deadline*.

For each applicant, we need to do more than just collect the application. We need to do the screening, interview, acceptance or rejection, etc. So, you might ask, why don't we put all activities related to one candidate in a single looping subprocess? It's legal in BPMN and it makes the diagram simple (Figure 13-4).

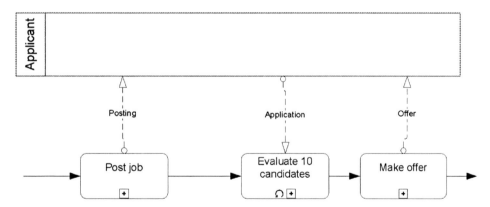

Figure 13-4. Encapsulating candidate evaluation in a looping subprocess is not the best solution

But it's not what you really want. Ask yourself this question: In your company, what is the typical time interval between receiving a job application and completing the interview? Two weeks? Six weeks? Whatever it is, Figure 13-4 says go through this entire sequence for the first candidate before even looking at the second candidate's application. How long do you think those applicants are going to wait? Originally we said we would collect applications for up to two weeks, so that loop condition won't even bother looking at applicant number two. No, this is not what you actually mean.

We need the loop to be fast. Let's say it just includes receiving the message and a quick screen by HR. That works. When that activity is complete, it means either 10 applications have arrived or 2 weeks have elapsed (Figure 13-5).

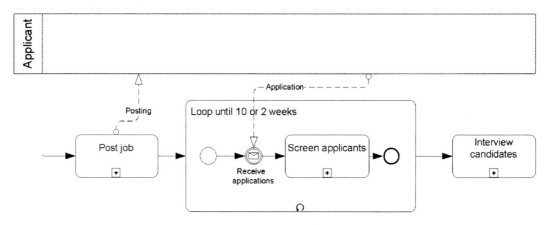

Figure 13-5. Each iteration of the loop should be fast

The activity exits with a *list* of possible candidates. There is another type of activity that BPMN provides to deal with lists, so let's look at that.

Multi-Instance Activities

A *multi-instance (MI) activity* is another type of repeating activity useful for performing actions on a list of items. In BPMN 1.1 and later its marker is three parallel bars at the bottom center of the activity, either a task or subprocess.[26]

An MI activity is equivalent to a *For-Each structure* in programming. The number of iterations is *known* when the activity starts. It is the number of items in the list. For example, in an order process you might have an MI activity *Check Stock*. It is MI because the order contains a list of order items, and the process needs to check the availability of each one independently. The number of items in the list is not the same for every order, but in each order instance the number is known.

Known vs. unknown number of iterations is one difference between MI and loop. Another difference is that the iterations of an MI activity can be performed in parallel, i.e., concurrently. You don't have to perform one to completion before starting the next. (You can specify through

---

[26] In BPMN 1.0 the marker was two bars, but its similarity to the Pause symbol on a media player was later seen as confusing.

an attribute that the iteration is sequential, but better to use loop for that and reserve MI for when you mean parallel.)

Normally the MI activity is complete when all of its instances are complete. Technically the BPMN spec allows other completion conditions, such as when the first one is complete, but these are seldom seen and not particularly useful. You should assume the completion condition for any MI activity is that all instances are complete unless otherwise indicated through a text annotation.

Any one instance of an MI activity can abort the activity as a whole through a Terminate or Error end event. This may be useful when the result of one instance of the MI indicates there is no need to continue processing the others.

Returning to the hiring exercise, we can use an MI activity to process the list of candidates coming out of our loop. That activity might be a subprocess that arranges and conducts the interviews. Each candidate's instance of the subprocess can be concurrent with the others, which is what we want. The resulting model looks something like this:

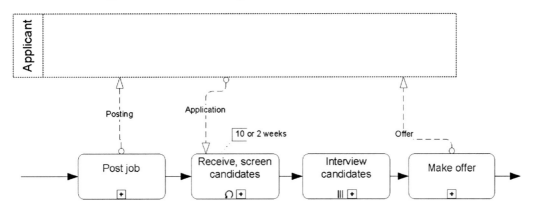

Figure 13-6. Using MI activity to act on a list of items

This is acceptable, but it has a small limitation. Interviewing cannot begin until all the applications have been collected, and once the MI interviewing activity begins no more applications can be received. This might be no problem at all. It could be how your company's hiring works in reality. But others might want to begin interviewing candidates as soon as they are screened, and keep collecting applications while other applicants are being interviewed. BPMN provides a way to do that, but not with repeating activities.

Multi-Instance Pools

The greatest flexibility comes from modeling your hiring process not as one pool but as two. This is harder for some people, especially those new to BPMN, to understand, but it allows the behavior we are trying to model.

Using this method, one pool represents the hiring process as a whole. An instance of that pool represents a job opening. This is essentially the main pool of our diagram. The other pool represents the processing of a single applicant. Each instance corresponds to an applicant. It looks like this:

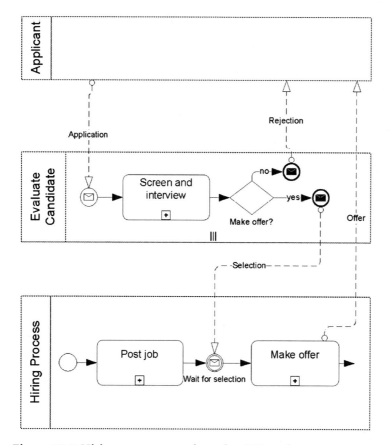

Figure 13-7. Hiring process exercise using MI pool

In Figure 13-7, each application triggers a new instance of *Evaluate Candidate*. Because these are instances of a pool, i.e., a process, it avoids the limitations imposed on repeating activities. Like a loop, the number of instances is unknown. It's whatever number are created by the arrival of new applications. But like an MI activity, the instances can run concurrently. So we can let each pool go all the way from receiving the application to completing the interview without delaying the processing of other applicants.

The possibility that a pool could represent multiple instances within a single diagram was implicit in BPMN 1.1, but BPMN 2.0 introduces the explicit notion of a *multi-instance pool*, which is what we have in our example. It is denoted by the same three-bar marker used by MI activity, placed at the bottom center of the pool, but, unlike MI activity, it does not necessarily process a list. The number of instances could be either known (For-Each) or unknown (Do-While). Our hiring exercise represents the unknown/Do-While case; a list of external providers of a service invoked in parallel by the process – for example, to seek the lowest price from a list of suppliers – could represent the known/For-Each case.

In this pattern, both pools are white-box, representing internal processes. While you should normally aim to create hierarchical models with a single top-level white-box pool, here is an example where multiple white-box pools in the top-level diagram works better. Even though the MI *Evaluate Candidate* pool is technically a top-level process, it behaves effectively as a child process. This pattern of a normal main pool plus a multi-instance "child" pool is often a convenient way to handle the situation where a single instance of the business process must act on N instances of some component, particularly when the value of N is unknown in advance and they are processed concurrently.

Modeling Batch Processing

Repeating activities and multi-instance pools are useful in modeling batch processing. While BPMN may pretend that business processes are fully service-oriented, real-time, and event-driven, in the real world many legacy systems still work in batch mode. In our order process examples, each instance of the process typically represents a single order. But posting that order to the MRP system or general ledger may not be real-time in practice. Orders may be accumulated and processed as batch updates one or more times a day. If there are parallel real-time paths in the process, the state of an order in those paths may not always match its state in the batch system. Careful Level 2 modeling can make this explicit and visible.

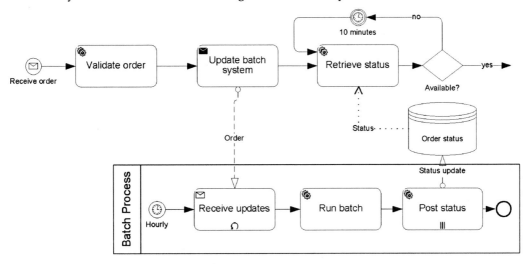

Figure 13-8. Modeling batch processing

Figure 13-8 illustrates the interaction between a real-time process and a batch process. Here the order process, shown without a visible pool boundary, is the real-time process. Each instance represents an order. As orders come in they are posted to a batch system, and downstream processing depends on the completion status of that batch process. In this example, the real-time process waits for the batch to complete, but real-world processes may not do this.

In the batch process, an instance is not an order but a batch of orders, specifically those accumulated since the last batch run. It is not triggered by a message from our order process, so it doesn't have a Message start event. We show it running on a predetermined batch schedule (hourly). Some batch processes may be run manually according to no fixed schedule. The first activity in the batch process is a looping Receive task. One of the few differences between a Receive task and a catching Message event is you can put a loop marker on the task. We don't indicate the loop condition but in this case it just accumulates Order messages until the next batch run. We use loop because it is Do-While, not For-Each. We don't know how many orders we are going to accumulate.

After the batch is run, the system posts the status of each order in the batch. This is MI, one status for each order. It would be nice if the system sent the order process a message, but here it makes us poll the system, modeled as a *data store*, for status. If it's not ready yet, we wait 10 minutes and try again.

CHAPTER 14

Transactions

What Are Transactions?

BPMN's outstanding ability to model exception handling is further enhanced by its support for transactions. The term *transaction* refers to the coordinated execution of multiple activities such that they either *all* complete successfully or the system is restored, or *rolled back*, to a state equivalent to *none* of them completing. An example familiar from everyday experience is electronic funds transfer in online banking or an automated teller machine. The transaction debits one account and credits another account, perhaps at another financial institution, an equal amount. This requires the coordinated action of databases at the two financial institutions. If, for some reason, the debit and the credit cannot both be executed, neither of them should be executed. What absolutely cannot happen is that one account is debited without the corresponding credit in the other account (or vice versa).

This example and similar distributed database operations are known in computer science as *ACID transactions*. Here ACID stands for:

- Atomic – indivisible, all-or-nothing behavior

- Consistent – preventing an inconsistent state of the system, such as a debit with no corresponding credit

- Isolated – the systems managing each account are locked during execution of the transaction

- Durable – the state of the participating systems is stored in a database, not just in memory, so it can be restored in case of a crash

In IT systems, ACID transactions are typically implemented using a special protocol such as *two-phase commit*. In two-phase commit, a piece of software called a transaction manager first communicates with the various systems performing, in this case, the debit and the credit, to ensure they are all available to execute their respective activities. Only if all systems report that they can is the transaction committed. Otherwise they are *rolled back* to the state before the transaction was initiated.

BPMN implements a similar idea for business processes. In BPMN, a subprocess marked as *transactional* means that its component activities must either all complete successfully or the subprocess must be rolled back to its original consistent state. However, these are usually not ACID transactions coordinated via two-phase commit. The reason is they fail the *I*, or isolation, requirement. In order to isolate, or lock, the resources performing the component activities of the transaction, those activities must complete almost immediately. For many business process activities you cannot make that assumption. Thus BPMN models what are called *long-running transactions* or *business transactions*, in which the activities are not locked while the transaction is in progress. Instead, each activity in the transaction executes normally in its turn, but if the transaction as a whole fails to complete successfully, each of its activities that has completed already is *undone* by executing a so-called *compensating activity*.

Examples of transaction recovery by compensation are familiar from everyday experience. Suppose you purchase some item online via credit card, but it turns out later that the item is unavailable from the company's suppliers. You will see on your credit card statement both a charge for the item and a subsequent matching credit cancelling the charge. The latter is the compensating activity for the charge. This is not the same as an ACID transaction that reserves the item in inventory before it charges the credit card. In that case you would see neither the charge nor the credit on your statement, because the transaction was never committed.

BPMN provides built-in support for business transactions. A subprocess with a double border (Figure 14-1) denotes it transactional. BPMN also provides notation to link activities within that subprocess to their compensating activities and to command compensation of a failed business transaction. Transaction compensation does not include the handling of the exception that caused the transaction to fail. It just means restoring the original consistent state of the system before the transaction began, by undoing those parts of the transaction that completed before the point of failure. Once compensation is complete, the normal BPMN exception handling semantics are executed.

Figure 14-1. Transactional subprocess

Compensation Events and Compensating Activities

The *Compensation boundary event* is used to link an activity to its undoing, or compensating, activity. It is not a normal boundary event, however. It has no exception flow coming out of it. Instead it has an association connector linking it to a single compensating activity (Figure 14-2). The purpose of the Compensation boundary event is simply to define the association between an activity and its defined compensating activity.

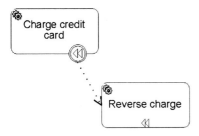

Figure 14-2. Compensating activity

Unlike a regular boundary event, a Compensation boundary event is only enabled after the activity to which it is attached completes successfully. If the activity has not started or is still running when the transaction fails, or if the activity itself completes unsuccessfully, its compensating activity is not run when the transaction fails.

Cancel Event

The *Cancel event* is a special form of the Error event used with transactional subprocesses (Figure 14-3) when the source of transaction failure is *within* the transaction subprocess, not after completion. Like Error, Cancel supports throw-catch from an end event of the transactional subprocess to a boundary event or event subprocess. Also, like Error it is always interrupting; there is no non-interrupting variant of Cancel. Its meaning is identical to Error except that before beginning the error handling, represented by exception flow or an event subprocess, Cancel implicitly commands compensation.

When the transaction is Canceled, all successfully completed activities within the subprocess that have defined compensating activities are undone by executing those compensating activities. Once compensation is complete, error handling commences by executing the exception flow or event subprocess associated with the Cancel event.

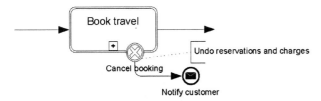

Figure 14-3. Cancel boundary event on transactional subprocess

Any other type of interrupting boundary event, such as Error, on a transactional subprocess aborts the transaction without compensation.

Compensation Throw-Catch

In addition to Cancel, BPMN provides an alternative way to directly command compensation. A throwing *Compensation intermediate event* or *Compensation end event* sends the command to a specific target activity within the pool. Unlike Cancel, the throw-catch is not to a boundary event.

In fact, the target is not an intermediate event at all, but the activity to be compensated, which does not need to be part of a transactional subprocess.

A use case for Compensation throw catch is when the need to undo the transaction is determined *after* the transaction is complete. The following examples illustrate the use of Cancel and Compensation events.

Using Compensation

To properly define compensating activities you need to think about the various points, either within the transactional subprocess or after its conclusion, where the transaction could possibly fail, and which possibly completed activities would need to be undone if that occurs.

Consider a simple travel booking example in which the transaction consists of two activities, reserving the seat and charging a credit card, always performed in that order (Figure 14-4). The only time this transaction requires compensation is if the credit card charge fails. In that case, the airline reservation must be undone using a compensating activity. If the activity reserving the seat fails (e.g., no seats available) there is no successfully completed activity to undo. Even though a compensating activity is defined, it is not executed unless the original activity completes successfully. Also, no compensating activity need be defined for the charge, since if it completes successfully the transaction as a whole completes successfully.

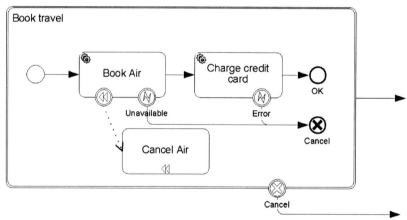

Figure 14-4. Transaction compensation, simple case

Now let's consider a more complex case, in which multiple flights and hotels must be booked to complete the itinerary (Figure 14-5). The order of booking each leg, hotel and air, is indeterminate. If any leg of the itinerary cannot be booked successfully, the transaction fails. If all legs of the itinerary can be booked, then the credit card is charged. If the credit card charge fails, the transaction also fails.

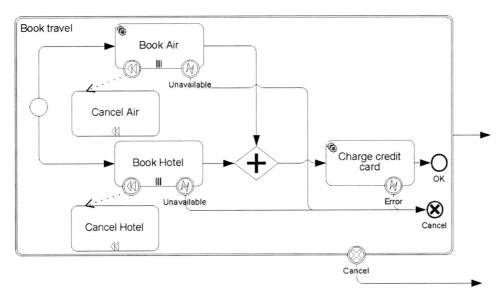

Figure 14-5. Transaction compensation, complex case

Here you can see the convenience of compensation, since there are many potential points of failure in this transaction. The state of each of the individual leg bookings at the point of failure cannot be known in advance. If you had to consider all the possible combinations and add paths to the diagram describing what to do if failure occurs in one state versus another, it would be a nightmare. With compensating activities, BPMN just applies a simple rule: if the activity has completed successfully when compensation is commanded, then execute its compensating activity; if it has not, do not execute the compensating activity.

In Figure 14-5, if any of the leg booking activities – that is, any *instances* of the multi-instance Book Hotel and Book Air activities – fail, the resulting Cancel throw-catch undoes just those instances that have already completed. If all of the leg booking instances complete but the credit card charge fails, then that Cancel undoes all of the bookings.

Now let's take it one step further. Suppose that after the transaction is complete, the customer for some reason decides to cancel the trip. This might not be modeled as part of the same process, but let's say in this case it was. The *Book travel* transaction is complete, but we want to undo it after the fact. This is a good use case for the *direct Compensation throw-catch*. We can't use Cancel because a Cancel throw must come from within the transactional subprocess.

Figure 14-6 illustrates. For argument's sake, we'll say that once all the bookings are complete, the travel agency requests final confirmation from the customer before charging the credit card.[27] The travel agency waits 24 hours before charging the customer in case of cancellation. To wait for

---

[27] Here we use an AND-join before the confirmation Message end event because we want to send the request only once. Connecting *Book Air* and *Book Hotel* directly to the end event would send it twice.

either 24 hours or the cancellation message, we use an event gateway. If a cancellation message is received, we can still undo the bookings using the previously defined compensating activities, but we cannot use a Cancel event because the transactional subprocess is already complete. Here we use a throwing Compensation event *Undo Book Travel*, targeted at the transactional subprocess, *Book Travel*. This triggers all of the compensating activities within that subprocess.

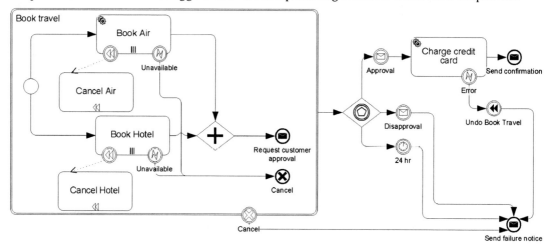

Figure 14-6. Throwing Compensation event

Note that compensation does not handle the exception. It merely rolls back the transaction to its initial state. The exception handling notifying the customer, perhaps adding a cancellation fee to the invoice, must be added in the exception flow.

CHAPTER 15

BPMN Method: Level 2

Level 2 modeling begins where Level 1 leaves off. As detailed in Chapter 5, that is with a hierarchical model leading to distinct success and fail end states represented by separate end events. The top-level process is typically linked to a pool representing Customer or other requester by request and response message flows.

Level 2 modeling introduces a richer palette of exception handling patterns and a more precise interpretation of BPMN semantics regarding starting and completing, sending and receiving, branching and merging, and repeating activities. But the Level 2 model is ideally a refinement of the Level 1, not a do-over, and generally speaking, the Level 1 method described in Chapter 5 remains a good way for Level 2 modelers to begin. The Level 2 method detailed in this chapter takes off from that point.

To review, the Level 1 method has five steps:

1. Define process scope

2. Create the top-level diagram for the happy path

3. Add top-level exception paths

4. Expand subprocesses to show detail at child level

5. Add intermediate message flows to Customer and other external pools (optional)

For Level 2 modeling, step 5 of the Level 1 method should be completed if it has not been done already. We will thus begin the Level 2 method with step 6.

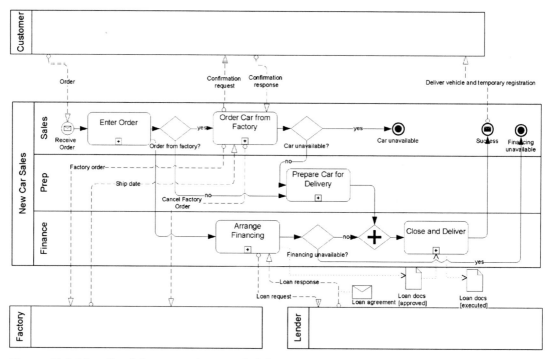

Figure 15-1. New Car Sales scenario as we left it at Level 1

We return to our *New Car Sales* scenario (Figure 15-1) as we left it back in Chapter 5. This is our starting point for Level 2. It is not uncommon that a large group of business users may create Level 1 models and a smaller group of BPMN experts "fixes up" those diagrams, refining them to Level 2 standards.

The steps described below may be performed in any order, or iteratively as the model is refined.

Step 6. Refine Branch/Merge Notation

In Level 1, we made a basic distinction between branching to an alternative exception path and splitting into parallel paths. At Level 2, we also have conditionally parallel splits and joins. Refining the branch and merge notation means re-examining the diagram to see whether it correctly reflects the distinction between exclusive alternative paths, unconditionally parallel paths, and conditionally parallel paths, and uses the appropriate joins.

Here we note that *Arrange Financing* may not be required for every instance. Some buyers may pay cash or arrange their own financing. So instead of unconditionally parallel flow out of *Enter Order*, we want a conditional split. That also means the join of *Arrange Financing* and *Prepare Car for Delivery* must be changed to an OR-gateway. The modifications are shown in Figure 15-2.

- Dealer-arranged financing may not be required

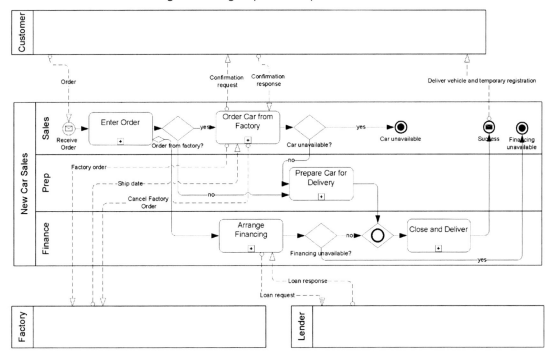

Figure 15-2. New Car Sales corrected for branch/merge notation

Step 7. Refine for Channel-Dependent Start

Another Level 2 refinement concerns specifying differences in front-end activities based on how the process is triggered, typically the *channel* of interaction. Our Level 1 model assumes the order is a paper form filled out by a customer in person at the dealer's location. This is the most common occurrence, but the dealer also accepts orders with a credit card deposit over the web.

Scenario: **New car sales** (continued)

- In-person orders: Buyer fills out and signs a paper form and gives it, together with deposit, to salesperson. Process activity keys in data from the form to the order system.

- Online orders: Buyer fills out a web form and provides deposit via credit card. Web application (external to process) validates data completeness. Process activity retrieves credit card confirmation.

- For both entry points, the form indicates whether the buyer requires dealer-arranged financing.

The channel-dependent start notation was discussed in Chapter 12. It is modeled with multiple Message start events (Figure 15-3). One Message event represents the paper order and another represents the web order. Each path leads to a different activity representing the channel-dependent processing.

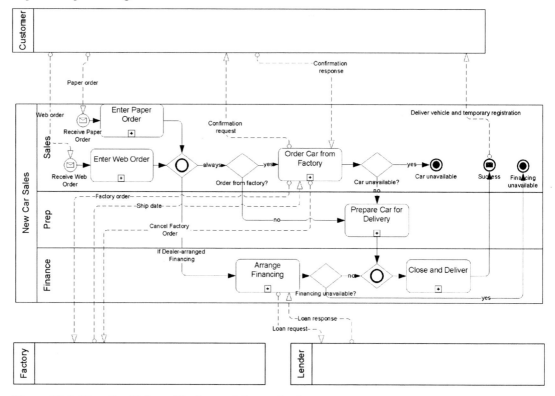

Figure 15-3. New Car Sales with channel-dependent start

These paths are exclusive alternatives so they can be merged downstream without a gateway. They merge here at an OR-gateway representing the conditional split of the financing and factory order paths. Because the conditional split does not come from an activity, we can no longer use the conditional sequence flow notation of Figure 15-2; we must use the OR-gateway. It is generally not best practice to have multiple inputs and multiple outputs on the same gateway, but it is allowable when the inputs are exclusive alternatives and space is at a premium, as in Figure 15-3. In such a situation, the gateway symbol reflects the branching (here, conditional split) not the merging behavior.

Step 8. Refine for Iterative Behavior

As discussed in Chapter 13, some refinement of iterative behavior using repeating activities or multi-instance pools may be required. Examples include:

- Handling multiple messages from or to external entities
- Assigning a task to multiple performers

- Iterating a business function over multiple items within the process instance, such as items in an order

Scenario: New car sales (continued)

- Arrange Financing: The customer's loan application is delivered to multiple lenders, and the best offer is selected.

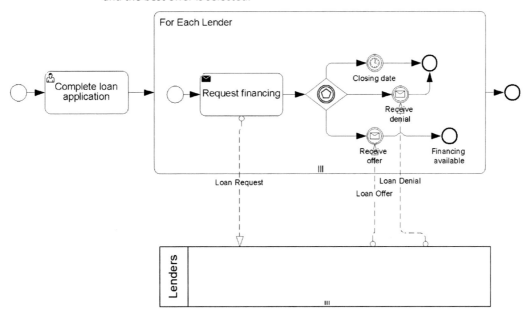

Figure 15-4. Expansion of *Arrange Financing,* **with iterative behavior**

Figure 15-4 illustrates the expanded view of *Arrange Financing* showing the iterative behavior. Each lender is represented as an instance of a multi-instance pool, and process interactions with that MI pool occur through a multi-instance subprocess labeled *For Each Lender.* Here a Send task is used to issue the request, but it could just as easily be modeled by a throwing Message event. An event gateway waits for the response. A loan offer received ends the instance in the *Financing Available* end state. If no response is received by the predetermined closing date, it is considered the same as a denial by the lender. Note we have changed the lender response to two alternative messages, *Loan Offer* and *Loan Denial.* We need to make that change in the top-level diagram as well.

Step 9. Refine Exception Handling Patterns

In Level 1 we had only one exception-handling pattern at our disposal, the internal business exception, modeled using the XOR gateway. But Level 2 modelers have a richer palette of patterns available, so their diagrams can distinguish a wide variety of exception types. It is up to the modeler to determine how many and what kind of exceptions to include in the diagram. Best practice is to include any exception significant to overall process performance, meaning its impact on aggregated metrics of time, cost, or quality. That significance is the product of the probability that the exception occurs and the additional time, cost, or error effect that results.

Start with your top level diagram and think about *what could go wrong* in each of the activities, typically subprocesses, shown at that level. Typical problems include:

- Incomplete or incorrect data is provided
- A request or approval is denied
- A process step cannot be performed (e.g., order item is out of stock so cannot be shipped)
- An activity is not completed in time, or is in danger of same
- An expected response does not arrive in time
- The process is cancelled or receives new relevant information while in flight

Then, for each exception identified, think about *how it should be handled*. Some possibilities, which may be used in combination, include:

- Abort the activity. (Unfortunately, BPMN does not currently support the notions of *suspending* and *resuming* an activity or process, even though many commercial process engines provide this function!)
- Restart the current activity, possibly after reassigning or delegating the performer
- Initiate a parallel action, from a simple reminder/notification to a long-running handler flow
- Branch to an alternative path
- Jump back to a previous step
- Jump ahead, skipping one or more steps
- Start a new process
- Cancel another activity occurring in parallel

Actually, these actions just describe the *local handling* of the exception, meaning within the subprocess where they originate. Local handling is usually followed by *propagation* to a parent-level diagram for additional exception handling at that level. For example, an out-of-stock error in a fulfillment subprocess would typically be propagated to end the overall order process at the top level. Given the myriad combinations of exception sources, local handling, and propagation, modeling exception handling in a way that is both expressive and clear may seem a daunting task. The following method tries to bring some order to it.

In our discussion of exception-handling patterns in Chapter 12, we began at the exception source and local handling, and then considered propagation. In our top-down method, however, we often start at the other end, with exception end states of the top-level diagram. For each exception end state, we need to ask the questions, *How does the process get here? What is the original source of the exception? Where is it first detected? How is it handled locally, and how is it propagated?*

At the top level, most activities are subprocesses. Propagation from exceptions occurring inside them can be modeled either using a gateway or an Error boundary event. The latter has the advantage of requiring less space on the page. Whether modeled using a gateway or Error boundary event, it is important to check that an end event with matching label is provided in the child-level diagram.

In addition to the exception paths modeled at Level 1, new exceptions may be considered in the Level 2 model. All exceptions significant to aggregated metrics of performance or quality should be included in the model.

> **Scenario: New car sales** (continued)
>
> In the Level 1 model we considered two exceptions, *Car Unavailable* and *Financing Unavailable*. At Level 2 we will detail those exceptions and add two more, *Bad Order* and *Customer Cancel*.
>
> 1. *Bad Order* results from a problem with web orders, either invalid data or inability to process the credit card deposit. If this exception is detected in *Enter web order*, we want to end the top-level process with a rejection message to the customer.
>
> 2. *Car Unavailable* results from the inability of the factory to deliver the selected configuration at a date acceptable to the customer. Here we are refining the Level 1 exception shown in Figure 5-6. As before, in this case we want to end the top-level process, including the parallel path to *Arrange Financing*, and send a *Cancel Factory Order* message to the factory.
>
> 3. *Financing Unavailable* results from the failure of obtaining any Loan Offer responses from lenders. In this case we want to end the top-level process, including the parallel path to *Prepare Car for Delivery*, and send a *Cancel Factory Order* message to the factory.
>
> 4. *Customer Cancel* results from receipt of an order cancellation from the customer. It could occur at any time following completion of the *Enter Order* subprocess and before *Close and Deliver*. In this case we want to end the top-level process, including both the *Arrange Financing* and *Prepare Car for Delivery* paths, and send a *Cancel Factory Order* message to the factory.

Here we will restructure our top-level diagram to reflect the fact that a single handler for the *Customer Cancel* message applies across a large scope, from the completion of *Enter Order* to just prior to *Close and Deliver*. We can enclose that fragment of the process in a subprocess, *Fulfill Order*, and attach the *Customer Cancel* Message event to its boundary. The exception flow goes to a *Cancel Factory Order* Message end event, which both ends the top-level process and sends the cancellation message to the factory.

In the new structure, both *Car Unavailable* and *Financing Unavailable* become exception end states of *Fulfill Order*. So we will make them Error end events, propagating the error to the *Fulfill Order* boundary. As with *Customer Cancel*, the exception flows from these go to the *Cancel Factory Order* Message end event.

This defines our overall exception handling structure. Now let's look at the local handling of each exception.

Enter Web Order is a sequence of three tasks: *Validate Order*, *Process Credit Card*, and *Update Order System*. If *Validate Order* has incomplete or invalid data (business exception), throw an *Invalid data* error. If *Process Credit Card* has invalid credit card for deposit (business exception), throw a *Bad card* error. We catch both errors on boundary and end the process, returning *Bad Order* message to customer. We can use a single Error boundary event to catch both errors, since the exception flow is the same.

Figure 15-5 illustrates the expansion of *Enter Web Order*, showing the business exceptions that throw the specified errors.

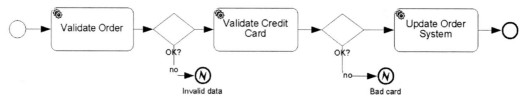

Figure 15-5. Child-level expansion of Enter Web Order throws error from internal business exceptions.

Car Unavailable occurs in the *Order Car from Factory* subprocess. After placing the factory order, wait for the *Ship Date* response message. If a ship date is provided, the dealer calculates a promised delivery date and sends a confirmation request message to the customer, who can respond either Accept or Decline. If Accept, end the subprocess in a *Confirmed* end state. If Decline, the dealer offers the customer available alternatives and waits for a response, again either Accept or Decline. If the customer accepts an alternative, loop back to place the factory order again, repeating the cycle. If the customer declines, throw a *Car Unavailable* error. If the factory responds that the requested configuration is unavailable, the dealer offers the customer alternatives, as above.

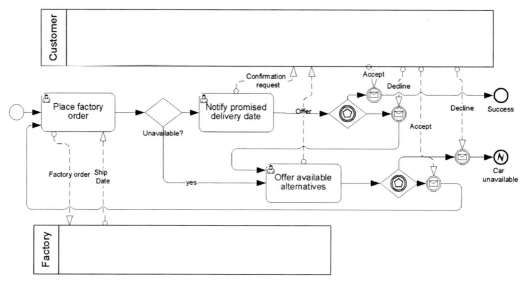

Figure 15-6. Expansion of Order Car from Factory

Figure 15-6 shows the expansion of *Order Car from Factory*. Notice that the external pools Customer and Factory, and the message flows between them and the process, are replicated in the child-level diagram. Here there are two cases of solicited response exceptions. The customer could decline the promised date, or the customer could decline the offer of available alternatives. Both are modeled as event gateways with one Message event representing the happy path response and another representing the exception response. We could have added a third timeout path as well. Declining the offer of alternatives leads to the *Car unavailable* end state; acceptance leads to the *Confirmed* end state. This subprocess can end only in one of those two end states.

Figure 15-7 shows our revised top-level diagram. Here we have inserted *Fulfill Order* in the expanded inline representation, for ease of comparison with Figure 15-1. All three of its boundary events have the same handling, simply ending the top-level process with a *Cancel Factory Order* message. However, by making them separate events, we could insert different activities in each handler.

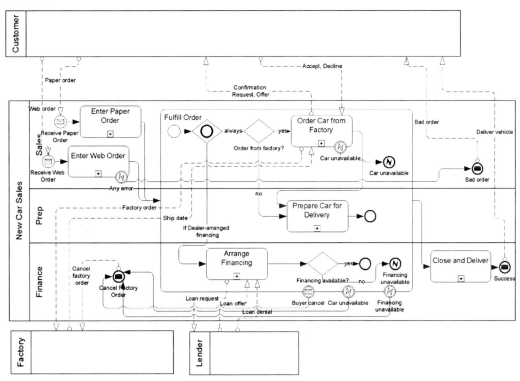

Figure 15-7. Buyer cancel handled with Message boundary events

CHAPTER 16

Elements of BPMN Style: Level 2

"Style" at Level 2 is about creating diagrams that can be shared effectively between business and IT. Even though business analysts and implementation designers might draw from the same palette of shapes and symbols, they cannot truly collaborate if they use different conventions and diagram patterns. Those are largely matters of style.

Adherence to a consistent modeling style is just as valuable at Level 2 as it is at Level 1. And the elements of Level 1 style presented in Chapter 6 remain just as important at Level 2, as well. This might be a good time to go back and review them before continuing. In this chapter are 13 more recommendations for a creating Level 2 diagrams that are expressive yet clearly understandable across the organization.

1. *Validate your diagrams, and fix the errors.*

Sure, this is a "motherhood" statement, like "eat your vegetables" or "be kind to strangers". But you would be surprised at how often modelers – especially beginners – ignore this advice. BPMN has rules, and real BPMN tools understand those rules and can automatically validate your diagrams (Figure 16-1). You wouldn't want to publish a business memo filled with spelling and grammar errors, and you shouldn't want to publish a process diagram filled with illegal BPMN constructs, either.

To be fair, the BPMN spec could have done a lot more to make following the rules easy. For starters, it could have at least listed the important ones, instead of sprinkling them throughout the narrative text. Here is my list of the important rules of BPMN for *non-executable* process models.

Sequence flow...
- Cannot cross boundary of pool or subprocess (process level)
- Cannot go into a start event, out of end event
- Cannot go into a boundary event
- Can attach only to activity, gateway, or event
- Conditional sequence flow (diamond on tail) can only come out of an activity (not gateway or event)

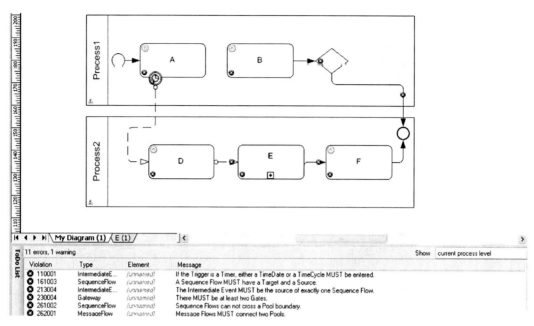

Figure 16-1. Diagram validation in Process Modeler for Visio from ITP Commerce

Message flow…
- Cannot connect objects in the same pool
- Should attach to boundary of black-box pool, and to activity or event in white-box pool

Gateway…
- Must have either 2+ incoming sequence flows, or 2+ outgoing sequence flows
- Cannot send or receive message flow
- Cannot be AND-join unless all incoming sequence flows are unconditionally enabled

Start event…
- Is required if an end event is used
- Must have None trigger in subprocess
- Cannot send message flow

End event…
- Is required if a start event is used
- Cannot receive message flow

Catching Intermediate event (in sequence flow)…
- May not have Error, Escalation, Multiple, or Cancel trigger
- Cannot be "floating", must have sequence flow in and out

Boundary event (except Compensation)…
- Must have one sequence flow out
- Must be Catching, not Throwing
- May not have None or Link trigger

2. *Model end-to-end process as a single pool, if possible.*

This recommendation elaborates on similar advice given back at Level 1. A common beginner mistake is to model each role or organizational unit as a separate pool rather than as a lane within a single process pool. At the other extreme, a modeler might stuff multiple processes within a single pool. Both of these are incorrect: A pool is a container for a single BPMN process. Part of the confusion comes from the spec's association of a pool with a *participant*, but a participant in BPMN does not mean the role or entity that performs a process activity. That term is *performer*. Participant here refers to a role or entity involved in a collaboration, such as the requester vs. the provider of a service.

You may be tempted to model your end-to-end process as top-level processes in separate pools chained together (Figure 16-2). This is not illegal, but in most cases it is not best practice. Chaining makes it more difficult to manage and measure end-to-end performance, and the "spirit" of BPM as a management discipline encourages conceptualizing the end-to-end business process as a single entity.

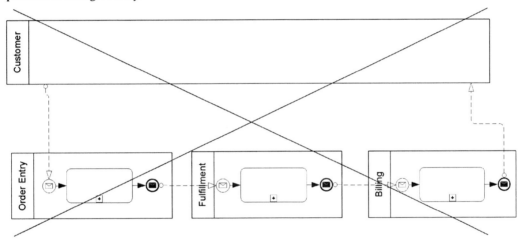

Figure 16-2. Process chaining is legal, but not best practice if there is one-to-one correspondence between the instances of each pool

Instead of chaining pools, use subprocesses within a single pool (Figure 16-3) to represent the major steps of the end-to-end process.

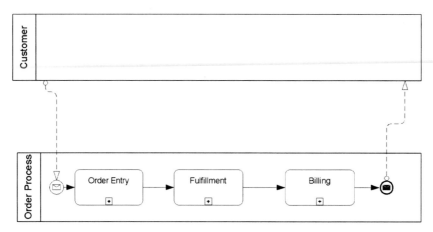

Figure 16-3. If you can, use subprocesses within a single pool

One reason modelers might give for avoiding Figure 16-3 is *modularity*. They want to maintain the internal flows of *Order Entry, Fulfillment,* and *Billing* as independent models. Each might use different business systems and different data models, and each might be reused in various other end-to-end processes. These are all valid reasons for not wanting to *embed* subprocess definitions within a single end-to-end process definition. But BPMN provides a better solution than chaining pools. It's called a *reusable subprocess*.

What we have been calling simply a subprocess was called in BPMN 1.x an *embedded subprocess,* meaning specified within the process definition, as opposed to *reusable subprocess,* which is specified externally as an independent process. There was no way to distinguish them in the notation, however.

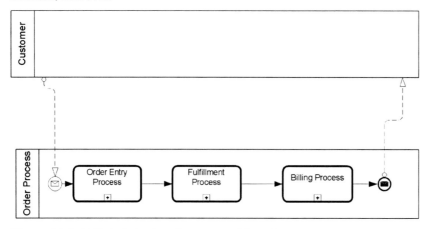

Figure 16-4. *Call Activity* invokes a reusable subprocess

In BPMN 2.0, embedded subprocess has become simply *Subprocess,* and the reusable subprocess has been renamed *Call Activity,* drawn with a thick border (Figure 16-4). Here *Call Activity* can be viewed as the call or invocation of an independently defined process within the context of a single BPMN process. This notion of modularity and reuse is not confined to subprocesses. *Global tasks*, drawn with a similar thick border plus a task type icon, represent reusable User tasks, Service tasks, Business Rule tasks, etc.

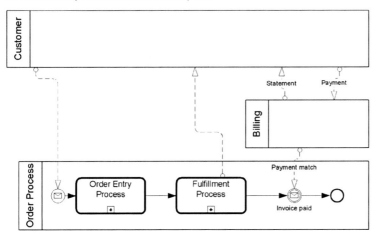

Figure 16-5. An end-to-end process may have multiple pools in special circumstances

An exception to the single-pool rule is when there is not a one-to-one correspondence between the instances of each major step in the process. For example, in Order-to-Cash, it may be that the customer does not pay separately for each order, but instead interacts with monthly statements from a separate Billing process (Figure 16-5). We saw a similar example in the discussion of batch processes (Figure 13-8). In such cases your internal process might involve two or more pools, but usually not in a chained arrangement.

3. *Propagate exceptions to parent level to show effect on the end-to-end process.*

When an exception occurs within a subprocess, in addition to any local handling defined within the subprocess, you need to propagate the exception to show the effect on the downstream process. This is normally accomplished using either a gateway following the subprocess that tests the end state (Figure 16-6) or error throw-catch to the boundary (Figure 16-7). In both of these examples, membership expiration inside the *Validation* subprocess is propagated to the parent level to end the overall process.

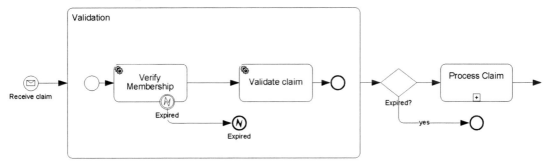

Figure 16-6. Exception propagation using a gateway to test subprocess end state

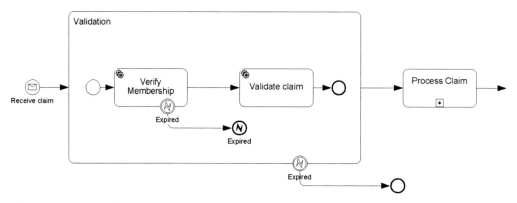

Figure 16-7. Exception propagation using error throw-catch

Note that a Terminate event does not end the overall process. It just ends the subprocess, so Figure 16-8 is incorrect.

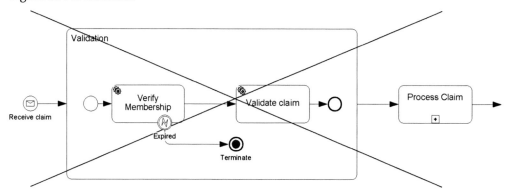

Figure 16-8. Terminate just ends the subprocess, not the overall process

4. *Show request/response at top level.*

This recommendation could be considered personal style, but I think it is helpful in creating that common language shared by business and IT. If the process is triggered by a request, use Message end events in the top-level diagram to return a response to the requester, such as a confirmation or rejection notice, for each distinct end state of the process. From a business perspective, this makes the end states of the process immediately visible and connected to the process's global context. From an IT perspective, this aligns your diagram with concepts from Service Oriented Architecture, and makes the process's *service interface* – its request and possible response messages – clear from the diagram itself.

That requires propagating terminating exceptions occurring in child level diagrams up to the top level *before* returning the process's end state response to the requester. For example, if *Credit Check* inside a *Fulfillment* subprocess fails, you could send a rejection notice directly from the point of failure (Figure 16-9), but this does not make it obvious that the message is a final response from the process. Propagating the exception one level and returning the rejection from the *Fulfillment*

---

subprocess (Figure 16-10) is no better. If *Fulfillment* is drawn collapsed, Figure 16-9 and Figure 16-10 look identical.

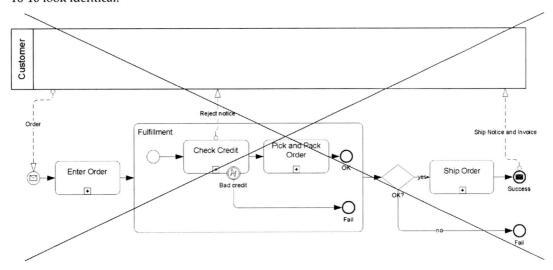

Figure 16-9. Returning final exception response from deeply nested subprocess is not best practice

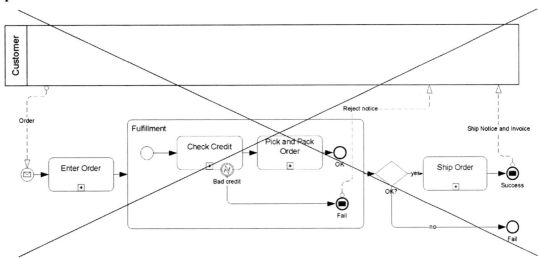

Figure 16-10. Propagating one level still sends response from child level

Here it's best to propagate the exception all the way up to the top level, and return the rejection notice from a top level Message end event (Figure 16-11). In this way, the process interface is clearly visible from the start and end events that "frame" the top-level diagram.

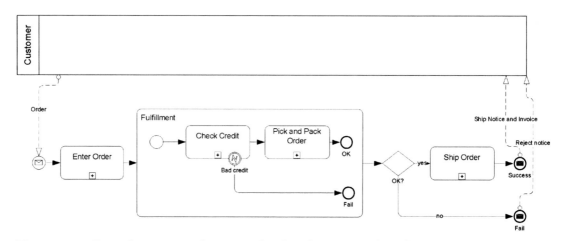

Figure 16-11. Exception propagation to top level makes process interface obvious from the diagram

> 5. *Do not use a task to forward work to another performer.*

In Level 2 modeling, sequence flow implicitly provides notification to the task performer and delivery of information required to perform the task. It is not necessary to use a task to forward work to a downstream performer (Figure 16-12), and unless you need to call special attention to the effort of sending the work, it is best practice to omit it.

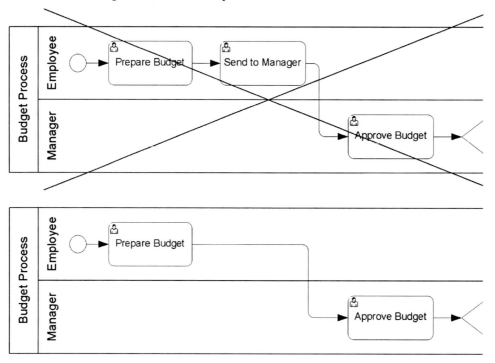

Figure 16-12. Sequence flow by itself implicitly forwards work downstream

6. *Reserve the keywords Send and Receive in task names for Send and Receive task types.*

You cannot use message flow to communicate within a pool, so any type of communication to another performer within the process must be something other than a "message." I think it is best practice to reserve the keywords Send and Receive in flow element names for activities or events that send and receive messages. If you need to show intra-pool communication, try a User task and a verb like Notify or Deliver.

7. *To iterate an activity, use Loop when the number of iterations is determined during performance of the activity; use Multi-instance when the number of iterations is known in advance.*

Many modelers are confused about the difference between Loop and Multi-Instance activities. Loop is like Do-While in programming. You perform the activity, and then evaluate a condition. If the condition is true, perform it again, and afterwards evaluate the condition again. You do not know, when starting the activity, how many times it will be performed.

Multi-Instance is like For-Each in programming. The process instance provides a list of something, like items in an order. An MI activity is performed once for each item in the list. Unlike Loop, you know when you start the activity how many times it will be performed. Also, unlike Loop, instances of the MI activity may be performed concurrently.

When using either Loop or MI, it is best to indicate the loop condition or the nature of the multiple instances somehow in the diagram, either in the activity name or via a text annotation.

8. *Use OR-gateway to join conditionally parallel paths.*

At Level 1, it is OK to use AND-gateway to join conditionally parallel paths, but the strict semantics of BPMN Level 2 say you must use an OR-gateway instead. Conditionally parallel paths may be split by an OR-gateway (Figure 16-13), conditional sequence flow, or a non-interrupting boundary event. In the join, an OR-gateway waits for all sequence flows that are enabled, ignoring those that are not enabled for that process instance.

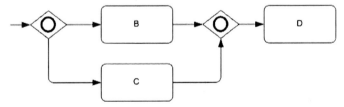

Figure 16-13. OR-gateway joins conditionally parallel paths

9. *Do not use default sequence flow to mean 'always'. It means 'otherwise'.*

Many modelers misunderstand the meaning of the sequence flow tickmark, which signifies *default flow*. It means "otherwise" – i.e., no other sequence flow has a condition that evaluates to True. It does not mean "always." The two diagrams shown in Figure 16-14 do *not* mean the same thing.

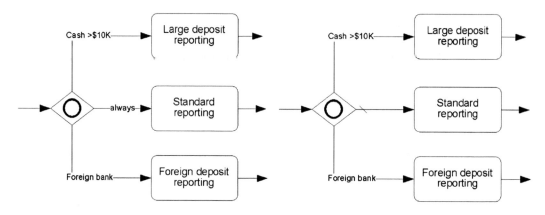

Figure 16-14. These diagrams do NOT mean the same thing

> 10. *Do not use conditional sequence flow to model exclusive alternative paths out of an activity.*

Modelers should get in the habit of using a gateway to model exclusive choice, not conditional sequence flow. Conditional sequence flow implies *independent* conditions, so one or more could be true. When there are only two paths and one uses the default condition, as in Figure 16-15, this is technically equivalent to an exclusive gateway. But if you have more than two paths, as in Figure 16-16, the left and right diagrams are no longer equivalent.

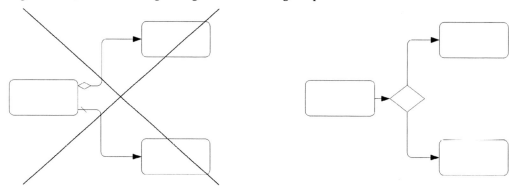

Figure 16-15. Left and right diagrams mean the same thing, but right one is preferred

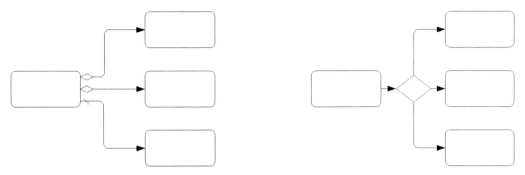

Figure 16-16. With more than two paths, left and right diagrams do *not* mean the same thing

11. *Use catching Message or Signal intermediate event (or Receive task), not Timer, to wait for something to happen. If an information request has a deadline, put Timer event on the receive (catch) not the send (throw).*

Beginning modelers often make the mistake of using a catching Timer event to represent a deadline when waiting for something to happen (Figure 16-17). That is incorrect. A catching Timer event is just a delay, so Figure 16-17 really says: Request info, wait 2 days, and then Process info. There is no activity or event to receive the requested info!

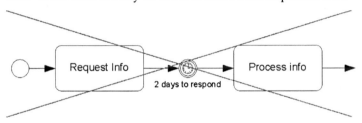

Figure 16-17. Timer event is just a delay; it does not wait for something to happen

Another common mistake is applying a Timer boundary event to the Send, i.e. the request, rather than to the Receive, the wait for response. Remember, sending is immediate; receiving means wait until you receive the message. So Figure 16-18 is incorrect as well.

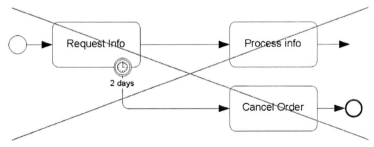

Figure 16-18. Requesting is immediate; the timeout applies to the receive, which waits for a response

The right way to apply a deadline to a wait is with an event gateway (Figure 16-19). Alternatively, you can attach a Timer boundary event to a Receive task.

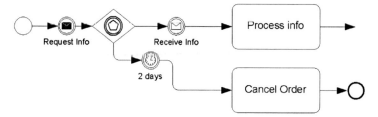

Figure 16-19. Waiting for a response uses event gateway

> 12. *Use matching labels for paired throw-catch events (Error, Escalation, Signal), in addition to any non-visual linking attributes.*

For executable processes, throw-catch event pairs are linked by reference to a common event definition element, but this is not visible in the diagram. To make the pairing obvious from the diagram, simply give the throwing and catching events matching labels. This is especially important with Signal throw catch, since you cannot indicate source and target with message flow. Unlike Message events, Signal is not sent to a specific process but broadcast (published) to any listener.

> 13. *Error and Escalation throw-catch is only allowed from child to parent level.*

You cannot throw an Error or Escalation signal to a catching event in sequence flow, to a start event, or to a boundary event in a parallel path or another process. Error and Escalation can only be thrown from a subprocess and caught on a boundary event of that same subprocess.

CHAPTER 17

Model Serialization and Interchange

The Model Interchange Problem

The success of BPMN 1.x in the marketplace is all the more remarkable considering it does not provide a standard XML *serialization*, or interchange format, for diagrams. People naturally assume that because BPMN is a standard supported by many tools, you can define a model in one tool and continue editing it in another. But that assumption is mostly mistaken.

BPMN 2.0 is OMG's long-awaited answer to an *official* interchange format for BPMN. In the absence of such a standard, a limited amount of tool interoperability has been available by mapping model elements to other serialization standards, notably BPEL from OASIS and XPDL from the Workflow Management Coalition (WfMC). Even once BPMN 2.0 takes hold as the serialization format, it is possible that BPEL and XPDL will continue to play an important role in assuring model portability between tools.

Model interchange is a thorny subject because it means different things to different people. It is helpful to distinguish the following use cases:

1. Create non-executable (Level 1 or Level 2) BPMN model in Tool A and import it to BPMN Tool B.

2. Create non-executable BPMN model in Tool A and import it to non-BPMN Tool B, such as an executable design tool based on BPEL or proprietary BPMS.

3. Create executable (Level 3) BPMN model in Tool A and execute it in BPMS environment B. Executable Level 3 modeling is a major focus of BPMN 2.0. As of this writing, no commercial implementations exist, so for now we will ignore this use case.

BPEL as an Interchange Format

BPEL is an execution language for processes based on automated orchestration of web services. That means it is an XML programming language that can be directly executed on a BPEL process engine such as IBM WebSphere Process Server or Oracle BPEL Process Manager. BPEL has two factors in its favor when used as an interchange format between BPMN-based modeling tools and BPEL-based executable design tools – use case 2 above.

First, BPEL is supported by most major middleware vendors, and it will continue to play an important role in SOA regardless of BPMN 2.0. Second, a BPEL tool must support the complete language. Unlike BPMN, where supposedly compliant tools can pick and choose the constructs they elect to support, BPEL tools must support all of the defined constructs in the language. That means if you can export the BPMN to standard BPEL, the importing BPEL tool can usually understand all of it.

That assumption does not apply when the BPEL export has been enhanced with vendor-specific extensions. For example, Oracle BPA Suite contains BPEL extensions to support specific services of Oracle BPEL Process Manager, like human tasks, notifications, and business rules. Those extensions would not necessarily be understood by other BPEL tools.

BPEL is not a good solution, however, for our use case 1, interchange between different BPMN modeling tools. It is not ideal even for use case 2, since it imposes business-unfriendly constraints on the process modeler. There are a few reasons for this:

First, BPEL's basic structure is *block-oriented*, while BPMN is *graph-oriented*. To be BPEL-compatible, every gateway split or branch in the BPMN diagram must have a corresponding merge or join gateway collecting all of the paths.[28] All of the nodes between the split and the merge constitute a *block*, and all blocks must be properly nested; they cannot overlap. Programmers are used to such constraints, but business people used to BPMN's more freeform flowcharting style are not.

In addition, certain other sequence flow patterns valid in BPMN are not easily mapped to BPEL. For instance, in BPMN a sequence flow can loop back arbitrarily to some prior step in the flow, but not in BPEL. Exception flows out of BPMN boundary events are similarly difficult to translate to BPEL. It's not that these BPMN patterns are *impossible* to serialize in BPEL, especially if you are willing to map them to multiple BPEL processes interacting via events. It's just that the round trip from BPMN to BPEL and back again is virtually impossible. The solution typically offered by BPMSs that combine BPMN and BPEL is to restrict the BPMN to patterns that map easily to BPEL. This technically "works," but is a problem for many business analysts.

A second problem is BPEL has no native construct for human tasks, which play a large role in BPMN models. That is because in BPEL every activity is implicitly a web service. While a BPMN User task is a type of process activity, its equivalent in BPEL *creates* a human task managed by a

---

[28] A few BPMN tools have built-in intelligence that can generate BPEL without requiring the BPMN to be drawn in block-structured fashion.

vendor-proprietary task management service. Task performers interact with that service, which notifies the process when it is complete.

A proposed add-on to BPEL, called BPEL4People, is trying to standardize the interaction of the process and the human task, but it is a far cry from BPMN, in which automated services and human tasks are peer flow elements. For that reason, BPEL has had its greatest adoption for processes in which human tasks play a minor role.

Third, the constructs of the BPEL language, both in name and in semantics, are different from BPMN. It has no equivalent, for example, to some of the BPMN event types.

Fourth, BPEL is concerned with executable processes, not with modeling the flow of abstract activities for analysis and documentation. It has no standard diagramming notation and no way to map graphical information from the BPMN diagram to and from the BPEL tool.

Finally, BPMN 2.0 used at Level 3 is quite similar to BPEL, except that its executable constructs map exactly to the graphical notation. In fact, this was an intentional design consideration of the BPMN 2.0 team, led by IBM, Oracle, and SAP, all major BPEL providers today.

All of these factors point to a diminishing role for BPEL as an interchange format for BPMN in the future.

XPDL as an Interchange Format

XPDL was originally developed as a format for interchange between process modeling tools and proprietary executable process design tools. Because it is intended to connect arbitrary process languages, XPDL's constructs are generic. The downside of this flexibility is that tool vendors are free to select which of them they support. That means while it is straightforward for any tool to export BPMN to XPDL, there is no guarantee the importing tool can understand all parts of the exported diagram.

Like BPMN, XPDL is graph-oriented, and thus does not suffer from BPEL's topology constraints. Also, XPDL does not assume that the execution environment is based on BPEL, or even that the model is executable. For that reason it is favored by a significant number of BPM Suites, most of which are not BPEL-based, as a way to import from third party BPMN tools, such as Business Process Analysis suites.

XPDL 2.0 was enhanced specifically to support BPMN, adding constructs wherever necessary to match all of the information elements defined in the BPMN spec. XPDL 2.1 updated that support to BPMN 1.1, and XPDL 2.2 is planned to support BPMN 2.0. The mapping between XPDL 2.2 and the new BPMN 2.0 format should be straightforward and bidirectional.

In addition to the semantic information, XPDL also allows graphic layout information – the position and size of the various diagram shapes and connectors – to be interchanged between tools. In fact, XPDL's approach to serializing the graphics information is in many ways superior to the approach taken by OMG in BPMN 2.0.

BPMN 2.0 as an Interchange Format

BPMN 2.0 at long last fulfills OMG's commitment to provide an official XML interchange format for BPMN models. The format is defined by an XML schema (xsd) generated from the UML-based BPMN metamodel. In the schema, the *semantic model* is separated from the *diagram interchange model*, the graphic elements as arranged on the page. Each shape and line in the diagram interchange model includes a reference to a corresponding element in the semantic model.

The semantic model has three top-level model types: *process, collaboration,* and *choreography*. In this book we are concerned only with the process and collaboration models. The *collaboration model* describes the interaction between pools via message flows. Each *process model* describes the orchestration of a single process. A single interchanged XML document could contain multiple processes, and possibly multiple collaborations. Also, BPMN models can reference externally defined processes, data, and messages via the *import* tag. This is important in practice because it supports modular process definition and governance without losing the ability to specify an end-to-end process as a single instance document.

BPMN and Model Portability

A standard serialization format is necessary but not sufficient to assure successful interchange of models from BPMN tool A to BPMN tool B. Here I use the term *model portability* to mean the ability to export a serialized Level 2 (non-executable) BPMN model from tool A and import it reliably into another BPMN tool B. Because tools will probably not support every last bit of the BPMN schema, guaranteeing model portability requires imposing some constraints on the interchanged instance. For example, portability might be assured only for a subset of BPMN elements. A practical approach to the portability problem is to define one or more *portability conformance classes* representing subsets of BPMN, with requirements that must be met by tools claiming to support the class.

In its initial release of BPMN 2.0, OMG does not support such model portability conformance classes. Process Modeling Conformance, according to the BPMN 2.0 specification, means only that a tool does not necessarily claim that it can define executable (Level 3) BPMN or Choreography models. Thus claims of Process Modeling Conformance by tools A and B do not imply portability of BPMN diagrams between those tools.

This was a missed opportunity by OMG. Interoperability between BPMN tools was a loud user demand going all the way back to BPMI.org days. For now, BPMN portability efforts are trying to build on WfMC's work in this area. That work, based on XPDL, defines SIMPLE, STANDARD, and COMPLETE conformance classes for BPMN 1.x, and includes an online tool that validates a BPMN instance document and lists elements falling outside the specified conformance class.

Led by Robert Shapiro, [29] this work is being extended to BPMN 2.0 and modified to work directly with the BPMN serialization instead of the XPDL mapping. I am trying to align the portability conformance classes with the Level 1 and "core" Level 2 palettes described in this book, and this work is ongoing as the book goes to press. Those interested in developments in this area are referred to the book's website, www.bpmnstyle.com, for updated information. Background on the work to date is provided below.

XPDL and Portable BPMN

XPDL has taken the lead in the area of BPMN model portability, providing conformance levels and rules of compliance so that users can know in advance – in theory – whether their non-executable (Level 2) model can be interchanged between two particular tools. The following is part of WfMC's XPDL 2.1 white paper:[30]

> BPMN can be used for both "abstract" activity flow modeling and for complete executable design. Many tools, however, make use of BPMN for the abstract modeling but add executable detail in tool-specific activity properties. One goal of XPDL 2.1 is to promote portability of abstract activity flow models between tools. This requires separating the elements and attributes of BPMN related to activity flow modeling from those related to executable design. The BPMN spec does not define this separation, but XPDL does, in the form of BPMN Model Portability conformance classes.

> In broad terms, the "abstract model" elements are those that represent BPMN constructs that are printable in the business process diagram, such as those defining the flow object type or subtype (e.g., looping User task, collapsed subprocess, exclusive gateway, Timer event), including only attributes specifying the subtype, label (Name attribute), and unique identifiers for the object itself and pointers to other identifiers in the diagram. Elements and attributes representing data, messages, or other implementation detail are omitted from the abstract process model. In other words, the model describes the "what" and the "when" of process activity flow, but not the "how" of flow object implementation.

> XPDL defines three Model Portability conformance classes, SIMPLE, STANDARD, and COMPLETE. A modeling tool asserting compliance to one of these classes means that the tool can import and understand all parts of a serialized BPMN instance conformant to the class. All three classes exclude implementation-related XPDL elements and attributes. All three classes exclude vendor specific extensions via the use of Extended Attributes or user name spaces. They differ only in the set of abstract modeling elements supported.

---

[29] http://blog.processanalytica.com/category/portability/

[30] See http://wfmc.org/xpdl-developers-center.html

The SIMPLE class includes the following BPMN objects: task, collapsed subprocess, gateway (exclusive data-based, inclusive, parallel), None start and None end events, pool, lane, data object, text annotation, sequence flow (uncontrolled, conditional, default), and association.

The STANDARD class includes the following BPMN objects: task (task type User, Service, Send, Receive); collapsed and expanded sub-process, looping or multi-instance activity, gateway (inclusive, exclusive data-based, exclusive event-based, parallel), start events (None, message, timer), catching intermediate events in sequence flow (timer, message), throwing intermediate events in sequence flow (message), attached intermediate events (timer, message, error), end events (None, error, message, terminate), pool, lane, data object, text annotation, sequence flow (uncontrolled, conditional, default), and association.

The COMPLETE class includes all task types, all event types, and all gateway types described by BPMN 1.1, message flow, transactional sub-process, and ad hoc sub-process.

Each class is described by a filter transform (xslt) that can be applied to the XPDL instance, leaving only the elements and attributes of the class. If the original XPDL is schema-valid, the filtered XPDL will also be schema valid. A second transform provides additional validation rules required for conformance. If the original XPDL is identical to the filtered XPDL and has no validation errors, the original instance is said to be conformant to the class. If the original XPDL is not identical to the filtered XPDL, but the filtered XPDL has no validation errors, the filtered XPDL represents the class-conformant portion of the original instance.

We will provide tools for validating BPMN abstract model portability conformance levels. We envision other BPMN portability conformance classes, and other levels of abstract model portability conformance may be introduced in the future.

In March 2009, WfMC announced[31] that three tools were able to successfully interchange models in the SIMPLE class: Fujitsu, ITP Commerce, and eClarus. A few other tools needed only minor technical changes to achieve SIMPLE class portability. Details are provided on the WfMC website.

---

[31] http://www.wfmc.org/workflow-management-announces-results-of-bpmn-model-portability-validation.html

PART IV.
LEVEL 3: EXECUTABLE BPMN

CHAPTER 18

What Is Executable BPMN?

To most of the team that developed it, BPMN 2.0 is really about *executable BPMN*. Honestly, many of them can barely imagine any use for it *other* than defining executable processes! And when I say executable BPMN, I don't mean executable in the way that processes modeled in BPMN 1.x are executable in BPM Suites from Adobe, Appian, Cordys, FlowCentric, Fujitsu, Lombardi, Oracle, SAP, Savvion, Singularity, SoftwareAG, TIBCO, Vitria, and others. That's because those tools, in their current incarnation, just use BPMN to define the *abstract activity flow*, the part that you can see in the diagram. By itself, BPMN 1.x is not executable, because it does not specify the data, messages, service interfaces, and similar detail that a process execution engine needs to run the process. BPMN 1.x actually provides attributes for those things, but they are universally ignored by the BPMS vendors in favor of their own vendor-specific implementation design languages.

Executable BPMN, as "reinvented" by BPMN 2.0, now means executable process design completely within the BPMN standard. This is what I call Level 3 modeling. The difference between Level 2 and Level 3 modeling is the difference between a process flow diagram, no matter how richly detailed, and an XML language describing an executable process. Level 3 modeling goes past what is in the diagram. Its focus is the XML details underneath.

Executable modeling in BPMN 2.0 is done by populating XML *metadata* in the model, not by writing code. You start by creating the flow diagram, just as in Level 2. But then you add all that executable detail by filling in the execution-related properties of each activity, gateway, event, and the data flows between them. This means defining the data definitions, the service interfaces, the messages, the gateway expressions, and task assignment rules, as specified by BPMN. Those details do not appear in the diagram, but they are present in the XML. If you are familiar with BPEL design tools, you might say this sounds a lot like them, with the addition of a standardized, more business-friendly, process diagram. And that would not be too far from the truth.

Level 3 modeling is not the principal focus of this book, which concentrates on method and style in creating the "abstract" Level 2 model. As this book goes to press, Level 3 modeling "in the wild" does not yet exist. BPMN 2.0-based BPM Suites are not yet even available. It is helpful, nevertheless, to take a look at the key features of executable BPMN to give a glimpse of the next generation of BPM technology. And we do just that in the next few chapters.

CHAPTER 19

Data

Executable BPMN begins with *process data*. BPMN 1.x had a way to specify data, but it was rarely used. Data and data flow, as represented in the diagram by the *data object* shape and *association*, were classified in BPMN 1.x as *artifacts*, meaning essentially annotations of the diagram with no defined semantics.

That has all changed in BPMN 2.0. Data has been elevated to a first-class semantic element. A data object, together with a handful of other types of *item-aware elements*,[32] now signifies a *process variable*, defined by an XML schema. It is no longer connected to flow elements by a regular association, which still just applies to artifacts, but with a new type of connector, a *data association*. In the XML, the data association actually defines the *mapping* of data from one flow element to the next.

BPMN does not provide its own model for data structure or an expression language for querying that data, but instead supports existing industry standard data definition and expression languages. BPMN designates XML Schema and XPath as its defaults, but tools are free to substitute other languages.

Data Objects, Properties, and Data Stores

The *data object* is the primary construct for modeling data within a process. Each data object is contained within a specific process or subprocess element, and its lifetime and visibility are constrained within that element. In other words, a data object could represent a *global variable* for the process or a *local variable* for a particular activity. The lifetime of a data object is limited to the lifetime of the process or activity instance.

---

[32] A BPMN *item* can represent either information or a physical item that is an input or output to a process or activity. In most cases an item refers to data.

The data structure represented by a data object is defined by its associated *itemDefinition* element, which specifies an XML schema. A data object representing a *collection* of variables is depicted in the diagram with the multi-instance marker (Figure 19-1).

Figure 19-1. A collection data object

A *property* of a process or activity, such as the process owner or task performer, can also be defined with an item definition and used in process logic. It has no visual representation in the diagram.

A *data store* (Figure 19-2) represents a data structure that the process can read or write but which persists beyond the lifetime of the process. For example, a process may interact with external systems via shared data, represented as data stores.

Figure 19-2. A data store

Data Inputs and Outputs

Processes, tasks, and global tasks specify their input and output parameters as *data inputs* and *data outputs* (Figure 19-3). A data input represents information needed to start an activity, and each data input can be defined as required or optional; it may have no incoming data associations. If a required data input is unavailable when a process or task is invoked, start is delayed until that data input becomes available. A data output represents information that may be output from an activity; it may have no outgoing data associations. Like data objects, data inputs and outputs reference XML schemas via item definitions.

Figure 19-3. Data input (left) and data output (right)

Even when data inputs and outputs are omitted from the diagram, as they frequently are, they may be specified in the XML.

The collection of data inputs and data outputs required by a particular activity is called an *inputSet* and *outputSet*, respectively, and together these comprise the *ioSpecification* for the activity or process. It is possible to define multiple inputSets and outputSets, in which case the implementation determines which ones apply.

Data Associations

A *data association*, depicted in the diagram using the dotted line connector, represents a mapping between a data object, property, or data store on one end and a data input or data output (i.e., parameter) on the other end (Figure 19-4). A data association connected to an activity or event in the process diagram represents a visual shorthand for connection to the data input or output of that activity or event. Activities have two types of data association, *dataInputAssociation* and *dataOutputAssociation*, respectively. A catching or throwing event has only one, as appropriate.

A data association defines a *source* and a *target*, and optionally a *transformation*. When a data association is executed, data is copied from the source to the target, and possibly transformed in the process. In the XML, each data association is actually a child of a particular activity or event.

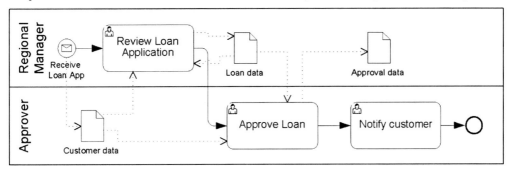

Figure 19-4. Process showing data flow

Data Mapping

 Data objects, inputs, and outputs are data structures defined by XML schema elements or complex types. Individual elements in those structures may be referenced for data mapping by XPath expressions using the *assignment* and *transformation* elements. Similar to BPEL, BPMN supports mapping with special XPath functions, *getDataObject*, *getDataInput*, and *getDataOutput* (and equivalent functions to access properties and data stores) to address specific information elements contained in these structures. The *transformation* element of data association could be used to apply an XSLT transform to perform the mapping.

Examples

The example shown in Figure 19-4 illustrates the use of data objects and data associations in executable BPMN. It is expected that BPMN tools will shield process modelers from some of the complexity of the underlying XML, and allow them to configure the process using point-click wizards. The XML, however, does provide more technical readers with an idea of how the various elements fit together. A snippet of the serialization of this diagram is provided below:

```xml
<?xml version="1.0" encoding="UTF-8"?>
<definitions id="def"
targetNamespace="http://www.example.org/Processes/LoanProcess"
typeLanguage="http://www.w3.org/2001/XMLSchema"
expressionLanguage="http://www.w3.org/1999/XPath"
xsi:schemaLocation="http://www.omg.org/bpmn20 ../schemas/bpmn20.xsd"
xmlns="http://www.omg.org/bpmn20" xmlns:xsi="http://www.w3.org/2001/XMLSchema-
instance" xmlns:sd="http://example.omg.org/Sample"
xmlns:tns="http://www.example.org/Fragments">
    <import importType="http://www.w3.org/2001/XMLSchema" location="SampleData.xsd"
namespace="http://example.omg.org/Sample"/>
    <!-- Declaration of structures -->
    <itemDefinition id="customerStructure" structure="sd:customer"/>
    <itemDefinition id="loanStructure" structure="sd:loan"/>
    <itemDefinition id="approvalStructure" structure="sd:approval"/>
    <!-- Process definition -->
    <process name="LoanProc" id="LoanProc1">
        . . .
        <!-- Data objects -->
        <dataObject id="customerDataObject" name="Customer Data"
itemSubjectRef="tns:customerStructure"/>
        <dataObject id="loanDataObject" name="Loan Data"
itemSubjectRef="tns:loanStructure"/>
        <dataObject id="approvalDataObject" name="Approval Data"
itemSubjectRef="tns:approvalStructure"/>
        <!-- Activities and control flow -->
        . . .
        <userTask id="reviewLoan" name="Review Loan Application"
implementation="humanTaskWebService">

        <ioSpecification>
            <dataInput id="reviewLoan-input1"
itemSubjectRef="tns:customerStructure" optional="false"/>
            <dataInput id="reviewLoan-input2" itemSubjectRef="tns:loanStructure"/>
            <dataOutput id="reviewLoan-output"
itemSubjectRef="tns:loanStructure"/>
            <inputSet id="reviewLoan-is">
                <dataInputRefs>reviewLoan-input1</dataInputRefs>
                <dataInputRefs>reviewLoan-input2</dataInputRefs>
                <outputSetRefs>reviewLoan-os</outputSetRefs>
            </inputSet>
            <outputSet id="reviewLoan-os">
                <dataOutputRefs>reviewLoan-output</dataOutputRefs>
                <inputSetRefs>reviewLoan-is</inputSetRefs>
            </outputSet>
        </ioSpecification>
        <dataInputAssociation id="dataInputAssociation_1">
            <sourceRef>customerDataObject</sourceRef>
            <targetRef>reviewLoan-input1</targetRef>
        </dataInputAssociation>
        <dataInputAssociation id="dataInputAssociation_2">
            <sourceRef>loanDataObject</sourceRef>
            <targetRef>reviewLoan-input2</targetRef>
        </dataInputAssociation>
        <dataOutputAssociation id="dataOutputAssociation_1">
            <sourceRef>reviewLoan-output</sourceRef>
            <targetRef>loanDataObject</targetRef>
        </dataOutputAssociation>
        . . .
    </userTask>
```

```
     .  .  .
   </process>

</definitions>
```

Examination of the XML illustrates the basic workings of data in BPMN:

1. The data structures may be defined in *external schema documents* and *imported* into the model. Here they are defined in a file called SampleData.xsd, using its own namespace.

2. The *structure definitions* for the three data objects in the diagram are declared as root elements in the model, referencing elements in the imported SampleData schema.

3. The three *data objects* are defined at the process level, referencing the structure definitions.

4. Each task's *ioSpecification* element defines *data inputs and outputs*, referencing structure definitions.

5. Each task's ioSpecification also defines an *input set* and an *output set*, referencing the needed data inputs and corresponding data outputs.

6. Each task's *dataInputAssociation* element maps a data object to one of the task's data inputs, and each *dataOutputAssociation* element maps a data output to a data object.

In the example above, the data mappings were simple references to the structure definition, but BPMN allows mapping using the assignment element as well. For example, instead of

```
<dataInputAssociation id="dataInputAssociation_1">
   <sourceRef>customerDataObject</sourceRef>
   <targetRef>reviewLoan-input1</targetRef>
</dataInputAssociation>
```

we can provide more specific element mappings such as this:

```
<assignment>
  <from>bpmn:getDataObject('customerDataObject')/sd:customer/sd:Name</from>
  <to>bpmn:getDataInput('reviewLoan-input1')/sd:loan/sd:CustomerName</to>
</assignment>
```

CHAPTER 20

Services and Messages

Automated tasks in BPMN are represented by *services* in the BPMN metamodel. If the process itself can be invoked as a service, the same constructs may be applied to the process as a whole.

A *service reference* names a callable service in BPMN. It may also define a *service endpoint*, the URL for invoking the service. Usually a service reference is understood to mean a web service specified by WSDL, but other implementations are allowed. Each service reference requires an *interface*, which specifies a set of *operations*, individually addressable actions provided by the service. Each operation in turn references a set of *messages*: an *input message* used to invoke the service, an *output message* used to return the result, and possibly a list of *errors* that may be returned if the operation fails. The information content of these messages is defined by a structure definition that typically references an imported WSDL document.

A simple example is shown below:

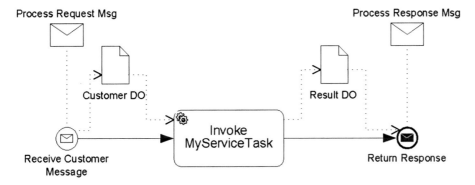

Figure 20-1. Simple service invocation

Here we have a simple process consisting of a single Service task called *InvokeMyServiceTask*. The process is also callable as a service called *ServiceTaskProcess*. Both the invoked service and the process thus advertise their interfaces through a WSDL document that is referenced by the BPMN.

The serialization snippets that follow illustrate how data flows from the process request message through the start event to the Customer data object, and from there to the data input of the Service task to the service's request message. Similarly, they illustrate the data flow from the service's response message to the Service task data output to the Result data object, continuing to the end event and the response message of the process.

The *definitions* root declares the separate namespaces used by the data, process client, the called service, and the process's own target namespace. In addition to *import* of the data definitions from SampleData.xsd, BPMN also needs to import the WSDL documents, as shown below:

```
<?xml version="1.0" encoding="UTF-8" ?>
<definitions xmlns="http://www.omg.org/bpmn20"
             targetNamespace="http://example.omg.org/BPMN"
             expressionLanguage="http://www/w3/org/1999/XPath"
             typeLanguage="http://www/w3/org/2001/XMLSchema"
             xmlns:xsi="http://www.w3.org/2001/XMLSchema-instance"
             xsi:schemaLocation="../schemas/Bpmn20.xsd"
             xmlns:tns="http://example.omg.org/BPMN"
             xmlns:sd="http://example.omg.org/Sample"
             xmlns:client="http://example.omg.org/ServiceTaskProcess"
             xmlns:tasksvc="http://example.omg.org/MyFirstTaskService">

  <!-- Import Sample XML-Schema -->
  <import importType="http://www.w3.org/2001/XMLSchema"
         location="xsd/SampleData.xsd"
         namespace="http://example.omg.org/Sample"/>

  <!-- Import WSDL Definition of the Process -->
  <import importType="http://schemas.xmlsoap.org/wsdl/"
         location="ServiceTaskProcess.wsdl"
         namespace="http://example.omg.org/ServiceTaskProcess"/>

  <!-- Import WSDL Definition of MyFirstTaskService -->
  <import importType="http://schemas.xmlsoap.org/wsdl/"
         location="MyFirstTaskService.wsdl"
         namespace="http://example.omg.org/MyFirstTaskService"/>
```

Now BPMN needs to define the *itemDefinition* elements that point to the imported data and message structures. Item definitions for the messages don't point to the WSDL message types directly. Instead they point to *message* elements in BPMN, and those in turn point to the WSDL. In BPMN 2.0, a message can have a graphical representation – an envelope shape – linked to an activity, Message event, or message flow in the diagram.

```
<!-- Process ServiceTaskProcess related structures -->
  <itemDefinition id="customerStructure" structure="sd:customer"/>
  <itemDefinition id="resultStructure" structure="sd:result"/>

  <!-- Structures referring to WSDL Messages of ServiceTaskProcess -->
  <itemDefinition id="clientCustomerMessageStructure"
                  structure="client:ServiceTaskProcessRequestMessage"/>
  <itemDefinition id="clientResultMessageStructure"
                  structure="client:ServiceTaskProcessResponseMessage"/>

  <!-- Structures referring to WSDL Messages of service MyFirstTaskService -->
  <itemDefinition id="tasksvcCustomerMessageStructure"
```

```
                        structure="tasksvc:MyFirstTaskServiceRequestMessage"/>
<itemDefinition id="tasksvcResultMessageStructure"
                        structure="tasksvc:MyFirstTaskServiceResponseMessage"/>

<!-- Input and Output Message of process ServiceTaskProcess  -->
<message id="processCustomerMessage"
        name="Service task Process Request Message"
        structureRef="tns:clientCustomerMessageStructure"/>
<message id="processResultMessage"
        name="Service Task Process ResponseMessage"
        structureRef="tns:clientResultMessageStructure"/>

<!-- Input and Output Message of service MyFirstTaskService -->
<message id="myServiceCustomerMessage"
        name="MyFirstTaskService Request Message"
        structureRef="tns:tasksvcCustomerMessageStructure"/>
<message id="myServiceResultMessage"
        name="MyFirstTaskService Response Message"
        structureRef="tns:tasksvcResultMessageStructure"/>
```

Next BPMN defines the *service reference* elements, one for the invoked service and one for the process itself, along with their *interfaces*. The service reference includes a pointer to its interface and possibly its endpoint.

```
<!-- Process Service -->
<serviceReference id="ServiceTaskProcessService"
            name="ServiceTaskProcess Service"
            implementation="WebService">
  <interfaceRef>tns:ServicetaskProcessInterface</interfaceRef>
  <endPointRef>tns:ServiceTaskProcessEndPoint</endPointRef>
</serviceReference>

<!-- MyFirstServiceTask service -->
<serviceReference id="MyFirstServiceTaskService"
            name="MyFirstServiceTask Service"
            implementation="WebService">
  <interfaceRef>tns:MyFirstServiceTaskInterface</interfaceRef>
  <endPointRef>tns:MyFirstTaskServiceEndPoint</endPointRef>
</serviceReference>

<!-- Interface of ServiceTaskProcess -->
<interface id="ServiceTaskProcessInterface"
            name="ServiceTaskProcess Client Interface">
  <operation id="ServiceTaskProcessInterfaceOperation"
            name="Operation exposed by ServiceTaskProcess Interface">
    <inMessageRef>tns:processCustomerMessage</inMessageRef>
    <outMessageRef>tns:processResultMessage</outMessageRef>
  </operation>
</interface>

<!-- Interface of MyFirstTaskService -->
<interface id="MyFirstServiceTaskInterface"
            name="MyFirstServiceTask Client Interface">
  <operation id="MyFirstServiceTaskInterfaceOperation"
            name="Operation exposed by the MyFirstServiceTask Interface">
    <inMessageRef>tns:myServiceCustomerMessage</inMessageRef>
    <outMessageRef>tns:myServiceResultMessage</outMessageRef>
  </operation>
</interface>
```

Now BPMN can define the process variables, represented in the diagram as *data objects*.

```
<!-- Process Variable Definitions -->
<dataObject id="CustomerDataObject"
            name="Data Object to store Customer Information"
            itemSubjectRef="tns:customerStructure"/>

<dataObject id="ResultDataObject"
            name="Data Object for the result of the process"
            itemSubjectRef="tns:resultStructure"/>
```

With the data defined, BPMN can at last describe the orchestration, beginning with the start event. The child element *messageEventDefinition* references the process's *interface* and request *message* (defined from the imported WSDL). The *data output* of the event, in turn, references the *structure definition* associated with that message. The *data output association* maps the data output to the *Customer data object*. Here that mapping uses *assignment*, similar to BPEL's assign construct. The BPMN special XPath functions *getDataOutput* and *getDataObject* allow the assignment to reference specific elements in the source and target data structures.

```
<!-- Process flow -->
<startEvent id="firstStep"
            name="Instantiate Process">
  <dataOutput id="EventOutput"
              name="Start Event Data"
              itemSubjectRef="tns:processCustomerMessage"/>
  <dataOutputAssociation sourceRef="EventOutput"
                         targetRef="CustomerDataObject">
    <assignment>
      <from>getDataOutput('EventOutput')/payload</from>
      <to>getDataObject('CustomerDataObject')</to>
    </assignment>
  </dataOutputAssociation>

  <messageEventDefinition messageRef="tns:processCustomerMessage">
    <operationRef>tns:ServiceTaskProcessInterfaceOperation</operationRef>
  </messageEventDefinition>
</startEvent>
```

With all this, we have only received the process request message and passed it to the Customer data object. The next step in the process is a Service task that invokes a web service. Its *ioSpecification* element defines the *data input* and *data output* for the task. In this case these are the *structure definitions* for the service's *interface*, which were originally defined in the imported WSDL.

In order to invoke the service, BPMN needs to populate the task's data input by mapping data from the Customer data object via the *data input association*. This example uses assignment to copy the customer address from the data object to the data input and also populates some other data input elements with literal values.

```
<serviceTask id="secondStep"
             name="InvokeMyServiceTask">
  <ioSpecification>
    <dataInput id="DataInput"
               name="Customer Data Input"
               itemSubjectRef="tasksvc:MyFirstTaskServiceRequestMessage"
```

```
                        optional="false"/>
    <dataOutput id="DataOutput"
                name="Result Output"
                itemSubjectRef= "tasksvc:MyFirstTaskServiceResponseMessage"/>
    <inputSet name="InvokeMyServiceTaskInputSet" dataInputRefs="DataInput"/>
    <outputSet name="InvokeMyServiceTaskOutputSet"
               dataOutputRefs="DataOutput"/>
  </ioSpecification>

  <dataInputAssociation name="Copy from DataObject to DataInput"
                        sourceRef="CustomerDataObject"
                        targetRef="DataInput">
    <assignment>
      <from>string('Scott')</from>
      <to>bpmn:getDataInput('DataInput')/payload/sd:customer/sd:firstName</to>
    </assignment>

    <assignment>
      <from>string('Tiger')</from>
      <to>bpmn:getDataInput('DataInput')/payload/sd:customer/sd:lastName</to>
    </assignment>

    <assignment>
      <from>bpmn:getDataObject('CustomerDataObject')/sd:customer/sd:address</from>
      <to>bpmn:getDataInput('DataInput')/payload/sd:customer/sd:address</to>
    </assignment>
  </dataInputAssociation>
```

The *data output association* then maps the service response, which is the task's *data output*, to another process variable, the *Result data object*. Here instead of *assignment* the example uses *transformation*, which can be any type of expression.

```
  <dataOutputAssociation name="Copy from DataOutput To ResultDataObject"
                         sourceRef="DataOutput"
                         targetRef="ResultDataObject">
    <transformation evaluatesToTypeRef="sd:result">
      bpmn:getDataOutput('DataOutput')/payload/sd:result
    </transformation>
  </dataOutputAssociation>

  <operationRef>tns:MyFirstServiceTaskInterfaceOperation</operationRef>
  <serviceRef>tns:MyFirstServiceTaskService</serviceRef>
</serviceTask>
```

The final step is to return the process response message from the end event. This works like the start event in reverse. Here the *Message event definition* references the process's *operation* and associated *response message*. The message is populated by the event's *data input*, which is mapped from the *Result data object* by a *data input association*.

```
<endEvent id="thirdStep"
          name="Return Response">
  <dataInput id="EventInput"
             name="Return Event Data"
             itemSubjectRef="tns:processResultMessage"/>

  <dataInputAssociation sourceRef="ResultDataObject"
                        targetRef="EventInput">
    <assignment>
      <from>bpmn:getDataObject('ResultDataObject')/sd:result</from>
```

```
        <to>bpmn:getDataInput('EventInput')/payload/sd:result</to>
      </assignment>
    </dataInputAssociation>

    <messageEventDefinition messageRef="tns:processResultMessage">
      <operationRef>ServiceTaskProcessInterfaceOperation</operationRef>
    </messageEventDefinition>
  </endEvent>

  <!-- Sequence Flows -->
  <sequenceFlow id="sf01" sourceRef="firstStep" targetRef="secondStep"/>
  <sequenceFlow id="sf02" sourceRef="secondStep" targetRef="thirdStep"/>
</process>

</definitions>
```

This is a lot of detail for a one-step process, but it is very similar to the structure of BPEL. Tools will hide most of the complexity under the covers. A simple process like this would typically only require the modeler to select the invoked service from a UDDI browser and define the data mappings, which is no different from a conventional BPMS today. While today's BPEL tools are oriented to developers who like to tweak the XML directly, most Level 3 BPMN tools will take a more business-empowering approach. The fact that messages, data objects, process-level data inputs and outputs, and data associations are graphical elements in the diagram should facilitate this.

CHAPTER 21

Human Tasks

BPMN 2.0 allows specification of executable human tasks. Technically, BPMN distinguishes two types of human tasks, called User and Manual (Figure 21-1). *User tasks* are assumed to be performed via a computer interface, as in a BPM Suite. Their details are presented to the assigned performer via a worklist, with completion signaled through the task user interface, which communicates with the process engine. A *Manual task* provides no system interface to the performer, so it is inherently not executable in a BPMS. Our focus here is on the User task and its reusable variant, *Global User task*.

Figure 21-1. User (left) and Manual (right) task

The User task specification is aligned with the BPEL4People and WS-HumanTask standards in OASIS. A key feature of those standards is that human tasks can be defined, assigned, and performed independently of a business process. For example, an ERP application can directly assign tasks and receive their results, and enterprise application vendors can provide a common worklist for tasks assigned from either an application or a process. BPMN's human task architecture supports this.

A User task's *implementation* attribute can specify WS-HumanTask, a generic web service, or other. Other attributes specify the task's *priority* (an integer) and the *rendering*, or task user interface. The main function, however, of the User task specification is to define *task assignment* to users or roles.

Any process activity can reference one or more *resource* elements defined in the model, such as a *performer*. For activities representing human interaction, such as a User task, models can specify a particular type of performer, such as *potential owner*, meaning a user who can claim the task from a shared queue. Other types of human performer types, such as supervisors or quality control roles, could be defined as well. For each performer element, the model specifies a task assignment rule, either a design-time *expression* that resolves to a particular user or group, or a *parameter-based query* evaluated at runtime.

The most flexible assignment method uses parameter-based query. The definition of a resource like "loan approver" can specify one or more *resource parameters* based on attributes of users, groups, and the process instance itself. Values of the process instance are passed to the parameters to resolve the task assignment at runtime.

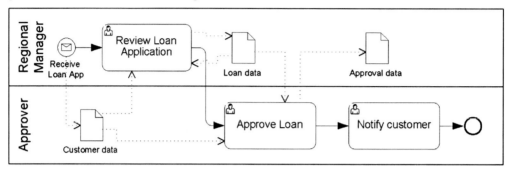

Figure 21-2. Human workflow example

Returning to our loan application example (Figure 21-2), we note the lanes labeled *Regional Manager* and *Approver*, which here represent resources. In the serialization, resources are declared as root elements, external to the process definition, and are referenced by the process. The Regional Manager role is defined by a required *country* parameter and an optional *city* parameter.

It is common to label lanes in the process diagram with the name of the assigned group or resource. However, lanes can be used to organize flow elements by any category, not just by resource. The lane set *ByPerformer* indicates the placement of the process tasks in lanes defined by the performer. Another lane set could be defined for this process that groups activities according to some other category.

```
      <!-- Resources (performers) -->
<resource id="regionalManagers" name="Regional Managers">
      <documentation>Group of managers responsible for the region.
      </documentation>
      <resourceParameter id="parmCity" isRequired="false" name="city"
                         type="xsd:string"/>
      <resourceParameter id="parmCountry" isRequired="true" name="country"
                         type="xsd:string"/>
</resource>
<resource id="loanApprovers" name="Loan Approvers">
      <documentation>Group of reviewers responsible for approving loans,
                    depending on the loan amount.</documentation>
      <resourceParameter id="parmAmt" isRequired="true" name="amount"
                         type="xsd:long"/>
</resource>

      <!-- The Process -->
<process name="Human Workflow" id="HumanWorkflow">
```

```
<!-- Lane set to organize flow elements by performers -->
<laneSet id="ByPerformer">
   <lane id="ByPerformer_lane1" name="Regional Manager">
      <flowElementRef>reviewLoan</flowElementRef>
   </lane>
   <lane id="ByPerformer_lane2" name="Approver">
      <flowElementRef>approveLoan</flowElementRef>
      <flowElementRef>notifyCustomer</flowElementRef>
   </lane>
</laneSet>
```

The User task *Review Loan Application* is specified below. The performer *Regional Manager* is defined by populating the query parameters *city* and *country* from the data inputs to the task:

```
<userTask id="reviewLoan" name="Review Loan Application"
implementation="humanTaskWebService">
    <ioSpecification>
        . . .
    </ioSpecification>
    <dataInputAssociation id="dataInputAssociation_1">
    . . .
    </dataInputAssociation>
    <dataOutputAssociation id="dataOutputAssociation_1">
        . . .
    </dataOutputAssociation>
    <performer name="Regional Manager" id="regionalManager"
            resourceRef="tns:regionalManagers"/>
       <resourceParameterBinding parameterRef="tns:parmCity">
         <formalExpression>
                getDataInput('reviewLoan-input1')/address/city
         </formalExpression>
       </resourceParameterBinding>
       <resourceParameterBinding parameterRef="tns:parmCountry">
         <formalExpression>
                getDataInput('reviewLoan-input1')/address/country
         </formalExpression>
       </resourceParameterBinding>
    </performer>
    . . .
</userTask>
```

CHAPTER 22

For Further Learning

BPMN News, Analysis, and Commentary

- www.bpmnstyle.com is the website for this book, with news and commentary about BPMN specification, BPMN tools, model portability, and best practices.

- BPMS Watch, www.brsilver.com/wordpress, is Bruce Silver's blog about BPMN and BPM Suites

- blog.processanalytica.com is Robert Shapiro's website covering the latest in BPMN model portability

- www.workflowpatterns.com/patterns/index.php is an academic research site about classifying and applying "patterns" in process modeling, including BPMN.

BPMN Training

- BPMessentials (www.bpmessentials.com) is the leading provider of BPMN training, which follows the method and style of this book. It is available through a variety of channels: online, in private group classes, and in two-day public classes from the BPM Institute (www.bpminstitute.org/index.php?id=523).

BPMN Specification

- BPMN 1.x spec and white papers can be found at www.bpmn.org, the official BPMN site, not yet updated to BPMN 2.0.

- BPMN 2.0 final public draft before ratification vote (document bmi/09-05-03) can be found at www.omg.org/cgi-bin/doc?bmi/2009-05-03. The most current version can also be found at this book's website, www.bpmnstyle.com.

Books on BPMN

- Stephen White and Derek Miers, *BPMN Modeling and Reference Guide*, www.amazon.com/Modeling-Reference-Guide-Stephen-White/dp/0977752720. A good digest of the BPMN 1.x specification.

- Alexander Grosskopf et. al., *The Process: Business Process Modeling using BPMN*, www.amazon.com/Process-Business-Modeling-using-BPMN/dp/0929652266. Introduction to BPMN process modeling for business people, in the form of an extended conversation.

Books on Process Modeling and Analysis

These books focus on techniques of process analysis and improvement, not on the diagram. They do not even use BPMN.

- Paul Harmon, *Business Process Change, Second Edition*, www.amazon.com/Business-Process-Change-Second-Professionals/dp/0123741521

- Dan Madison, *Process Mapping, Process Improvement and Process Management*, www.amazon.com/Process-Mapping-Improvement-Management/dp/1932828044

- Alec Sharp and Patrick McDermott, *Workflow Modeling: Tools for Process Improvement and Application Development, 2nd Edition*, www.amazon.com/Workflow-Modeling-Improvement-Application-Development/dp/1596931922

Index

activity, ix, xiii, xvii, 3, 4, 5, 6, 7, 8, 13, 14, 15, 16, 18, 19, 20, 23, 25, 27, 30, 33, 34, 35, 36, 41, 42, 43, 45, 46, 47, 48, 49, 50, 53, 54, 55, 57, 60, 63, 68, 69, 70, 72, 73, 75, 76, 79, 80, 81, 82, 83, 84, 87, 90, 91, 92, 93, 96, 97, 98, 99, 100, 101, 104, 105, 108, 109, 112, 114, 115, 116, 118, 119, 121, 122, 123, 125, 127, 128, 130, 131, 132, 133, 137, 138, 140, 141, 142, 143, 144, 145, 146, 147, 149, 150, 153, 154, 156, 159, 160, 161, 162, 166, 167, 168, 171, 172, 173, 174, 175, 176, 177, 178, 179, 181, 182, 183, 184, 185, 186, 189, 191, 192, 194, 195, 197, 199, 200, 201, 202, 207, 208, 209, 210, 215, 217, 218, 223, 225, 226, 227, 233, 239, 240

ad-hoc subprocess, ix, 83, 84, 218

AND-join, 19, 27, 33, 42, 43, 46, 132, 133, 134, 137, 186, 200

AND-split, 19, 33, 42, 133, 158

annotation, 34, 37, 51, 60, 137, 139, 173, 175, 208, 218, 225

artifact, xviii, 34, 37, 51, 225

boundary event, 69, 70, 76, 91, 93, 96, 97, 98, 99, 100, 101, 102, 104, 105, 106, 107, 108, 109, 111, 112, 114, 115, 116, 117, 118, 119, 120, 121, 123, 131, 132, 136, 142, 143, 144, 145, 146, 149, 150, 151, 154, 155, 156, 159, 161, 164, 183, 184, 195, 196, 197, 198, 199, 201, 208, 210, 211, 214

BPEL, xv, 18, 116, 119, 213, 214, 215, 223, 227, 235, 237

BPMN 1.x, viii, x, xiv, xv, xvi, xvii, 20, 28, 29, 34, 35, 36, 50, 51, 82, 83, 84, 91, 93, 96, 97,

107, 112, 120, 121, 122, 123, 124, 175, 177, 202, 213, 215, 217, 218, 223, 225

BPMN 2.0, viii, ix, x, xii, xiii, xiv, xvi, xvii, xviii, 8, 19, 28, 29, 30, 34, 35, 36, 47, 51, 53, 68, 76, 79, 81, 82, 83, 84, 87, 88, 91, 94, 96, 97, 99, 105, 107, 108, 116, 120, 121, 122, 123, 128, 136, 142, 177, 202, 213, 214, 215, 216, 217, 223, 224, 225, 233, 239

Business rule task, 76, 203

Call Activity, 81, 82, 202

Cancel event, 6, 89, 92, 93, 98, 120, 122, 123, 183, 184, 186, 194, 195, 196, 197, 201

choreography, x, 20, 216

collaboration, x, xiii, xvi, 3, 19, 20, 28, 201, 216

compensating activity, 182, 183, 184, 186

compensation, 84, 92, 182, 183, 184, 185, 186, 187, 201

complex gateway, 137

Conditional event, 25, 76, 77, 86

data association, 34, 35, 51, 72, 225, 226, 227, 238

data input, 35, 226, 227, 229, 233, 236, 237, 238, 241

data object, 34, 35, 36, 51, 59, 72, 218, 225, 226, 227, 228, 229, 233, 235, 236, 237, 238

data output, 226, 227, 229, 233, 235, 236, 237

data store, 36, 37, 51, 179, 226, 227

default flow, 129, 130, 131, 208

discriminator pattern, 136, 137

end event, 13, 14, 15, 17, 18, 19, 20, 28, 31, 32, 33, 41, 42, 44, 45, 46, 47, 48, 50, 58, 59, 60, 62, 69, 70, 71, 87, 88, 89, 90, 91, 92, 93, 95,

96, 98, 99, 105, 107, 108, 110, 111, 118, 119, 120, 131, 136, 141, 146, 150, 154, 156, 158, 163, 164, 175, 183, 184, 186, 189, 195, 196, 199, 200, 205, 206, 218, 233, 237

Error event, 89, 90, 91, 92, 93, 96, 99, 105, 106, 107, 108, 109, 110, 111, 112, 114, 117, 118, 119, 120, 140, 142, 143, 154, 155, 156, 160, 162, 164, 165, 175, 183, 184, 195, 196, 201, 211

Escalation event, 91, 92, 99, 105, 108, 109, 110, 111, 112, 114, 115, 140, 142, 154, 156, 157, 158, 160, 162, 164, 165, 201, 211

event, vii, xi, xiv, xvii, 3, 4, 5, 7, 8, 14, 16, 19, 20, 21, 22, 23, 27, 31, 32, 33, 34, 35, 37, 38, 40, 41, 42, 43, 44, 45, 47, 49, 50, 53, 57, 58, 59, 60, 63, 69, 70, 71, 72, 73, 74, 75, 76, 81, 85, 86, 87, 88, 89, 90, 91, 92, 93, 94, 95, 96, 97, 98, 99, 100, 101, 102, 103, 104, 105, 106, 107, 108, 109, 110, 111, 112, 113, 114, 115, 116, 117, 118, 119, 120, 121, 122, 123, 124, 125, 126, 127, 128, 130, 131, 136, 139, 140, 141, 142, 143, 144, 145, 146, 147, 148, 149, 150, 151, 152, 153, 154, 155, 156, 157, 158, 159, 160, 161, 162, 163, 164, 166, 172, 173, 178, 179, 183, 184, 186, 187, 192, 193, 195, 196, 197, 199, 200, 204, 206, 207, 210, 211, 214, 215, 217, 218, 223, 227, 233, 235, 237

event gateway, 73, 74, 75, 89, 103, 104, 105, 108, 111, 112, 125, 126, 127, 131, 147, 148, 151, 152, 153, 186, 193, 197, 211

event subprocess, 81, 91, 96, 99, 100, 109, 116, 117, 118, 119, 120, 121, 122, 143, 144, 145, 146, 149, 150, 154, 155, 156, 157, 158, 159, 161, 164, 166, 183

event, interrupting, 70, 92, 93, 96, 97, 98, 99, 101, 104, 105, 108, 111, 114, 115, 117, 119, 120, 121, 122, 123, 131, 136, 140, 142, 143, 144, 145, 149, 156, 159, 162, 168, 183, 184, 208

event, non-interrupting, xiv, 91, 93, 96, 97, 98, 99, 101, 102, 104, 105, 108, 111, 115, 117, 118, 120, 121, 122, 123, 124, 136, 142, 143, 144, 145, 149, 150, 155, 156, 159, 162, 164, 168, 183, 208

exception flow, 69, 70, 81, 91, 92, 96, 97, 98, 99, 101, 104, 107, 109, 110, 114, 115, 116, 117, 118, 119, 120, 131, 133, 134, 135, 136, 142, 143, 145, 150, 156, 166, 183, 187, 196, 214

exceptions, viii, ix, x, xi, 5, 6, 7, 8, 13, 14, 18, 44, 45, 46, 58, 61, 67, 69, 70, 71, 81, 87, 91, 92, 96, 97, 98, 99, 100, 101, 104, 105, 106, 107, 109, 110, 114, 115, 116, 117, 118, 119, 120, 126, 127, 131, 132, 133, 134, 135, 136, 139, 140, 141, 142, 143, 145, 146, 147, 148, 149, 150, 151, 152, 153, 154, 155, 156, 158, 159, 160, 161, 162, 163, 164, 165, 166, 169, 171, 181, 182, 183, 187, 189, 190, 193, 194, 195, 196, 197, 203, 204, 205, 206, 214

exceptions, propagating, 99, 117, 118, 119, 120, 153, 154, 155, 156, 157, 158, 160, 162, 163, 164, 166, 167, 169, 194, 195, 196, 204, 205, 206

exclusive (XOR) gateway, 32, 103, 125, 126, 129, 131, 132, 138, 141, 153, 194, 209, 217

fault, 106, 119, 142, 156, 158

gateway, 3, 7, 8, 14, 16, 17, 18, 19, 27, 32, 33, 34, 35, 42, 43, 45, 46, 47, 50, 53, 57, 58, 60, 62, 63, 64, 69, 73, 76, 87, 90, 101, 103, 104, 106, 110, 125, 126, 127, 128, 129, 130, 131, 132, 133, 135, 136, 137, 138, 139, 141, 147, 151, 152, 163, 164, 172, 192, 195, 199, 200, 203, 204, 208, 209, 214, 218, 223

Global activity, 31, 79, 80, 82, 205, 225, 226

hierarchical style, xiii, 16, 17, 30, 47, 82, 83, 178, 189

inclusive (OR) gateway, 129, 130, 135, 190, 192, 208

intermediate event, 70, 71, 73, 74, 76, 81, 83, 87, 95, 96, 97, 99, 100, 102, 104, 105, 108, 110, 112, 121, 123, 126, 128, 147, 152, 158, 172, 184, 200, 210, 218

internal business exception, 140, 141, 142, 143, 154, 156, 158, 162, 193, 196

join, ix, 18, 19, 33, 34, 42, 43, 90, 125, 132, 133, 134, 135, 136, 137, 190, 208, 214

lane, 14, 16, 18, 19, 22, 24, 25, 28, 29, 30, 40, 41, 46, 47, 55, 62, 70, 72, 113, 201, 218, 240, 241

Link event, 16, 28, 37, 38, 60, 61

loop, 18, 132, 134, 141, 172, 173, 174, 175, 177, 179, 197, 208, 214, 217, 218

Manual task, 239

merge, xvi, 33, 43, 90, 125, 128, 131, 132, 135, 136, 137, 138, 141, 172, 189, 190, 191, 192, 214

message, ix, xi, xii, xiv, 19, 20, 27, 28, 29, 31, 32, 34, 35, 36, 40, 41, 42, 44, 47, 48, 49, 50, 51, 53, 54, 55, 56, 57, 59, 60, 62, 63, 69, 70, 71, 72, 73, 74, 75, 76, 81, 85, 86, 87, 90, 97, 98, 99, 102, 103, 104, 105, 109, 111, 112, 116, 122, 123, 126, 127, 146, 147, 151, 152, 153, 158, 171, 172, 173, 174, 179, 186, 189, 193, 195, 196, 197, 200, 205, 207, 210, 211, 216, 217, 218, 223, 232, 233, 234, 235, 236, 237

Message event, x, 20, 28, 31, 32, 34, 35, 41, 42, 44, 48, 49, 50, 54, 57, 59, 62, 63, 64, 70, 71, 72, 73, 74, 75, 76, 85, 86, 87, 88, 90, 96, 97, 100, 102, 103, 104, 111, 112, 116, 122, 123, 126, 146, 147, 148, 149, 150, 151, 152, 153, 154, 155, 158, 159, 160, 172, 173, 179, 186, 192, 193, 196, 197, 198, 200, 205, 206, 210, 211, 233, 234, 237

message flow, x, 19, 20, 27, 28, 29, 31, 32, 34, 35, 36, 40, 41, 42, 44, 47, 48, 49, 50, 51, 53, 54, 55, 56, 57, 59, 60, 62, 63, 64, 69, 70, 71, 85, 86, 90, 98, 102, 111, 112, 116, 123, 146, 147, 152, 158, 171, 189, 197, 200, 207, 211, 216, 218, 233

method, ix, x, xi, xii, xiii, 1, 4, 7, 8, 9, 17, 22, 28, 39, 40, 48, 71, 88, 123, 139, 176, 189, 195, 223, 240

multi-instance, 137, 175, 176, 177, 178, 179, 186, 192, 193, 207, 208, 218, 226

normal flow, 70, 91, 92, 93, 96, 97, 98, 99, 101, 107, 109, 117, 118, 119, 131, 133, 135, 140, 142, 144, 145, 149, 150, 154, 156

Object Management Group (OMG), ix, x, xi, xiii, xv, xvi, xviii, 3, 4, 6, 8, 213, 216, 217

orchestration, 5, 6, 7, 34, 51, 60, 70, 73, 75, 87, 214, 216, 235

OR-join, 134, 135, 136, 150

OR-split, 128, 129, 134, 135, 165, 190, 192

parallel (AND) gateway, 19, 33, 127, 128, 132, 133, 135, 157, 208

patterns, x, xi, xiii, 3, 8, 20, 91, 92, 97, 99, 109, 112, 113, 114, 125, 128, 129, 132, 136, 137, 139, 140, 141, 142, 146, 148, 151, 152, 154, 160, 161, 163, 164, 166, 167, 169, 178, 189, 193, 195, 199, 214

pool, 14, 16, 18, 19, 22, 23, 24, 25, 26, 28, 29, 31, 32, 34, 36, 38, 40, 41, 46, 47, 48, 49, 54, 55, 56, 60, 61, 62, 63, 70, 71, 72, 74, 85, 86, 102, 109, 110, 111, 112, 116, 123, 126, 141, 146, 152, 158, 159, 160, 171, 176, 177, 178, 184, 189, 192, 193, 197, 199, 200, 201, 202, 203, 207, 216, 218

Receive task, 73, 74, 75, 102, 126, 173, 179, 207, 210, 211

Script task, 73, 74

Send task, 70, 71, 72, 74, 102, 193

sequence flow, xi, 14, 15, 17, 18, 19, 27, 29, 32, 33, 34, 35, 37, 38, 41, 42, 43, 46, 57, 60, 61, 62, 68, 69, 70, 72, 73, 76, 81, 83, 85, 87, 88, 90, 91, 96, 97, 100, 101, 102, 104, 105, 112, 113, 125, 126, 127, 128, 129, 130, 132, 133, 134, 135, 136, 137, 138, 140, 141, 143, 147, 152, 156, 157, 172, 173, 192, 199, 200, 201, 206, 207, 208, 209, 211, 214, 218

Service task, 28, 30, 68, 69, 70, 72, 73, 74, 75, 76, 106, 109, 141, 143, 203, 232, 233, 234, 236

Signal event, xiv, 72, 76, 86, 90, 111, 112, 113, 114, 115, 116, 140, 146, 148, 149, 150, 154, 160, 161, 166, 167, 210, 211

start event, 13, 15, 20, 25, 28, 31, 41, 42, 47, 48, 54, 57, 58, 59, 60, 69, 72, 76, 85, 86, 87, 88, 89, 90, 95, 96, 99, 111, 112, 116, 117, 119, 120, 128, 146, 147, 148, 158, 179, 192, 199, 200, 211, 218, 233, 235, 237

style, ix, x, xi, xii, xiii, 3, 4, 7, 8, 9, 18, 28, 51, 53, 54, 71, 80, 82, 89, 90, 91, 96, 97, 131, 139, 161, 199, 205, 214, 223

Subprocess, 15, 16, 17, 18, 19, 28, 30, 31, 32, 33, 38, 42, 46, 47, 49, 50, 53, 56, 57, 58, 59, 60, 61, 62, 69, 70, 79, 80, 81, 82, 83, 84, 85, 87, 88, 89, 90, 91, 93, 95, 97, 98, 99, 107, 108, 109, 110, 111, 113, 114, 116, 117, 118,

119, 120, 121, 123, 131, 136, 141, 144, 145,
149, 150, 151, 153, 154, 155, 156, 160, 161,
163, 164, 165, 172, 173, 174, 175, 182, 183,
184, 186, 193, 194, 195, 196, 197, 199, 200,
202, 203, 204, 205, 211, 217, 218, 225
task, xii, xviii, 6, 9, 14, 15, 20, 27, 30, 40, 68,
69, 70, 71, 72, 73, 74, 76, 81, 82, 97, 99, 105,
106, 109, 116, 119, 121, 131, 141, 142, 143,
144, 151, 161, 162, 172, 175, 179, 193, 195,
196, 203, 206, 207, 214, 215, 218, 223, 226,
229, 232, 233, 234, 236, 237, 239, 240, 241
Terminate event, 28, 32, 44, 45, 89, 93, 114,
120, 121, 160, 163, 175, 204
throw-catch, 91, 92, 107, 108, 110, 111, 112,
113, 114, 115, 116, 119, 120, 149, 154, 156,
157, 158, 159, 160, 161, 162, 164, 165, 166,
167, 168, 183, 184, 186, 203, 204, 211
timeout, 69, 73, 74, 81, 101, 103, 126, 127, 143,
144, 145, 152, 156, 158, 162, 197, 211

Timer event, 25, 28, 31, 41, 58, 69, 73, 81, 85,
86, 96, 100, 101, 104, 119, 121, 126, 143,
144, 145, 147, 152, 153, 155, 156, 210, 211,
217
top-level process, 16, 31, 32, 40, 44, 45, 46, 47,
48, 49, 52, 53, 56, 80, 81, 85, 88, 90, 108,
178, 189, 193, 194, 195, 196, 197, 201, 205,
206, 216
transactions, 40, 84, 92, 181, 182, 183, 184,
185, 186, 187
user action, ix, 140, 142, 162
User task, 28, 30, 68, 69, 71, 72, 101, 106, 107,
109, 126, 142, 143, 203, 207, 215, 217, 239,
241
voting pattern, 136, 137
WSDL, xv, 232, 233, 234, 235, 236
XPDL, 213, 215, 216, 217, 218
XSD, 216, 228, 229, 233, 240

About the Author

Bruce Silver, well-known BPM industry analyst and consultant, is founder and principal at BPMessentials, the leading provider of BPMN training and certification. He is currently a member of the BPMN 2.0 development team in OMG, and was a developer of OMG's OCEB BPM certification exam. He writes the popular blog BPMS Watch (www.brsilver.com/wordpress), which covers the world of BPMN and BPM Suites, and is the author of the BPMS Report series of detailed product evaluations.

As principal consultant at Bruce Silver Associates (www.brsilver.com), he advises most of the leading vendors of BPM tools and technology in product strategy and design. Prior to founding Bruce Silver Associates in 1994, he was Vice President in charge of workflow and document management at the analyst firm BIS Strategic Decisions, which became Giga (now part of Forrester Research). He has Bachelor and PhD degrees in Physics from Princeton and MIT, and four US Patents in electronic imaging.

To contact the author, email bruce@brsilver.com.

Printed in the United States
151330LV00006BA/136/P

9 780982 368107